GOVERNMENT: Servant or Master?

Exposing America's Runaway Bureaucracy and Abuse of Its Citizens

Sandra Joy Adams

Copyright © 2025 by Sandra Joy Adams

All rights reserved.

ISBN: 978-1-5710248-8-6

Publishing services provided by Fitting Words LLC

All rights reserved. No part of this book may be reproduced or transmitted in any form or by any means, electronic or mechanical, including photocopying, recording or any other information storage and retrieval system, without the written permission of the publisher.

Scripture quotations marked CSB have been taken from the Christian Standard Bible®, Copyright © 2017 by Holman Bible Publishers. Used by permission. Christian Standard Bible® and CSB® are federally registered trademarks of Holman Bible Publishers.

Printed in the United States of America

1 2 3 4 5 6 7 8 9 10

To my husband, Melvin, who is fighting alongside me for God and Country.

To Congressman Bob Good, who has given me the opportunity to serve.

To my colleagues who work with me to serve the constituents.

To all those who work in government and truly fight for the American people.

To all Americans who want to be free.

Sandy Adams is taking up the fight for every American. She's seen and heard the despair of too many. Her insights are an inspiration for all of us to fight harder.

Bob McEwen, Former United States Congressman, Ohio

Sandy Adams does an excellent job identifying and exposing how hundreds of federal agencies are defiling the Constitution, abusing their power, and assaulting our fundamental freedoms. She provides examples both from her work helping citizens suffering under the heavy hand of the administrative state and from the neglect of thousands of disinterested federal employees. Most importantly, she is calling our nation back to its constitutional foundation and calling on Congress to reassert its Article I authority and responsibility as the representatives of the people.

Bob Good, United States Congressman, Virginia

Sandy Adams speaks truth to the real power in America: the citizens who value liberty, are grateful for all the wise men and women who gave so much to establish and build our nation, and simply wish to live in a free society where opportunity, peace, and security flourish. Her rallying cry to stand against the growing tyranny of a national government that violates our Constitution with abandon is one that requires us to answer with prayers and actions. To vote is one essential action that every citizen must take.

Becky Norton Dunlop, Former Deputy Assistant to President Ronald Reagan, Former Vice President of the Heritage Foundation, and Ronald Reagan Distinguished Fellow

Sandy Adams's book GOVERNMENT: Servant or Master? is long overdue. Why has no one else ever written a comprehensive, readable explanation of America's two founding documents, what the Founding Fathers were working to achieve, and the insidious, modern trend to undermine the system of checks and balances and separation of powers that the Founders established? Liberty-loving parents and good teachers will find this book a godsend.

Morton Blackwell, President, Leadership Institute

Sandy Adams's book is an eye-opening compilation of the bureaucratic agencies that have led to our bondage as a people, as entrepreneurs, and as taxpayers. Her book will be a powerful tool in helping everyday Americans see that we do have a path forward in restoring our rightful place as We the People. It's time to slay the bureaucratic behemoth that's brought bondage for far too many people in the land meant to be free! Homeschoolers to PhDs will benefit from this comprehensive, easy-to-read resource.

Tamara Scott, RNC National Committeewoman of Iowa and Host of *The Tamara Scott Show*

Sandy Adams has written an incredible book that, in my view, does two important things for the American reader. First, she reflects on founding US history in a most unique way. She has made it clear to the reader that America is living under much of the same tyranny that existed under King George III, the British King against whom the Declaration of Independence articulated twenty-seven grievances. And secondly, Sandy gives us a very clear picture of where we are headed as a nation by sharing her experience of living in Ukraine for eight years. You will be astounded to see the similarities between Communist/Marxist nations and America today. She not only tells us what the future holds if we continue down this path but also gives us a game plan for how to turn things around before it is too late. This is a must-read for all patriotic Americans.

LTG (Ret.) Jerry Boykin, US Army

In her well-researched work, GOVERNMENT: Servant or Master?, Sandy Adams goes there with the hard-hitting truth that the monsters abusing our government and citizens aren't necessarily those whose names are on the ballot, but the faceless—and too often soulless—bureaucrats whose function is to perpetuate power at the expense of real people while never being accountable to the electorate. Few discuss it for fear of generating hopelessness that we can ever overcome the leviathan, but Sandy's knowledge of our founding documents combined with her godly worldview have produced a treatment of the subject that convinces me that there is indeed a way back to freedom. I highly recommend this book to every patriot of every political stripe, and especially to young people.

Patti Lyman, Esq., Constitutional Attorney and RNC National Committeewoman for Virginia

Contents

Introduction	9
Chapter One: Government: Servant or Master?	13
Chapter Two: The Founding Fathers' Design	19
Part One: The Declaration of Independence	19
Part Two: The Constitution	41
Chapter Three: Evolution from Limited Government to the Administrative State	94
Chapter Four: The Behemoth	113
Chapter Five: Real Stories of Agency Abuse	174
Chapter Six: What Can You Do?	202
Chapter Seven: What Can Congress Do?	209
Chapter Eight: Final Thoughts—Is There Still Hope?	222
Endnotes	227
About the Author	238

Introduction

In recent years, I have been given the privilege and opportunity to work for a congressional office. As district director, it has been my responsibility and joy to serve all the constituents of the district along with my team. While serving, I have witnessed the realities of the US federal government and its hundreds of agencies as they exercised overwhelming control and, sometimes, abused the citizens of our district. I have seen the suffering and neglect of Americans caused by the burden of excessive regulations and penalties being forced upon them. When citizens finally called us, they were desperate and feeling helpless against the power and control that the government was wielding against them. I found that there were thousands of people in our district alone that were having this experience, and it angered me!

That's when I decided to write this book.

As I began to witness this abuse, I was often taken back to a time where I, with my husband and our six children, witnessed firsthand the oppressive government control and abuse of the people living in the former Soviet Union.

In the early 1990s, when the Soviet Union was breaking apart, we landed in Kyiv, Ukraine, to begin what would be an eventful eight years of service. We immediately felt we had entered a time machine and been sent back in time fifty years. Our suitcases were removed from the plane and placed on long, wooden hay wagons pulled by common farm tractors into a dimly lit building, where we searched among the bags to find our own. We were overwhelmed by the police presence and control that was everywhere.

As we settled into life in Kyiv, we observed people standing in long lines with their government-issued ration cards for everyday staples such as flour, sugar, bread, and fuel. Each family was given a certain ration based on their family size; they could only get more on the black market. However, they could be arrested if caught buying or selling there.

As I tried to make friends and get to know neighbors, it was apparent they were extremely cautious of interacting at all. Some seemed afraid, others suspicious; they obviously did not trust easily. Sitting outside our high-rise apartment one day, I offered an elderly neighbor a Bible in her language. She immediately said, "No! No! Hide it! I'm afraid I'll go to prison! Please bring it to my apartment tonight." We soon learned that government informants were constantly following us and that this was a way of life for everyone. We were cautioned by people with whom we did business to be careful of everything we said and did. It became clear in meetings with government officials that our movements, associations, and many conversations were already known by them.

I also learned the extent of the government's control over parents and their children. Mothers were allowed maternity leave for up to two years but were then expected to return to their government jobs and put their young children in government daycare until they were placed in government schools. There was no school choice or homeschool option. In the summer, children were taken to "pioneer camps" run by the government. The government had more control over the children than the parents did. Almost everyone worked for the government. The government controlled all media at that time. The people were allowed to watch or hear only what the government approved.

Why am I telling you this?

I am telling you this because we are in danger of losing our freedom to an ever-expanding government in our own country!

After our family returned to the United States in 2000, we noticed that major things had changed in American society during our eight years in Ukraine. While America was and still is the greatest nation on earth, we were sad to see an increased breakdown of traditional American values, a decline in education, and a political shift toward socialism and greater government control. We were appalled when we found that our elementary-aged children were not being taught nutrition in health class. Instead, they were being presented graphic details of sexual behaviors, both heterosexual and homosexual. Traditional values of abstinence were replaced with ideas of experimentation and use of condoms. American society had shifted both morally and socially to a greater dependence on government and an increased emphasis on criticism of free markets, capitalism, and even patriotism, encouraging a disdain for the US Constitution and acceptance of increased government handouts. And, let's be honest, it's worse today!

My husband and I were very concerned, so we began to get involved and do everything we could to prevent the decline of our country by supporting and electing leaders committed to the Constitution and the liberty of the American people. But it wasn't until I got a job working for Congress that I realized the magnitude of the US government's control and sometimes abuse of its citizens.

During our years in Ukraine, we saw the impact of a new constitution patterned after the US Constitution. It called for a more limited government and provided increased liberty for the people. It offered significant change to personal freedoms, free markets, and media. This created much more openness in the society, which was reflected in the faces, countenances, and outlook of Ukrainians as they became free to flourish. They were no longer afraid to express their opinions; they were allowed to start their own businesses; they could travel freely; and they could assemble without fear. We understand why they are fighting so hard right now: they have experienced freedom for the past thirty years and don't want to go back to tyrannical government control!

The United States was birthed out of our citizens' desire to be free from the tyrannical rule of Great Britain and King George III. We have experienced freedom for nearly 250 years because of the willingness of our ancestors to fight for it. We have enjoyed phenomenal opportunities because of the Constitution our founders gave us, but we have also seen attacks on the Constitution over the past hundred years that are threatening to destroy us. If we hope to continue to enjoy the liberties we have known and pass them on to future generations, we need to understand the battle we are in for the soul of this country and know how to take our own actions today to remain free.

In this book I share:

- Some alarming facts about our government that most Americans know nothing about, including the Administration Procedures Act, which essentially launched the current administrative state,
- What you can do as a citizen and what Congress can do to make government accountable again, and
- What you can do to get help if you find yourself personally encountering abuse from the government.

The purpose of this book is to bring awareness to Americans about how the government is controlling their lives through agencies that were put in place to "serve" them, to show the scope and control of these agencies, and to help citizens and our elected representatives get more involved in getting their government back to working for the American people!

For freedom,
Sandra Joy Adams

Chapter One
Government: Servant or Master?

Government is not reason; it is not eloquence. It is force. And force, like fire, is a dangerous servant and a fearful master.[1]

George Washington

Can you imagine living in a country such as the Ukraine of thirty years ago, as I described in the introduction—a country where your government tells you what you can and cannot do, down to the minute details of your life? Why would you want that? Why would *anyone* want that?

Before living in Ukraine, I could not have imagined living in that kind of world. It was a world where we were stopped by police on every corner. They accused us of any infraction just to get bribe money to put in their own pockets, whether we were guilty or not.

I was stopped by the police one day while driving. They accused me of running a red light, which I had not done. I had waited at the red light for it to turn green. Then they pulled me over because they saw my foreign tag and wanted to make some easy money. I had been in Ukraine long enough to speak the language, and I knew the cops would want a bribe in dollars instead of "coupons" (their local currency at the time). I decided that this time I would not just "go along to get along." I was going to force them to give me a ticket. The policeman informed me my fine would be five dollars. (The average salary there at that time was the equivalent of twenty dollars per month.) I asked him to give me a ticket and told him I would pay in Ukrainian currency. He did not want to give me a ticket; instead, he wanted to pocket the dollars, which were worth a lot more. If he gave me a ticket, he would have to record it and would not be able to hide his acceptance of the money.

He was not happy! The officer finally took the tags off my car and threw them in the back of his car. He then tried to take my car keys from me. I patiently waited and told him that I would call the US embassy if he did not give my tags back. He finally returned my tags to me, and then I was given a properly written ticket, which I paid for but didn't deserve.

While in Ukraine, I experienced many other situations that made me so thankful for my own country that was free from this kind of control, where we had a constitution protecting people from government overreach and tyranny.

When we returned to the US in 2000, my husband and I knew that we should be more actively involved in helping to elect government leaders who respect and follow the Constitution, and the guidelines laid out by our Founding Fathers. Because my husband was an educator and I was a mother of six children, we saw many worrisome changes in education, a decline in morals and patriotism, and a growing dismissal of the great ideals of capitalism and free markets that have made our country thrive and prosper. We also recognized that it wasn't just leaders in Washington, DC, we needed to focus on, but every office down to the local level, especially our school boards. We felt so strongly that my husband and I founded Noah Webster Educational Foundation to inform citizens and equip school boards to help them shape the next generation of leaders.

In his senior year of high school, our oldest son was honored to be nominated by his civics teacher and our state legislator to join several hundred students from across the US to visit Washington, DC, for a young leaders' congress. They were chosen as the cream of the crop and the potential next leaders of our country. They went to learn how government works. They even had the opportunity to write bills and have mock debates.

Our son called us from DC one evening and told us that he had expected to meet students who were serious and interested in serving our country to make it a better place to live. He was disappointed to find out that the large majority were more interested in talking about sex, the drugs with which they had experimented, and the next party they were going to. Yes, they obviously had the grades to receive the honor of being there, but our son made this statement that we have not been able to get away from since: "Mom and Dad, if this is the next group of leaders that will be leading our country, we are in serious trouble!" He was not trying to be a Goody Two-shoes, but he sensed their lack of values and appreciation for our country and what it represented. Of course, he had grown up in Ukraine, and by his senior year in high school he had visited almost every country in Europe. He had visited Auschwitz and seen the horrors of what a tyrannical government can do to a people if given too much power or if the people turn a blind eye to what is happening under their noses. He understood the freedom Americans have that others around the world only dream of.

Our idea and vision for Noah Webster Educational Foundation (NWEF), which Melvin and I founded to reclaim education and culture through foundational principles and sound policy, came to us one day while we were in a Golden Corral. We started writing our ideas on a napkin and brainstorming about what could be done to rescue our country by shaping the next generation of leaders—our children. We knew we had to focus on five things: the role of instruction, the role of parents, the role of government, the role of ethics and moral values, and the role of appropriations in education. Our country is spending more money on education than ever before, but we are not producing a better product.

As we studied each state's constitution and statutes on education, we realized that school boards have more authority and power to bring positive change in educating our children than they realize. Most school boards have not exercised that authority, and have simply followed the guidance of teachers' unions, superintendents, and school board associations and their lawyers, many of whom are advancing a radical, progressive ideology in education.

In recent years, during COVID, as classrooms moved into our homes via online video conferencing, Americans became more aware of the failure of our schools and the agenda that was being forced upon the hearts and minds of our children. We could all now see what was being taught! Who would have thought that we would have to address an issue of boys and girls being given the choice, sometimes even encouraged, to change their mind about their gender while school authorities kept this from the parents? In some cases, parents were being charged with crimes and losing their children to Child Protective Services (CPS), a federal government agency. In the past, an expressed need for gender reassignment would have been treated as a mental illness and attended to with reality orientation and sensible advice as the parents saw fit. Noah Webster Educational Foundation provides resources for parents, grandparents, educators, and school board members. Our goal is to impact the next generation of leaders by reclaiming America's education and culture. (Join us at nwef.org.)

Many of our concerns compelled us to also become more active in the political world, supporting and working for candidates who embrace constitutional and traditional values. We have worked with campaigns and seen some great constitutional leaders elected.

In 2020, I was asked to take a position that allowed me to work for Congress. I had worked on a congressional campaign helping with fundraising. When the candidate won, he asked if I would be willing to be the district director and run the district on his behalf. This opportunity opened my eyes to see exactly how the government works in relation to the American people. To be honest, I have been shocked, horrified, and angered to realize that, in many ways, our government no longer has the interest of the American people at heart. It is more interested in growing itself and having more control over us. That might be shocking to hear and might even sound melodramatic, but it's true!

I'll never forget wondering what it would be like to work directly with the federal government on behalf of our constituents. I have a nursing background, so I have always enjoyed serving and caring for people and was anticipating the joy and reward that helping others brings.

What I didn't expect, and had not thought about, was that by the time the constituents reached out to our office, they had been trying to get help from the appropriate federal agency for a long time. Instead of hearing that cheerful voice on the other end of the line saying, "How can I help you?" most people had waited on hold for one to four hours. Then, if and when the call was answered, they usually were connected to someone who was in a hurry or gave them another number to call because they had reached the wrong department. If the constituent seemed upset in any way, the agent would often hang up on them, and they would have to start the process over! The decisions or judgments made by the agencies were rarely in the constituents' favor. When mistakes were made by the agency, the penalty was often placed on the constituent. I had interacted with the IRS, of course, but was unaware of all the other agencies that also have control over our lives.

I received the shock of my life when I found out that on January 20, 2021, President Biden had, by executive order, sent 75 percent of the federal workforce home due to COVID concerns. How in the world did they think that the work of the people was to be accomplished when only 25 percent of the federal employees were working? We were told they were working remotely from home, but that couldn't be true, because they weren't answering phone calls or emails. This affected how we were able to do or not do our work. It was extremely frustrating to be at the mercy of a government agency that was only concerned about the well-being of the federal workers and not that of the American people. We also learned that 100 percent of Social Security offices were closed across the nation. You could only do business if you made an appointment. However, it was nearly impossible to get anyone to answer the phone or an email to make an appointment!

There are many good people working in federal positions. Some have worked there for many years and are truly there to serve the public. But in many cases, federal employees are just blindly following orders without realizing what is happening and are convenient pawns in the system that has been created.

I am very concerned about the elected and unelected people who no longer respect and obey the constitutional rule of law in our founding documents. The elected people are our representatives in Congress, sometimes passing legislation that is in contradiction to the Constitution and our rights set forth there. For example, Congress has passed laws that give the unelected people who work in federal agencies the ability to make rules or "laws" that we are required to follow. The Constitution specifically gave lawmaking authority to Congress, not to unelected bureaucrats. I go into more detail on this matter in chapter 3.

Some of the unelected people aren't following the constitutional rule of law because they might not even know what it is. They have just landed a job in the federal government that pays good money and gives them security for retirement. They are just working in one of these federal agencies and doing what they're told to do. Because the Constitution is many times ignored, laws get passed or rules are created, and our constitutional rights and freedoms are eroded. We are slowly being weighed down with regulations and laws not created by our representatives. Our government is systematically being changed with each rule or "law" to be our *master* instead of our *servant*!

How has this happened? What is going on? Where did we go wrong in this wonderful country of ours, and is there any way we can fix it?

While I don't claim to have all the answers, I hope that by the time you are finished reading this book, you will have a better understanding of the following:

1. How our Founding Fathers designed our government to work,
2. How the government functions today,
3. The size and scope of government,
4. What needs to be done to change it,
5. What you can do to help, and
6. What Congress must do to preserve our liberty and get the government back to working for the American people.

Finally, please understand that the government should be your servant and *not* your master.

When the righteous are in authority, the people rejoice; but when a wicked man rules, the people groan.

Proverbs 29:2 (NKJV)

Chapter Two
The Founding Fathers' Design

I am well aware of the Toil and Blood and Treasure that it will cost us to maintain this Declaration and support and defend these States. Yet through all the gloom, I can see the rays of ravishing light and glory. I can see that the end is worth more than the means.

John Adams to his wife Abigail July 3, 1776.[2]

Part One: The Declaration of Independence

At the time of this writing, I am in my fourth year working for a congressional district office. A Congressman has two offices. One is in Washington, DC, which mostly handles policy and legislation. He also has one or more offices in his home district that handle all constituent services, which includes representing constituents for any problem they might have with a federal agency. The district office also handles outreach for the Congressman and celebrates with local organizations at ribbon cuttings, grand openings, school functions, veteran events, and any other event deemed important to the people of the district. My job is to oversee such work in the district.

While I have learned so much about the federal government and its operations, it never ceases to amaze me how many ways it bypasses the Constitution and Congress to impose its power over the American people. It does this without any fear of retribution or consequence because it knows it has total control.

If you're like most people, you've probably found yourself frustrated with the government at some point, particularly with federal agencies that you are required to have contact with, such as the Internal Revenue Service (IRS) and the Social Security Administration (SSA).

We live in the greatest nation on earth, and our system of government has lasted almost 250 years, thanks to our wise Founding Fathers. As time has passed, however, our government has grown into an almost unrecognizable behemoth. It is now putting an ever-increasing burden on the American people. Most of us are not aware anything is wrong until we deal with a federal agency that has been given extreme power over us.

Are you aware, for example, that when Congress passed the Inflation Reduction Act (IRA), signed into law by President Joe Biden on August 16, 2022, it gave the IRS enough money to hire eighty-seven thousand more agents to be "weaponized against hardworking Americans via increased taxes and more aggressive enforcement"?[3] I know we were told that its purpose was to pursue millionaires and billionaires, but they are not telling the whole truth.

According to the *Congressional Record*, Representative Adrian Smith of Nebraska's Third District stated the following on the House floor on January 9, 2023, in opposition to the Inflation Reduction Act (IRA), when proposing the Family and Small Business Taxpayer Protection Act:

> The overwhelming majority of Americans, about 85 percent, follow the law and pay their taxes. The last thing they need is more IRS agents knocking on doors to conduct audits.
>
> Yet, this IRS funding is part of the broad Biden administration strategy to tax and audit exponentially more Americans by looking into their bank accounts, requiring online payment services to report them when they split a dinner check with friends or pay their babysitter after a night out, and then target them using eighty-seven thousand new IRS employees. Americans deserve to know their government is working for them, not against them.

Today, Mr. Speaker, you are going to hear Democrats claim there really won't be eighty-seven thousand new IRS employees. I imagine that they will say that new employees aren't going to target middle-class families and small businesses, and that Republicans don't care about IRS's customer service failings.

Let's focus on the facts. When a federal agency hires a new employee to replace one who retires, it does not increase the agency's head count. Yet, the Biden administration's own documents say they are increasing the head count by eighty-seven thousand over the next decade with these funds.

Treasury Secretary Janet Yellen's own instructions to IRS stated audit rates of families earning less than $400,000 should continue to be audited at historically similar rates. Under those instructions, nine out of every ten new audits can target families earning less than $400,000.[4]

The government already takes a large portion of our money from every paycheck we receive, and now they want to harass us and find reasons to take more. This is unacceptable!

As I began working closely with these federal agencies, my team and I tried to help the thousands of constituents calling our office for assistance. I realized they were seeking our help because their calls and emails were not being answered by the agencies put in place by Congress to serve them. One gentleman who came into the office was a veteran who had sustained injuries during combat that had required surgery and a lengthy hospitalization. He had many complications from these injuries and had been trying for thirty-one years to get a copy of his hospital records from the Veterans Administration (VA). He needed these to prove he had been injured. This veteran was not able to work to the level a healthy individual could. His ability to continue working to provide for his family was becoming more difficult. He was trying desperately to get full disability.

This gentleman spoke to anyone and everyone he could at the VA to see if there was anything else he could do to get those records, but to no avail. He had even gone through another congressional office in the beginning, only to be told the hospital paperwork could not be found. I have a medical background and knew that his records had to be somewhere. So, I called the National Archives, and they immediately told me I would need to contact the Missouri division with very specific dates and the names of the hospitals where he had been treated. Thankfully, our constituent had that information. Within two weeks, I received the package with all his records in our office! When I called him with the good news, he didn't believe me. But when he came to my office and looked at the records, he cried and was so grateful.

This is a story with a nice ending, but the sad thing is that the agency that should have done everything in their power to help a gentleman who had sacrificed so much of his life and health for his country had let him down for thirty-one years. My staff and I watch failures such as this take place every day across many different federal agencies. We often feel helpless because we are up against a behemoth, often indifferent even to a Congressional inquiry.

Just recently, a sweet ninety-two-year-old lady who had lived in the same house with her husband for fifty years called our office for help. After her husband passed away, someone had talked her into doing a reverse mortgage. She was left with a large loan that had to be paid off. Years later, when she realized she could no longer take care of the property, and with no children or family to help her, she tried to sell her house but was unsuccessful. She recognized she needed to move into assisted living but wasn't sure what to do about her house, especially since she still owed money on it.

I don't know how this happened, but Housing and Urban Development (HUD) contacted this elderly woman and asked if she would like to sign a Deed in Lieu of Foreclosure (DIL) form, which meant HUD would take charge of the property. At ninety-two years of age, she wanted to be free of the worry. She just wanted to live peacefully in her new home where she could make friends and not worry about who would take care of her or her house. So much for that!

This nice lady contacted us to tell us that several months after signing the necessary paperwork to receive the DIL form, she still hadn't received her copy despite her efforts to obtain it. She had been told by HUD that she was required to pay taxes and carry insurance on the house until she received the signed documents from them. But we found out that HUD had already taken possession of the property and changed the locks right after she moved to the assisted living facility. After going through the regular portal and channels required by HUD without success, I called someone I knew personally at HUD to rattle some cages. My friend at HUD was amazing. She managed to get all the signed documents needed to give this dear lady peace of mind. It should not have been that difficult. HUD is an agency that is supposed to serve the people and should not be allowed to cause this kind of stress and delay! But it happens every day.

When I took this job, I began seeing an extremely broken federal government that was no longer serving the people. Instead, it was bringing trouble, hardship, and unbearable burdens upon them at every turn of their lives, often at no fault of their own but because of mistakes made by the agencies themselves.

To understand what was happening, I asked myself some questions:

1. What is the government's role supposed to be in relation to the American people?
2. Is the government supposed to have total control over our lives in every area, or did our Founding Fathers lay out a specific and limited role for those who govern?
3. From whom do these agencies receive their authority?
4. Does Congress have the constitutional authority to start and empower an agency to create rules and regulations that inhibit our liberty?
5. When agencies infringe on the liberty of the American people, who provides oversight and correction to ensure they are not abusing the people with unconstitutional rules and regulations?
6. Does the American citizen have any say in how the government functions?
7. Do Americans still have the right to "petition the government for a redress of grievances," as stated in the First Amendment, or is that simply ignored today?

To answer these questions adequately, let's examine the government our Founding Fathers gave us and consider why they gave it to us. To do that properly, we need to read the first documents they wrote. This is so we can understand what they were experiencing under the governmental system at that time, and why they felt so strongly about breaking away from it.

Let's begin with the Declaration of Independence, written in 1776, and then examine the Constitution, which followed in 1787.

Allow yourself now to go back 250 years and imagine what the colonists must have been experiencing personally, emotionally, physically, financially, and spiritually that inspired their representatives to write these words to King George III.

The Declaration of Independence

> The unanimous Declaration of the thirteen United States of America, When in the Course of human events, it becomes necessary for one people to dissolve the political bands which have connected them with another, and to assume among the powers of the earth, the separate and equal station to which the Laws of Nature and of Nature's God entitle them, a decent respect to the opinions of mankind requires that they should declare the causes which impel them to the separation.

Sandy's Note: This first statement in the Declaration shows that the colonists had come to a point where they had no other choice but to break the ties they had with Great Britain after recognizing that all men were entitled by God to their natural rights. Because they were dissolving their ties with Great Britain, they wanted to declare what was compelling them to do so.

> We hold these truths to be self-evident, that all men are created equal, that they are endowed by their Creator with certain unalienable Rights, that among these are Life, Liberty and the pursuit of Happiness.

Sandy's Note: The colonists declared what they believed to be not just their rights, but the rights of all mankind given to them by God and not man. Among many of those were Life, Liberty, and the Pursuit of Happiness.

> —That to secure these rights, Governments are instituted among Men, deriving their just powers from the consent of the governed,

Sandy's Note: They express their beliefs that to secure these rights, men create governments, but they receive their powers from the people they govern.

> — That whenever any Form of Government becomes destructive of these ends, it is the Right of the People to alter or to abolish it, and

to institute new Government, laying its foundation on such principles and organizing its powers in such form, as to them shall seem most likely to affect their Safety and Happiness.

Sandy's Note: When a government fails to fulfill its obligations in protecting the fundamental rights of the people, it loses its right to govern, and the people then have the right to install a new government in its place to protect themselves.

> Prudence, indeed, will dictate that Governments long established should not be changed for light and transient causes; and accordingly, all experience hath shewn, that mankind are more disposed to suffer, while evils are sufferable, than to right themselves by abolishing the forms to which they are accustomed. But when a long train of abuses and usurpations, pursuing invariably the same Object evinces a design to reduce them under absolute Despotism, it is their right, it is their duty, to throw off such Government, and to provide new Guards for their future security.

Sandy's Note: A government that has been around for a long time should not be flippantly thrown off. Generally, though, people who are being abused or oppressed by a government will put up with it rather than try to change it. But because they had had enough and the abuses had become so egregious that the king had too much power and was exerting that power in cruel and oppressive ways, they had no choice. If they wanted to have a future where they and their children could be free from this tyranny, they had to throw it off.

> — Such has been the patient sufferance of these Colonies; and such is now the necessity which constrains them to alter their former Systems of Government.

Sandy's Note: They spoke of their patience in enduring this tyranny, but they could no longer tolerate the abuse and were being forced to change from their former system of government to a new one.

> The history of the present King of Great Britain is a history of repeated injuries and usurpations, all having in direct object the establishment of an absolute Tyranny over these States. To prove this, let Facts be submitted to a candid world.

Sandy's Note: They wanted to state the historical facts of the repeated abuses and tyrannical control of the king, and state what they were accusing him of by detailing his offenses.

> (1) He has refused his Assent to Laws, the most wholesome and necessary for the public good.

Sandy's Note: King George III was refusing to sign laws that would protect the natural rights of the people.

Example: After the French and Indian War, the population and economic growth of the colonies caused them to want to go west, expand, create their own laws, and govern their own people, but they needed permission from Britain to do so. The Royal Proclamation of October 7, 1763, banned the colonists from settling west of the Appalachian Mountains, and even though their desires to go west would have caused no harm, their requests were denied by the king and the governors and ministers representing England.[5,6]

> (2) He has forbidden his Governors to pass Laws of immediate and pressing importance, unless suspended in their operation till his Assent should be obtained; and when so suspended, he has utterly neglected to attend to them.

Sandy's Note: King George III would not allow local authorities to pass laws that were important and pressing for the people until they had received his permission. And while they waited, he would ignore the issues without addressing them. Sometimes these laws would be neglected by the king for years.

Example: "In 1764, New York wanted to pass a law to include some Indian tribes among the colonies. The British Governor agreed privately, but the King sent back instructions to all his governors to stop pursuing this notion until further notice. The colonists waited, but the King 'utterly neglected to attend to them.'"[7]

> (3) He has refused to pass other Laws for the accommodation of large districts of people, unless those people would relinquish the right of Representation in the Legislature, a right inestimable to them and formidable to tyrants only.

Sandy's Note: Here again he was refusing to allow the laws to be passed unless the people would give up their rights of representation. He wanted to be the sole power, making all decisions and neglecting the people's natural rights.

Example: In 1774, the British Parliament passed the Quebec Act, which changed the form of government in Canada from a representative government to a legislative council that would be under the control of the king.[8] Many English settlers were concerned and petitioned the king, but their concerns were ignored. The king was also proposing this type of government in Massachusetts. The colonists objected but the king ignored them. The Quebec Act proved to American colonists what they already believed: the British were not afraid to restrict colonial governments to secure their possessions in North America.[9]

> (4) He has called together legislative bodies at places unusual, uncomfortable, and distant from the depository of their public Records, for the sole purpose of fatiguing them into compliance with his measures.

Sandy's Note: King George III was forcing the colonial legislatures to meet at locations that were far away, inconvenient, uncomfortable, and where they did not have their official documents and records. He did this to exhaust them and force them into compliance with his demands.

Example: Following the Boston Tea Party (December 16, 1773), the Boston Port Bill went into effect in June of 1774. This was written in response to the Boston Tea Party uprisings but included an order that the legislative body be moved from Boston to Salem. This made no sense to the colonists, since the public records were kept in Boston. Instead of just crossing over the river, Bostonians would have a twenty-mile journey to get to legislative sessions! This was half a day's ride for most.[10]

> (5) He has dissolved Representative Houses repeatedly, for opposing with manly firmness his invasions on the rights of the people.

Sandy's Note: He would issue orders to disband entire legislative bodies because they were opposing him for his abuse of the people.

Example: In January 1768, on behalf of the Massachusetts Legislature, Samuel Adams wrote the "Massachusetts Circular Letter," stating that Great Britain had no right to tax the thirteen colonies without their consent and without the colonies having representation. The king's response was to declare that when the assembly next met, they must change their position or be dissolved immediately. They refused to reverse their position and were disbanded.[11]

> (6) He has refused for a long time, after such dissolutions, to cause others to be elected; whereby the Legislative powers, incapable of Annihilation, have returned to the People at large for their exercise; the State remaining in the meantime exposed to all the dangers of invasion from without, and convulsions within.

Sandy's Note: King George III would refuse to allow others to be elected, creating a very dangerous vacuum of leadership and exposing the colonies to invasions from outside and chaos within because there was no leadership.

Example: In 1768, New York's assembly announced it would resist the requirements that the Quartering Act enforced and sent an earnest petition to the king telling him why. As a result, they were told they had to comply or be disbanded. *The Boston Gazette* printed the following statement after news arrived of the threatened suspension of the New York Assembly: "If our legislative authority can be suspended whenever we refuse obedience to laws we never consent to, we may as well send home our representatives and acknowledge ourselves slaves; for a Parliament can be of no use to a people who are subject to laws they do not make."[12]

> (7) He has endeavoured to prevent the population of these States; for that purpose, obstructing the Laws for Naturalization of Foreigners; refusing to pass others to encourage their migrations hither, and raising the conditions of new Appropriations of Lands.

Sandy's Note: The king blocked immigration to the colonies because he didn't want its population to grow, and he changed the rules of new distributions of land.

Example: The king was opposed to various colonial laws passed for the purpose of encouraging immigration to America, so he sent agents to America to report back to him. They reported that the colonies were growing numerically and economically. The British government feared that such encouragement would reduce the population of England and lure away workers who would otherwise be employed in its domestic industries. He didn't want immigrants to gain any positions of power, so he placed barriers to prevent them from owning land.[13]

> (8) He has obstructed the Administration of Justice, by refusing his Assent to Laws for establishing Judiciary powers.

Sandy's Note: The king removed judiciary powers from the people, causing the judges to work for the king instead of the people.

Example: In early fall of 1772, news arrived in Massachusetts that colonial judges would no longer receive their salaries from colonial legislatures. Instead, all judicial salaries would be paid by the king. This came to be called "The Affair of the Royal Salary"; the colonists responded with widespread anger. In Massachusetts the judges had traditionally been appointed and paid by the legislature and the governor, and their salaries were paid by funds raised by the legislators. When the new salary plan was forced on the colony, the colonists feared that judges would no longer act impartially, especially in those cases concerning disputes between colonists and the king, such as the highly contentious issues of taxes and standing troops.[14]

> (9) He has made Judges dependent on his Will alone, for the tenure of their offices, and the amount and payment of their salaries.

Sandy's Note: The king forced judges to do what he said, and if they refused, they would lose their jobs and their salaries.

Example: The British Parliament passed an act that said judges' salaries would come directly from England rather than from money raised by local legislatures. The concern was that the judges would rule in favor of who was paying them instead of the people. In 1774, the Massachusetts Assembly asked Chief Justice Oliver if he intended to receive his salary from the king. He said he did. Chief Justice Oliver was not concerned about the potential conflict of being beholden to the king in cases between the colonial policies and the Crown or Parliament, but the people were very concerned.[15,16]

> (10) He has erected a multitude of New Offices and sent hither swarms of Officers to harrass our people and eat out their substance.

Sandy's Note: The king sent officers from England to the colonies, including tax collectors, to enforce new laws passed, and the colonists had to provide for them.

Example: The Townshend Acts created new taxes on numerous consumer goods. They authorized and funded the hiring of legions of royal tax collectors and customs officers arriving from England to establish new or expanded operations in every major colonial trading center. In 1765, after the Stamp Act was passed, officers were placed in every port, additional officers called "Collectors of the Customs" were added, a board of commissioners was established without the colonists' approval, and Admiralty and Vice Admiralty courts were established—and the colonists were forced to foot the bill. The ever-expanding and intrusive presence of tax collectors and customs officers merited several mentions in the "Petition to the King," one of the documents issued by the First Continental Congress in 1774, and became one of the grievances within the Declaration of Independence in 1776.[17]

> (11) He has kept among us, in times of peace, Standing Armies without the Consent of our legislatures.

Sandy's Note: The king forced people to house military personnel without the legislatures' consenting to this action. Through his actions he showed his disregard for the colonial people. He believed the independent spirit of the colonies was a threat to England, and he wanted to assert control over them.

Example: "In America during 1754, using his military authority, Lord Loudoun decreed that if barracks were not available, then the owners of both public and private houses would have to provide accommodations for his men. Loudoun left it up to local civilian officials to make the necessary arrangements and to secure reimbursement from their colonial legislatures. The most serious confrontation took place in the summer of 1756 in Albany, New York, the center of military activity against the French. Lord Loudoun ordered the people of Albany to take officers and common soldiers into their homes until regular military barracks could be constructed. When the townspeople objected, Loudoun took private houses by force and even seized a church to store his gunpowder."[18]

> (12) He has affected to render the Military independent of and superior to the Civil power.

Sandy's Note: The king effectively placed his military over the local civilian government.

Example: The king ordered that the colonists had to obey the authority of the British commander in chief (General Gage, at the time) and his generals. At one point Gage ordered Regulars (British soldiers) to capture several rebel leaders, including Samuel Adams and John Hancock, and seize a cache of weapons rumored to be in Lexington, Massachusetts.[19]

> (13) He has combined with others to subject us to a jurisdiction foreign to our constitution, and unacknowledged by our laws; giving his Assent to their Acts of pretended Legislation:

Sandy's Note: The king and Parliament continued to force laws upon the colonists. The Colonists recognized that the power of their own legislatures was slowly being taken away.

Example: From Founding.com: "The Founders believed that the colonists in each of the colonies had voluntarily consented to be governed by their own elected representatives; The colonies acknowledged King George as their 'chief executive,' and were in this sense British citizens. However, the colonists had not consented to be governed by the British Parliament, and it therefore had no authority over them. Accordingly, when King George gave his consent to the acts of 'pretended Legislation' of Parliament, he had given the colonists the justification for dissolving their allegiance to him, and thus for declaring their independence."[20]

> (14) For Quartering large bodies of armed troops among us:

Sandy's Note: The king placed armed troops in towns, and the colonists were required to take care of them.

Example: In 1775, just months after the war began at Lexington and Concord, about forty members of the Massachusetts provincial troops approached the Brookline home of William Thompson. The troops insisted that Mr. Thompson offer them a place to stay. He refused, claiming that his home was his castle, and suggested the troops should take shelter at a nearby public house. The soldiers rejected this offer and used a musket to break the lock on the front door and entered the home by force.

Although the colonists were upset about British quartering policies, the issue did not come up in the United States Constitution. However, when members of Congress began to draft a Bill of Rights, it received significant attention. The Third Amendment to the Constitution states, "No Soldier shall, in time of peace be quartered in any house, without the consent of the Owner, nor in time of war, but in a manner to be prescribed by law."[21]

(15) For protecting them, by a mock Trial, from punishment for any Murders which they should commit on the Inhabitants of these States:

Sandy's Note: The British troops were protected by the king with sham trials if they committed any crimes, including murder, against the colonists.

Example: The Boston Massacre is one of the most notable instances of this abuse. According to the Library of Congress, "the arrival of troops in Boston provoked conflict between citizens and soldiers. On March 5, 1770, a group of soldiers surrounded by an unfriendly crowd opened fire, killing three Americans and fatally wounding two more. A violent uprising was avoided only with the withdrawal of the troops to islands in the harbor. The soldiers were tried for murder but convicted only of lesser crimes."[22]

(16) For cutting off our Trade with all parts of the world:

Sandy's Note: England tried to make sure that the colonists traded only with Britain. America had enjoyed trade with the Spanish and French colonies, but England wanted to destroy the trade and isolate the colonists.

Example: This grievance refers to the Navigation Acts, which were passed in the 1660s to regulate trade between the colonies and England, and with other countries like Spain and France. Britain passed these acts to generate revenue for the British, but they also prohibited the colonists' ability to trade, which was a key source of income for them. The Founding Fathers believed in free trade, and exports like tobacco, flour, and rice were essential to the success of the American Revolution.[23]

(17) For imposing taxes on us without our Consent:

Sandy's Note: The king taxed the people in excess without their consent.

Example: The French and Indian War had cost England an enormous amount of money, and they wanted to raise revenue to replenish the funds that had been used. They did this by passing several Acts: the Sugar Act of 1764, which taxed refined sugar and molasses imported into the colonies; the Stamp Act, which required the colonists to pay a tax for stamps used on papers and documents and playing cards; and the Declaratory Act, which declared that Parliament had the same power over the colonies as in Great Britain. Taxes were placed on glass, paper, paint colors, and tea. The colonists complained intensely, and the British got rid of all taxes except the one on tea. This eventually led to the Boston Tea Party. [24]

(18) For depriving us in many cases, of the benefits of Trial by Jury:

Sandy's Note: The colonists had no recourse when accused of breaking the law because they did not have the privilege of being tried by a jury of their peers.

Example: There were many unfair matters that colonists took to court. Among the worst were the British Navigation Acts. Under these laws, only British-owned ships could bring imported goods to the colonies. Likewise, American businesses could only export goods using British ships. These ship owners charged enormous fees, and the British government handed the entire market to them. The colonists were at their mercy. After years of these abuses, Americans said no more. They used their own ships and traded with foreign countries and territories directly. British authorities arrested them, but colonial juries refused to convict. Great Britain responded by taking away the right to trial by jury—even though that right had been established in the 1215 Magna Carta and reaffirmed in the 1689 British Bill of Rights. The 1765 Stamp Act forced colonists who violated that law to appear in admiralty courts with no juries. Colonists issued a formal response to Parliament stating that "trial by jury is the inherent and invaluable right of every British subject of these colonies."[25]

(19) For transporting us beyond Seas to be tried for pretended offences.

Sandy's Note: The king would force the colonists to be taken far away to be tried for frivolous offenses.

Example: In 1774, Great Britain decided to use brute force to deal with the rebellious American colonies, particularly Massachusetts, due to the Boston Tea Party uprising. Parliament passed four acts, called the Coercive Acts. These quickly became known in America as the "Intolerable Acts" because they were perceived as being particularly cruel and severe. The Administration of Justice Act removed the colonists' ability to try British officials in the colonies. This bill also allowed the governor or the lieutenant governor to order colonists to be taken to another colony or Great Britain for trial.[26]

> (20) For abolishing the free System of English Laws in a neighbouring Province, establishing therein an Arbitrary government, and enlarging its Boundaries so as to render it at once an example and fit instrument for introducing the same absolute rule into these Colonies:

Sandy's Note: The Quebec Act of 1774 did away with the colonies' English system of government and set up an alternative system.

Example: The Quebec Act was a deliberate attempt on the part of British Parliament, ministry, and crown to overwhelm Americans with absolute power and control. The British Parliament did this by establishing the Catholic Church in Canada, extending that colony's territory into western lands, and instituting a civil government appointed by and serving at the pleasure of the Crown. John Adams declared that the Act was "not only unjust to the people in that Province, but dangerous to the interests of the Protestant Religion and of these Colonies."[27] The colonists feared that what the British government had done in Canada, it would do in America. This act is what solidified the Americans' resolve to move towards complete and total separation from Great Britain.

> (21) For taking away our Charters, abolishing our most valuable Laws, and altering fundamentally the Forms of our Governments:

Sandy's Note: The king changed their constitution and took away their ability to choose their own leaders.

Example: The Massachusetts Act, passed on May 20 of 1774, was one of the Coercive or "Intolerable" Acts. This act effectively restructured the Massachusetts government by giving the military governor, General Thomas Gage, the power to do away with the colony's charter. Colonial control over the government was diminished, and the king was given sole power to appoint and dismiss members of the Massachusetts Council, who were previously elected by the colonists with the governor's approval. Judges and county sheriffs were now chosen by the royal governor without the council's approval, and town meetings were forbidden unless the governor consented.[28]

> (22) For suspending our own Legislatures, and declaring themselves invested with power to legislate for us in all cases whatsoever.

Sandy's Note: This was another complaint about the colonists' legislatures being suspended and power conferred on royal governors to suspend colonial legislatures and enact royal proclamations that would then become law.

> (23) He has abdicated Government here, by declaring us out of his Protection and waging War against us.

Example: In October of 1775, King George addressed the opening of Parliament and declared the thirteen American colonies to be in open rebellion against the government and that he was committing British military forces to put down the rebellion. He basically declared war on the colonies, which meant he no longer recognized them as being under English rule or under the protection of English law.[29]

> (24) He has plundered our seas, ravaged our Coasts, burnt our towns, and destroyed the lives of our people.

Sandy's Note: Thomas Jefferson is referring to Thomas Paine's accusations of King George III's tyranny.

Example: King George declared war on the colonies. This complaint refers specifically to the burning of several American towns by British troops. The British considered the colonists in open rebellion against their lawful rulers. But for the colonists, their "lawful rulers" were the very colonial legislatures and town meetings that were declared closed by British decrees and under attack by British troops.[30]

> (25) He is at this time transporting large Armies of foreign Mercenaries to compleat the works of death, desolation and tyranny, already begun with circumstances of Cruelty & perfidy scarcely paralleled in the most barbarous ages, and totally unworthy the Head of a civilized nation.

Sandy's Note: This is referring to the treachery of King George III when he ordered his army and thirty thousand German mercenaries to crush the rebellion of the colonists.

Example: Early in 1776, King George consented to the hiring of thousands of Hessian (German) mercenaries to assist the British troops already in America in crushing the rebellion. The Revolutionary War lasted nearly eight years, largely because King George refused to surrender the colonies.[31]

> (26) He has constrained our fellow Citizens taken Captive on the high Seas to bear Arms against their Country, to become the executioners of their friends and Brethren, or to fall themselves by their Hands.

Sandy's Note: This complaint refers to how the British recruited the colonists into the navy by force, making them fight fellow colonists.

Example: In December 1775, the British Parliament passed a law which gave the British navy permission to capture ships and cargoes of other countries that traded with the American colonies, as if they were enemies of Great Britain. The law also said that anyone captured when these ships were taken was to be compelled to fight for the British, even though this meant that those captured would be fighting against their own countrymen.[32]

> (27) He has excited domestic insurrections amongst us, and has endeavoured to bring on the inhabitants of our frontiers, the merciless Indian Savages, whose known rule of warfare, is an undistinguished destruction of all ages, sexes and conditions.

Sandy's Note: King George III turned the colonists against each other, especially the Tories against the Patriots, and was now also using Native Americans against the colonists.

Example: In April 1775, John Murray, the Earl of Dunmore and Virginia's royal governor, threatened to free slaves and reduce the capital, Williamsburg, to ashes if the colonists rebelled against British authority. On November 7, 1775, Dunmore issued a proclamation that established martial law and offered freedom to slaves who would leave patriotic owners and join the British army: "I do hereby farther declare all indented servants, Negroes, or others (appertaining to rebels) free, that are able and willing to bear arms, they joining his Majesty's troops, as soon as may be, for the more speedily reducing this colony to a proper sense of their duty, to his Majesty's crown and dignity."[33]

> In every stage of these Oppressions We have Petitioned for Redress in the most humble terms: Our repeated Petitions have been answered only by repeated injury. A Prince whose character is thus marked by every act which may define a Tyrant, is unfit to be the ruler of a free people.

Sandy's Note: The colonists had tried to "humbly" petition their government many times but had been abused or ignored each time. They believed that any ruler who abused their people was not worthy to be their leader.

> Nor have We been wanting in attentions to our British brethren. We have warned them from time to time of attempts by their legislature to extend an unwarrantable jurisdiction over us. We have reminded them of the circumstances of our emigration and settlement here. We have appealed to their native justice and magnanimity, and we have conjured them by the ties of our common kindred to disavow these usurpations, which would inevitably interrupt our connections and correspondence. They too have been deaf to the voice of justice and of consanguinity. We must, therefore, acquiesce in the necessity, which denounces our Separation, and hold them, as we hold the rest of mankind, Enemies in War, in Peace Friends.

Sandy's Note: The colonists had done their part by letting the British citizens know about their concerns. They also reminded them why they had left Great Britain and that they had made a "clean break." They appealed to their common ties and reminded them that those ties would be broken if they didn't acknowledge their requests. They were ignored, so they had no other choice but to separate.

> We, therefore, the Representatives of the United States of America, in General Congress, Assembled, appealing to the Supreme Judge of the world for the rectitude of our intentions, do, in the Name, and by Authority of the good People of these Colonies, solemnly publish and declare, That these United Colonies are, and of Right ought to be Free and Independent States; that they are Absolved from

all Allegiance to the British Crown, and that all political connection between them and the State of Great Britain, is and ought to be totally dissolved; and that as Free and Independent States, they have full Power to levy War, conclude Peace, contract Alliances, establish Commerce, and to do all other Acts and Things which Independent States may of right do. And for the support of this Declaration, with a firm reliance on the protection of divine Providence, we mutually pledge to each other our Lives, our Fortunes and our sacred Honor.[34]

Sandy's Note: They declared who was writing the letter and that they had written it prayerfully on the authority and in the name of the people of the Colonies. They declared they had a right to be free and absolved themselves from any allegiance or obligation to the British king. They declared their freedom and ability to do all things that any other free state or country might lawfully do. They then signed their names, knowing the consequences could bring death.

So, there you have it, the first formal document of the United States of America.

What are some significant thoughts to take away from this important document?

- Individual human dignity and rights are given by God, not man.
- These principles and rights are applicable to all humankind, not just Americans.
- These principles are permanent and applicable throughout time.
- The government must be responsive and accountable to its citizens.
- The government should never be allowed to impose hardships, burdens, or limitations on its people without the consent of the governed.
- The people need to have representation.
- Citizens should always be able to challenge and address the government when they have a grievance against those who govern them.
- When the government abuses its citizens, they have a right to throw off that oppressive government if it does not hear or fix the abuse.

- Long-standing governments should not be changed for insignificant or temporary reasons.
- People will often tolerate the suffering and abuse from their government rather than throw it off because they are used to it.
- The Declaration accuses King George III and exposes his specific abuses of the colonists.
- It details how the king tried to control all aspects of society for the colonists, from controlling the law to disbanding their legislatures, which removed representation, to taking the citizens' personal property to use as he saw fit. He wanted to have the final say in every situation.
- It declares that the United States would have the power to declare war, negotiate peace, form alliances, establish commerce, and do all other acts and things that independent states have a right to do.
- It declared absolute independence from any power that would seek to control them.
- It shows the serious dedication and commitment of the men who signed this document; they believed in it so much that they were willing to risk everything for it to succeed.

When King George III received the Declaration of Independence from the Colonists, he responded in this manner:

- He referred to the colonists as "my colonies," "my kingdoms," and "my subjects";
- Accused the colonists of treason and "arbitrary tyranny";
- Dismissed the Declaration as a trivial document issued by disgruntled colonists;
- Praised the British victory over General George Washington at the Battle of Long Island;
- Warned that the British needed to prepare for another campaign;
- Reassured Parliament that England was still united; and

- Ended his speech by singing his own praises, saying, "No people ever enjoyed more Happiness, or lived under a milder Government, then those now revolted Provinces."

Once again, the king ignored the colonies. To him, they were an annoyance and inconvenience.

King George III elevated himself above everyone else as if he were different from all other humans, but the Colonists believed, as stated in the Declaration, that "all men are created equal and endowed by their Creator with certain unalienable rights," and they were no longer willing to endure tyranny.

The Declaration of Independence was written by a determined and desperate people who yearned to be free from the tyranny and oppression of a king who cared nothing for their well-being. Its writing was the catalyst for and the beginning of the greatest nation mankind has ever known! The main purpose of the Declaration of Independence was to present a compelling case that King George III and the British Parliament were tyrants and lawbreakers and that they had left the American colonists no choice but to throw off the British rule. While this declaration sparked war and many battles over America's right to exist separate from Britain, our Founding Fathers prevailed.

As you read the grievances our ancestors endured, did you notice offenses similar to what our government imposes on us today? As you continue to read this book, you may want to give it more thought.

A king's terrible wrath is like the roaring of a lion; anyone who provokes him endangers himself.

Proverbs 20:2

Part Two: The Constitution

The Constitution is not an instrument for the government to restrain the people but for the people to restrain the government.

Patrick Henry, Governor of Virginia from 1776–1779 and 1784–1786

The Founding Fathers had taken a bold stand against the king and now needed to create a new system of government so that their new freedoms could survive.

The first system was called the Articles of Confederation.[35] This document was the United States' first constitution. The Continental Congress adopted the Articles of Confederation on November 15, 1777. It was in force from March 1, 1781, until 1789, when the Constitution was enacted.[36] However, this document had many weaknesses that hindered the central government from getting anything done because of its limited powers over states or individuals in America. Weaknesses of the Articles of Confederation included

- No central leadership (executive branch);
- Congress had no power to enforce its laws;
- Congress had no power to tax;
- Congress had no power to regulate trade;
- No national court system (judicial branch); and
- Changes to the Articles required the unanimous consent of the thirteen states.[37]

These weaknesses motivated the Founding Fathers to write the Constitution, which was not easy, since it did require the cooperation of all thirteen states. The main goal for writing the Constitution was to create a government with enough power to act on a national level, but without so much power that fundamental rights would be at risk.

Finally, after much pleading with state leaders, the Framers of the United States Constitution (a group of authorized delegates) met in Philadelphia between May and September at the Constitutional Convention of 1787 and wrote the

Constitution of the United States. The delegates were a diverse group, including lawyers, planters, merchants, and physicians. These are some of the key delegates:

James Madison

Known as the "father of the Constitution," Madison was a driving force behind the convention and wrote the first ten amendments.

Gouverneur Morris

A skilled writer, politician, and diplomat, Morris wrote the Preamble to the Constitution, including the famous phrase "We the People of the United States." He also drafted the final version of the Constitution.

George Mason

Although he was one of only three delegates not to sign the Constitution, he had a unique role in its creation. He was deeply concerned with the amount of power being given to the federal government and said "I would sooner chop off my right hand" than sign the Constitution without a Bill of Rights, which was later ratified in the Constitution in 1791.[38]

Other delegates included Alexander Hamilton, John Jay, and James Wilson. On September 17, 1787, thirty-nine of the fifty-five delegates signed the Constitution. In 1788, this document replaced the Articles of Confederation and created a strong central government that still exists today.

So, what did our Founding Fathers give us in the Constitution, and why is it important for us to read and understand it today? To answer those questions, we need to read it and break it down.

In Part Two of "The Founding Fathers Design," you will find the complete Constitution with its twenty-seven amendments. This document has been America's guide since it went into effect in 1789.[39] It is significant to note that the United States Constitution is the world's longest-surviving written charter of government.

The Constitution of the United States

We the People of the United States, in Order to form a more perfect Union, establish Justice, ensure domestic Tranquility, provide for the common defense, promote the general Welfare, and secure the Blessings of Liberty to ourselves and our Posterity, do ordain and establish this Constitution for the United States of America.

Sandy's Note: Why did our Founding Fathers write the Constitution?

1. To "form a more perfect union," that is, to improve and strengthen the government they had formed: The Founding Fathers were united around some important principles that we will look at together.

2. To "establish justice," that is the judicial system, which the Founding Fathers designed to ensure equal justice for all people.

3. To ensure "domestic tranquility": The framers of our Constitution wanted their families and every citizen to live in peace without the oppression of abusive government.

4. To "provide for the common defense": The Founders wanted safety and security for all Americans, which would involve having a common military force that would protect all the colonies.

5. To "promote the general welfare": Dr. Larry P. Arnn, President of Hillsdale College, made the following statement about the meaning of this phrase:

The great Preamble of our Constitution states that the purpose of the document is, in part, to promote the general welfare. Contrary to the modern understanding of that term, the Founders understood welfare to mean public good or happiness. This was understood in accordance with the principles of the Declaration of Independence. Such happiness is contingent on securing to each citizen his natural rights to life, liberty, and the pursuit of happiness. Because this requires the government to be limited, the powers of the federal government were enumerated, and local matters were reserved to State authority. This was precisely intended to secure these inalienable rights and, in turn, promote the general welfare.[40]

Article. I.

Section. 1.

All legislative Powers herein granted shall be vested in a Congress of the United States, which shall consist of a Senate and House of Representatives.

Sandy's Note: Congress (the House and Senate) was created and given authority to establish laws.

Section. 2.

The House of Representatives shall be composed of Members chosen every second Year by the People of the several States, and the Electors in each State shall have the Qualifications requisite for Electors of the most numerous Branch of the State Legislature.

Sandy's Note: Every two years the citizens of the states selected their congressional representatives, and the state legislators selected the senators.

No Person shall be a Representative who shall not have attained to the Age of twenty-five years and been seven Years a Citizen of the

United States, and who shall not, when elected, be an Inhabitant of that State in which he shall be chosen.

Sandy's Note: A Representative must be at least twenty-five years of age to be elected, a citizen of the United States for seven years, and live in the state where they are elected.

> Representatives and direct Taxes shall be apportioned among the several States which may be included within this Union, according to their respective Numbers, which shall be determined by adding to the whole Number of free Persons, including those bound to Service for a Term of Years, and excluding Indians not taxed, three fifths of all other Persons.

Sandy's Note: Representatives and taxes were to be determined by the number of people in each state, which included, at the time, free people and people who were "bound to service" but would be free by the next census (and would therefore be allowed to vote).

The Constitution excluded the "Indians not taxed" because most Native Americans had nothing to do with the new nation except to trade with it. They were excluded from a state's population because they weren't US citizens, couldn't vote, and didn't pay taxes.

The phrase "three-fifths of all other persons" addresses the issue of the slave population:

> The three-fifths figure came from a debate that had taken place within the Continental Congress in 1783. The Articles of Confederation had apportioned taxes not according to population but according to land values. The states consistently undervalued their land to reduce their tax burden. To rectify this situation, a special committee recommended apportioning taxes by population. The Continental Congress debated the ratio of slaves to free persons at great length. Northerners favored a 4-to-3 ratio, while southerners favored a 2-to-1 or 4-to-1 ratio. Finally, James Madison suggested a compromise: a 5-to-3 ratio. All but two states—New Hampshire and Rhode Island—approved this recommendation. But because the Articles of Confederation

required unanimous agreement, the proposal was defeated. When the Constitutional Convention met in 1787, it adopted Madison's earlier suggestion.[41]

> The actual Enumeration shall be made within three Years after the first Meeting of the Congress of the United States, and within every subsequent Term of ten Years, in such Manner as they shall by Law direct.

Sandy's Note: The Constitution requires a census be taken every ten years. This was and is done to determine each state's number of representatives. Many times, congressional district maps are redrawn because of population growth, and sometimes a state may add or lose representatives.

> The Number of Representatives shall not exceed one for every thirty Thousand, but each State shall have at Least one Representative; and until such enumeration shall be made, the State of New Hampshire shall be entitled to chuse three, Massachusetts eight, Rhode-Island and Providence Plantations one, Connecticut five, New-York six, New Jersey four, Pennsylvania eight, Delaware one, Maryland six, Virginia ten, North Carolina five, South Carolina five, and Georgia three.

Sandy's Note: These numbers were determined for the states and their populations at the time of the writing of the Constitution. We now have fifty states with 435 Congressional seats and 100 Senate seats. Each Congressional member now represents approximately seven hundred thousand constituents, and each Senator represents the entire state.

There are also six "non-voting" members of Congress called *delegates* or *resident commissioners*. The delegates represent the District of Columbia, American Samoa, Guam, the Northern Mariana Islands, and the US Virgin Islands. Puerto Rico is represented by a Resident Commissioner.

The non-voting members do not vote on legislation but have floor privileges and participate in other House functions. They may vote in a House committee of which they are a member and introduce legislation.

> When vacancies happen in the Representation from any State, the Executive Authority thereof shall issue Writs of Election to fill such Vacancies.

Sandy's Note: This describes how vacancies are to be handled. A vacancy could be for many reasons: death, resignation, crime committed by the representative, etc. When a Congressional member vacates his seat, the governor of the state represented writes an order to hold a special election.

> The House of Representatives shall chuse their Speaker and other Officers; and shall have the sole Power of Impeachment.

Section. 3.

> The Senate of the United States shall be composed of two Senators from each State, chosen by the Legislature thereof, for six Years; and each Senator shall have one Vote.

Sandy's Note: This was the original rule of the Constitution that was changed in the 17th Amendment. The Senators are now elected by the people. There are differing opinions to whether this was a good amendment or not. Senators were originally chosen by their state's legislature so there would be representation of the state, while the Representative was a direct representative of the people.

> Immediately after they shall be assembled in Consequence of the first Election, they shall be divided as equally as may be into three Classes. The Seats of the Senators of the first Class shall be vacated at the Expiration of the second Year, of the second Class at the Expiration of the fourth Year, and of the third Class at the Expiration of the sixth Year, so that one third may be chosen every second Year; and if Vacancies happen by Resignation, or otherwise, during the Recess of the Legislature of any State, the Executive thereof may make temporary Appointments until the next Meeting of the Legislature, which shall then fill such Vacancies.

Sandy's Note: This section describes how the first elected Senate was divided into three classes and how the seats were vacated at different times, so the entire

Senate would not change at the same time. Of the original Senate, the first class served two years, the second class four years, and the third class six years. Two years after the initial Senate was elected, the first class was up for reelection or contest. The winners of that election and every subsequent election until now have been elected for a six-year term. This section also describes how vacancies are to be handled: when a senator vacates his seat, the governor of the state represented makes a temporary appointment to fill the seat until the next election.

> No Person shall be a Senator who shall not have attained to the Age of thirty Years and been nine Years a Citizen of the United States, and who shall not, when elected, be an Inhabitant of that State for which he shall be chosen.

> The Vice President of the United States shall be President of the Senate, but shall have no Vote, unless they be equally divided. The Senate shall chuse their other Officers, and also a President pro tempore, in the Absence of the Vice President, or when he shall exercise the Office of President of the United States.

Sandy's Note: This section explains the leadership structure of the Senate.

> The Senate shall have the sole Power to try all Impeachments. When sitting for that Purpose, they shall be on Oath or Affirmation. When the President of the United States is tried, the Chief Justice shall preside: And no Person shall be convicted without the Concurrence of two thirds of the Members present.

Sandy's Note: If the Senate is called upon to try an impeachment, the function and leadership structure of the Senate changes.

> Judgment in Cases of Impeachment shall not extend further than to removal from Office, and disqualification to hold and enjoy any Office of honor, Trust or Profit under the United States: but the Party convicted shall nevertheless be liable and subject to Indictment, Trial, Judgment and Punishment, according to Law.

Sandy's Note: We have seen impeachments played out with former president Donald Trump and most recently Secretary Alejandro Mayorkas. Reminder:

President Trump was impeached in the House and tried and acquitted (found not guilty) in the Senate. Secretary Myorkas was impeached in the House, but the Senate Majority Leader Chuck Schumer refused to bring the impeachment to trial.

Section. 4.

The Times, Places and Manner of holding Elections for Senators and Representatives, shall be prescribed in each State by the Legislature thereof; but the Congress may at any time by Law make or alter such Regulations, except as to the Places of chusing Senators.

Sandy's Note: The Constitution generally gives the states the power and authority to hold and manage their own elections.

The Congress shall assemble at least once in every Year, and such Meeting shall be on the first Monday in December, unless they shall by Law appoint a different Day.

Sandy's Note: These guidelines have since been modified from a part-time legislature to a full-time legislature due to the growth of our country. Today, each new Congress begins at noon on January 3 of each odd year, following a general election, unless it designates a different day by law.

Section. 5.

Each House shall be the Judge of the Elections, Returns and Qualifications of its own Members, and a Majority of each shall constitute a Quorum to do Business; but a smaller Number may adjourn from day to day, and may be authorized to compel the Attendance of absent Members, in such Manner, and under such Penalties as each House may provide.

Each House may determine the Rules of its Proceedings, punish its Members for disorderly Behaviour, and, with the Concurrence of two thirds, expel a Member.

Sandy's Note: Expelling a member is a serious thing and should not be done lightly. The people of each state elect the representative of their choosing, and Congress should not have sole power to choose on the people's behalf! However, the framers of the Constitution obviously foresaw there might be a need for Congress to expel a member, though it requires two-thirds of the members to do so. A recent example of this was when Congress expelled Representative George Santos of New York's 3rd District on December 1, 2023, because of charges that were brought against him. There are differing opinions about this decision because Rep. Santos had not been convicted but only charged with the crimes.

> Each House shall keep a Journal of its Proceedings, and from time to time publish the same, excepting such Parts as may in their Judgment require Secrecy; and the Yeas and Nays of the Members of either House on any question shall, at the Desire of one fifth of those Present, be entered on the Journal.

> Neither House, during the Session of Congress, shall, without the Consent of the other, adjourn for more than three days, nor to any other Place than that in which the two Houses shall be sitting.

Sandy's Note: Here we have basic rules and processes for both houses of Congress.

Section. 6.

> The Senators and Representatives shall receive a Compensation for their Services, to be ascertained by Law, and paid out of the Treasury of the United States. They shall in all Cases, except Treason, Felony and Breach of the Peace, be privileged from Arrest during their Attendance at the Session of their respective Houses, and in going to and returning from the same; and for any Speech or Debate in either House, they shall not be questioned in any other Place.

Sandy's Note: The section specifies privileges for members. The Supreme Court has interpreted this provision that the phrase "treason, felony, and breach of the peace" encompasses all criminal offenses. Consequently, members are only privileged from arrests arising from civil suits, which were common in America at the time the Constitution was ratified. This rule was instituted because, when a Representative is withdrawn from his seat by a summons, the people he represents lose their voice in debate and vote (as they do in his voluntary absence).[42]

No Senator or Representative shall, during the Time for which he was elected, be appointed to any civil Office under the Authority of the United States, which shall have been created, or the Emoluments whereof shall have been encreased during such time; and no Person holding any Office under the United States, shall be a Member of either House during his Continuance in Office.

Sandy's Note: This section above contains the Incompatibility and Ineligibility Clauses. The Incompatibility Clause forbids concurrent officeholding, and the Ineligibility Clause forbids a member of Congress from being appointed to a federal office that was created during his term and from having their compensation increased by a law passed during his term. The late US Supreme Court Justice Antonin Scalia explained it this way: "The Framers' experience with post-revolutionary self-government had taught them that combining the power to create offices with the power to appoint officers was a recipe for legislative corruption. The foremost danger was that the legislators would create offices with the expectancy of occupying them themselves. This was guarded against by the Incompatibility and Ineligibility Clauses."[43]

Section. 7.

All Bills for raising Revenue shall originate in the House of Representatives; but the Senate may propose or concur with Amendments as on other Bills.

Every Bill which shall have passed the House of Representatives and the Senate, shall, before it become a Law, be presented to the President of the United States; If he approve he shall sign it, but if not he shall return it, with his Objections to that House in which it shall have originated, who shall enter the Objections at large on their Journal, and proceed to reconsider it. If after such Reconsideration two thirds of that House shall agree to pass the Bill, it shall be sent, together with the Objections, to the other House, by which it shall likewise be reconsidered, and if approved by two thirds of that House, it shall become a Law. But in all such Cases the Votes of both Houses shall be determined by yeas and Nays, and the Names of the Persons voting for and against the Bill shall be entered on the

Journal of each House respectively. If any Bill shall not be returned by the President within ten Days (Sundays excepted) after it shall have been presented to him, the Same shall be a Law, in like Manner as if he had signed it, unless the Congress by their Adjournment prevent its Return, in which Case it shall not be a Law.

Every Order, Resolution, or Vote to which the Concurrence of the Senate and House of Representatives may be necessary (except on a question of Adjournment) shall be presented to the President of the United States; and before the Same shall take Effect, shall be approved by him, or being disapproved by him, shall be repassed by two thirds of the Senate and House of Representatives, according to the Rules and Limitations prescribed in the Case of a Bill.

Sandy's Note: This section speaks to the process by which legislation involving revenue is made. The Framers wanted all revenue bills to begin in the House to ensure that the power of the purse would lie with the legislative body closest to the people. Every order, resolution, or vote that is not approved by the President must be repassed by two-thirds of the House and the Senate before it goes into effect. This is a check and balance to prevent one man, the President, from cancelling out laws that representatives of the people present to him. However, if the President vetoes a bill, it must go back to the House and Senate and pass by two-thirds vote to be passed into law.

Section. 8.

Sandy's Note: Article I Section 8 lists all the specific powers given to Congress. This list is long, and as we go through it you will see that Congress has managed it poorly.

The Congress shall have Power To lay and collect Taxes, Duties, Imposts and Excises, to pay the Debts and provide for the common defense and general Welfare of the United States; but all Duties, Imposts and Excises shall be uniform throughout the United States;

Sandy's Note: This is where Congress gets its power to collect taxes from us.

To borrow Money on the credit of the United States;

Sandy's Note: Unfortunately, our government has almost borrowed our country "over the cliff." We now have almost thirty-five trillion dollars of debt to pass to our children and grandchildren! We must hold our Representatives accountable for this.

> To regulate Commerce with foreign Nations, and among the several States, and with the Indian Tribes;
>
> To establish an uniform Rule of Naturalization, and uniform Laws on the subject of Bankruptcies throughout the United States;

Sandy's Note: We must address our immigration problem immediately. Our country is being overwhelmed because of our open borders and broken immigration system. We are a country of immigrants, but we have always had law and order for how we allow people to come into our country. I can't think of another country in the world today that allows unfettered access to their country with the promise of provisions of money, phones, lodging, education, healthcare, and more, with little to *no* vetting of the people coming in. We don't leave our personal home doors open for anyone to come in, day or night! That privilege is reserved for those we trust and allow into our homes. I blame the Administration and Congress for this massive and dangerous problem, since the President takes the responsibility and oath to defend the Constitution, and members of Congress take an oath to defend the Constitution against all enemies both foreign and domestic. The Constitution is what provides us with our rights and protections. Our government *must* defend and protect it!

The Framers addressed bankruptcy to ensure that someone who had filed bankruptcy in one state to discharge their debts could not be put in prison in another state for not paying their debt. Congress did work quickly to enact federal bankruptcy laws. The first bankruptcy law was passed in 1800. There have been many changes since then, but the last significant change was in 2005.

> To coin Money, regulate the Value thereof, and of foreign Coin, and fix the Standard of Weights and Measures;

Sandy's Note: These are very broad powers that were given to Congress. It makes for an interesting read if you want to research it.

> To provide for the Punishment of counterfeiting the Securities and current Coin of the United States;
>
> To establish Post Offices and post Roads;

Sandy's Note: The Post Office had actually been established by the Continental Congress on July 26, 1775, so it is older than America itself. It was permanently established by the Postal Service Act of February 20, 1792, and signed into law by President George Washington.

> To promote the Progress of Science and useful Arts, by securing for limited Times to Authors and Inventors the exclusive Right to their respective Writings and Discoveries;

Sandy's Note: This clause is what brought about the US Patent and Copyright systems. Creators of scientific discoveries and art were granted a monopoly for a limited time, after which it would become free to all citizens, enriching the public domain.

> To constitute Tribunals inferior to the supreme Court;

Sandy's Note: This refers to the establishment of the lower federal courts subordinate to the Supreme Court of the United States. The inferior courts are put in place by Congress to adjudicate cases across the nation, but if a person believes their constitutional rights were violated in the inferior court, they can appeal to a higher court. A recent example was *Masterpiece Cakeshop v. Colorado Civil Rights Commission* in 2018, when owner Jack Phillips declined to do a wedding cake for a gay couple's wedding due to his deeply held religious beliefs.

> To define and punish Piracies and Felonies committed on the high Seas, and Offences against the Law of Nations;

Sandy's Note: This statement refers to international law and the crime of piracy, as well as the set of rules or normal standards that countries feel an obligation to obey in their mutual relationships.

> To declare War, grant Letters of Marque and Reprisal, and make Rules concerning Captures on Land and Water;

Sandy's Note: This is one of the enumerated powers that I find very interesting. The Constitution clearly gave the power to declare war to Congress and yet, while we have had many conflicts and our men and women have gone to war and some are still overseas fighting, a war has not been declared since 1942 when President Franklin D. Roosevelt declared war against Hungary, Bulgaria, and Romania. Since that time, every American president has used military force without a declaration of war. Some argue that if Congress authorizes funding, that is the same as a declaration of war, but it is clear in the Constitution that Congress must declare war, not the President. Incidentally, all the wars that Congress has declared, we have won. Of all the wars we've engaged in without a declaration—I will let you decide if we've won those wars.

> To raise and support Armies, but no Appropriation of Money to that Use shall be for a longer Term than two Years;

Sandy's Note: Congress is responsible to support our military by providing for them so that they will always be ready to defend our country.

> To provide and maintain a Navy;

> To make Rules for the Government and Regulation of the land and naval Forces;

Sandy's Note: The Supreme Court recognized that "The military is, by necessity, a specialized society separate from civilian society and is governed by a separate discipline from that of the civilian."[44] It also recognizes that "Congress is permitted to legislate with greater breadth and with greater flexibility when prescribing the rules by which the Military society will be governed than it is when prescribing rules for civilian society."[45] That doesn't mean they are free to disregard the Constitution.

> To provide for calling forth the Militia to execute the Laws of the Union, suppress Insurrections and repel Invasions;

> To provide for organizing, arming, and disciplining, the Militia, and for governing such Part of them as may be employed in the Service of the United States, reserving to the States respectively, the Appointment of the Officers, and the Authority of training the Militia according to the discipline prescribed by Congress;

To exercise exclusive Legislation in all Cases whatsoever, over such District (not exceeding ten Miles square) as may, by Cession of particular States, and the Acceptance of Congress, become the Seat of the Government of the United States, and to exercise like Authority over all Places purchased by the Consent of the Legislature of the State in which the Same shall be, for the Erection of Forts, Magazines, Arsenals, dock-Yards, and other needful Buildings;

Sandy's Note: After exclusive jurisdiction over lands within a state has been ceded (given) to the US, Congress alone has the power to punish crimes committed within the ceded territory. Private property located on the ceded land is not subject to taxation by the state. The local laws that were in force when the land was ceded that protect private rights continue in force until done away with by Congress.[46]

To make all Laws which shall be necessary and proper for carrying into Execution the foregoing Powers, and all other Powers vested by this Constitution in the Government of the United States, or in any Department or Officer thereof.

Sandy's Note: Finally, the Framers chose to follow the Articles by listing specific federal powers as opposed to giving Congress "general federal power." They included the Necessary and Proper Clause to make it clear that, as long as Congress stays within the scope and power given to it under the Constitution, it is authorized to employ any means appropriate to accomplish its task.

Section. 9.

The Migration or Importation of such Persons as any of the States now existing shall think proper to admit, shall not be prohibited by the Congress prior to the Year one thousand eight hundred and eight, but a Tax or duty may be imposed on such Importation, not exceeding ten dollars for each Person.

Sandy's Note: Article I Section 9 addresses the migration or importation of "such persons," which was understood at the time to mean primarily enslaved African persons. Congress was not allowed to prohibit this where the existing government allowed it, although they said they may impose a tax of no more than ten dollars per person on this activity.

> The Privilege of the Writ of Habeas Corpus shall not be suspended, unless when in Cases of Rebellion or Invasion the public Safety may require it.

Sandy's Note: The privilege of habeas corpus is used to bring a prisoner or other detainee (such as a mental patient) before the court to determine if their imprisonment or detention is lawful. Habeas corpus was originated in 1215 by the 39th clause in the Magna Carta. In 1789, James Madison argued for the Bill of Rights, including habeas corpus.[47]

> No Bill of Attainder or ex post facto Law shall be passed.

Sandy's Note: A Bill of Attainder is a law that imposes criminal liability or increases a criminal punishment retroactively. This is not allowed.

> No Capitation, or other direct, Tax shall be laid, unless in Proportion to the Census or enumeration herein before directed to be taken.

Sandy's Note: This clause prohibited any taxation on individuals, but this was later modified in the 16th Amendment.

> No Tax or Duty shall be laid on Articles exported from any State.

> No Preference shall be given by any Regulation of Commerce or Revenue to the Ports of one State over those of another: nor shall Vessels bound to, or from, one State, be obliged to enter, clear, or pay Duties in another.

Sandy's Note: Discrimination between individual ports is prohibited. Under the Commerce Clause, Congress may do many things that benefit particular ports, such as establishing ports of entry, erecting and operating lighthouses, improving rivers and harbors, and providing structures for the convenient and economical handling of traffic. Also, goods cannot be taxed that are exported from a state to foreign countries or from one state to another state.

No Money shall be drawn from the Treasury, but in Consequence of Appropriations made by Law; and a regular Statement and Account of the Receipts and Expenditures of all public Money shall be published from time to time.

Sandy's Note: The restriction on drawing money from the Treasury was a restriction on the executive branch to prevent them from paying any money out unless it had been approved by Congress.[48]

No Title of Nobility shall be granted by the United States: And no Person holding any Office of Profit or Trust under them, shall, without the Consent of the Congress, accept of any present, Emolument, Office, or Title, of any kind whatever, from any King, Prince, or foreign State.

Sandy's Note: This clause is often referred to as the Title of Nobility Clause, which forbids the United States from conferring titles such as prince or knight on any person. The second half, referred to as the Foreign Emoluments Clause, prohibits certain federal officers from accepting any salary, fees, payments, or honors from any foreign leader or state without approval from Congress.[49]

Section. 10.

No State shall enter into any Treaty, Alliance, or Confederation; grant Letters of Marque and Reprisal; coin Money; emit Bills of Credit; make any Thing but gold and silver Coin a Tender in Payment of Debts; pass any Bill of Attainder, ex post facto Law, or Law impairing the Obligation of Contracts, or grant any Title of Nobility.

Sandy's Note: In this clause we find a diverse list of prohibitions on the power of the states, just as we saw prohibitions put on Congress in the previous section. This statement guarantees that matters of war and diplomacy belong primarily or exclusively to the national government. The states are prohibited from forming compacts with foreign nations or with each other without the permission of Congress.

No State shall, without the Consent of the Congress, lay any Imposts or Duties on Imports or Exports, except what may be absolutely necessary for executing [its] inspection Laws: and the net Produce of all Duties and Imposts, laid by any State on Imports or Exports, shall be for the Use of the Treasury of the United States; and all such Laws shall be subject to the Revision and Controul of the Congress.

Sandy's Note: The Import-Export Clause was designed to limit the states' ability to interfere with commerce. For that reason, the States are prohibited from imposing taxes on imports and exports without congressional consent.

No State shall, without the Consent of Congress, lay any Duty of Tonnage, keep Troops, or Ships of War in time of Peace, enter into any Agreement or Compact with another State, or with a foreign Power, or engage in War, unless actually invaded, or in such imminent Danger as will not admit of delay.

Sandy's Note: This clause, again, prohibits states from engaging in matters of war and diplomacy without Congressional consent unless there is imminent danger. A good example of this today is how Texas and the federal government are suing each other over the border issue. Governor Greg Abbott believes the millions of people coming across the border is an "imminent threat of disaster for a number of Texas counties and state agencies."[50] He is fighting the federal government because he believes it is not doing its job to protect the American people living there. He recently renewed his declaration of disaster in June 2024 for sixty-one counties and for all state agencies affected by this disaster.

Article. II.

Section. 1.

The executive Power shall be vested in a President of the United States of America. He shall hold his Office during the Term of four Years, and, together with the Vice President, chosen for the same Term, be elected, as follows:

Sandy's Note: The executive power consists of the authority to enforce laws and to "appoint the agents charged with the duty of such enforcement."[51] Generally, the US Supreme Court has recognized that the Constitution contains not only expressed authority for the President but also implied authorities. Those include the ability to supervise and remove executive officials and the power to recognize foreign governments. The President is not a lawmaker.

> Each State shall appoint, in such Manner as the Legislature thereof may direct, a Number of Electors, equal to the whole Number of Senators and Representatives to which the State may be entitled in the Congress: but no Senator or Representative, or Person holding an Office of Trust or Profit under the United States, shall be appointed an Elector.
>
> The Electors shall meet in their respective States, and vote by Ballot for two Persons, of whom one at least shall not be an Inhabitant of the same State with themselves. And they shall make a List of all the Persons voted for, and of the Number of Votes for each; which List they shall sign and certify, and transmit sealed to the Seat of the Government of the United States, directed to the President of the Senate. The President of the Senate shall, in the Presence of the Senate and House of Representatives, open all the Certificates, and the Votes shall then be counted. The Person having the greatest Number of Votes shall be the President, if such Number be a Majority of the whole Number of Electors appointed; and if there be more than one who have such Majority, and have an equal Number of Votes, then the House of Representatives shall immediately chuse by Ballot one of them for President; and if no Person have a Majority, then from the five highest on the List the said House shall in like Manner chuse the President. But in chusing the President, the Votes shall be taken by States, the Representation from each State having one Vote; A quorum for this Purpose shall consist of a Member or Members from two thirds of the States, and a Majority of all the States shall be necessary to a Choice. In every Case, after the Choice of the President, the Person having the greatest Number of Votes of the Electors shall be the Vice President. But if there should remain two or more who

have equal Votes, the Senate shall chuse from them by Ballot the Vice President.

The Congress may determine the Time of chusing the Electors, and the Day on which they shall give their Votes; which Day shall be the same throughout the United States.

No Person except a natural born Citizen, or a Citizen of the United States, at the time of the Adoption of this Constitution, shall be eligible to the Office of President; neither shall any Person be eligible to that Office who shall not have attained to the Age of thirty five Years, and been fourteen Years a Resident within the United States.

In Case of the Removal of the President from Office, or of his Death, Resignation, or Inability to discharge the Powers and Duties of the said Office, the Same shall devolve on the Vice President, and the Congress may by Law provide for the Case of Removal, Death, Resignation or Inability, both of the President and Vice President, declaring what Officer shall then act as President, and such Officer shall act accordingly, until the Disability be removed, or a President shall be elected.

The President shall, at stated Times, receive for his Services, a Compensation, which shall neither be encreased nor diminished during the Period for which he shall have been elected, and he shall not receive within that Period any other Emolument from the United States, or any of them.

Before he enter on the Execution of his Office, he shall take the following Oath or Affirmation:—"I do solemnly swear (or affirm) that I will faithfully execute the Office of President of the United States, and will to the best of my Ability, preserve, protect and defend the Constitution of the United States."

Sandy's Note: The remainder of Article II Section 1 covers the election of the President, including the establishment of the Electoral College. There are those today who would love to do away with the Electoral College and just have a popular vote. The Framers of our Constitution had robust debate about this as well. Many suggestions, such as the popular vote, were thrown out because they believed that people would tend to support candidates from their own states, which would give an advantage to the larger states, and might cause a few areas with higher populations of voters to dominate. James Madison spoke well of the idea of an Electoral College, believing that there would be very little opportunity for corruption with that system. The plan was presented on September 4 and adopted with minor changes. It is found in Article II, Section 1 of the Constitution and has worked well for nearly 250 years.[52]

Section. 2.

> The President shall be Commander in Chief of the Army and Navy of the United States, and of the Militia of the several States, when called into the actual Service of the United States; he may require the Opinion, in writing, of the principal Officer in each of the executive Departments, upon any Subject relating to the Duties of their respective Offices, and he shall have Power to grant Reprieves and Pardons for Offences against the United States, except in Cases of Impeachment.
>
> He shall have Power, by and with the Advice and Consent of the Senate, to make Treaties, provided two thirds of the Senators present concur; and he shall nominate, and by and with the Advice and Consent of the Senate, shall appoint Ambassadors, other public Ministers and Consuls, Judges of the supreme Court, and all other Officers of the United States, whose Appointments are not herein otherwise provided for, and which shall be established by Law: but the Congress may by Law vest the Appointment of such inferior Officers, as they think proper, in the President alone, in the Courts of Law, or in the Heads of Departments.
>
> The President shall have Power to fill up all Vacancies that may happen during the Recess of the Senate, by granting Commissions which shall expire at the End of their next Session.

Sandy's Note: The President commands the army, navy and militia. The Commander in Chief Clause gives the President the exclusive power to command the military in operations approved by Congress. (A more difficult question is how much authority the Clause gives the President beyond operations approved by Congress.) Presidents have claimed authority over a range of military actions, such as attacking pirates, rescuing US citizens abroad, and making military deployments. He has the power to grant pardons or cancel punishment for those who have committed crimes against the United States. With permission of two thirds of the Senate, he can make treaties and appoint ambassadors, federal judges, US marshals, attorneys, and members and heads of independent agencies.

Section. 3.

> He shall from time to time give to the Congress Information of the State of the Union, and recommend to their Consideration such Measures as he shall judge necessary and expedient; he may, on extraordinary Occasions, convene both Houses, or either of them, and in Case of Disagreement between them, with Respect to the Time of Adjournment, he may adjourn them to such Time as he shall think proper; he shall receive Ambassadors and other public Ministers; he shall take Care that the Laws be faithfully executed, and shall Commission all the Officers of the United States.

Sandy's Note: This section addresses additional responsibilities and privileges of the President. We are all familiar with the State of the Union address given by our many Presidents over the years. They are attended by many special guests with much clapping and pomp and circumstance. The first State of the Union was given on January 8, 1790, by President George Washington in the first year of his first term before a joint session of Congress in New York City. His speech was the shortest of any President, speaking only 1089 words. He outlined his priorities and what he wanted the House and the Senate to carefully consider: funding the common defense, challenges presented by "hostile" Native Americans, the need to build new roads, and the importance of a uniformed currency.[53]

Section. 4.

> The President, Vice President and all civil Officers of the United States, shall be removed from Office on Impeachment for,

and Conviction of, Treason, Bribery, or other high Crimes and Misdemeanors.

Sandy's Note: This section simply addresses what happens when the President, Vice President, or any civil officer of the United States is convicted of treason, bribery, or other high crimes and misdemeanors. Sometimes when I see the corruption of our federal government, it is hard to understand why there are so many people still in office when we have this law.

Article. III.

Section. 1.

The judicial Power of the United States shall be vested in one supreme Court, and in such inferior Courts as the Congress may from time to time ordain and establish. The Judges, both of the supreme and inferior Courts, shall hold their Offices during good Behaviour, and shall, at stated Times, receive for their Services, a Compensation, which shall not be diminished during their Continuance in Office.

Sandy's Note: The US Supreme Court is the highest court in the federal judiciary of the United States. "Inferior Courts" simply refers to lower-level courts.

Section. 2.

The judicial Power shall extend to all Cases, in Law and Equity, arising under this Constitution, the Laws of the United States, and Treaties made, or which shall be made, under their Authority;—to all Cases affecting Ambassadors, other public Ministers and Consuls;—to all Cases of admiralty and maritime Jurisdiction;—to Controversies to which the United States shall be a Party;—to Controversies between two or more States;—<u>between a State and Citizens of another State,—between Citizens of different States,—between Citizens of the same State claiming Lands under Grants of different States, and between a State, or the Citizens thereof, and foreign States, Citizens or Subjects.</u>*

In all Cases affecting Ambassadors, other public Ministers and Consuls, and those in which a State shall be Party, the supreme Court shall have original Jurisdiction. In all the other Cases before mentioned, the supreme Court shall have appellate Jurisdiction, both as to Law and Fact, with such Exceptions, and under such Regulations as the Congress shall make.

The Trial of all Crimes, except in Cases of Impeachment, shall be by Jury; and such Trial shall be held in the State where the said Crimes shall have been committed; but when not committed within any State, the Trial shall be at such Place or Places as the Congress may by Law have directed.

Sandy's Note: Section 2 of Article III describes the jurisdiction of the federal courts. *Jurisdiction* is the power of a court to hear a case, so this section tells us what kinds of cases the Supreme Court and other federal courts will hear.

*The underlined portions were changed by the 11th Amendment, which states that the judicial power of the United States does not allow a state to be sued by citizens of another state, or by citizens or subjects of any foreign state.

Section. 3.

Treason against the United States shall consist only in levying War against them, or in adhering to their Enemies, giving them Aid and Comfort. No Person shall be convicted of Treason unless on the Testimony of two Witnesses to the same overt Act, or on Confession in open Court.

The Congress shall have Power to declare the Punishment of Treason, but no Attainder of Treason shall work Corruption of Blood, or Forfeiture except during the Life of the Person attainted.

Sandy's Note: Article III Section 3 addresses treason against the United States and its punishment by Congress. "Corruption of Blood" is a reference to an English practice of law where the family member of someone guilty of treason was also punished for their family member's crime by "being barred from inheriting, retaining, or transmitting any state rank or title."[54] This is forbidden in the US Constitution; only the guilty party can be punished for their crime.

Article. IV.

Section. 1.

Full Faith and Credit shall be given in each State to the public Acts, Records, and judicial Proceedings of every other State. And the Congress may by general Laws prescribe the Manner in which such Acts, Records and Proceedings shall be proved, and the Effect thereof.

Sandy's Note: Article IV Section 1 addresses states and their responsibility to honor other states' laws and court orders, even when their laws differ.

Section. 2.

The Citizens of each State shall be entitled to all Privileges and Immunities of Citizens in the several States.

A Person charged in any State with Treason, Felony, or other Crime, who shall flee from Justice, and be found in another State, shall on Demand of the executive Authority of the State from which he fled, be delivered up, to be removed to the State having Jurisdiction of the Crime.

No Person held to Service or Labour in one State, under the Laws thereof, escaping into another, shall, in Consequence of any Law or Regulation therein, be discharged from such Service or Labour, but shall be delivered up on Claim of the Party to whom such Service or Labour may be due.

Sandy's Note: All the states generally cooperate with each other in extraditing a person who has committed a crime back to the state in which the crime was committed. The person being extradited is always given a court hearing. If the judge deems that extradition is appropriate, the decision is reviewed by the governor's office. It is still the practice today for states to cooperate with each other.

Section. 3.

New States may be admitted by the Congress into this Union; but no new State shall be formed or erected within the Jurisdiction of any other State; nor any State be formed by the Junction of two or more States, or Parts of States, without the Consent of the Legislatures of the States concerned as well as of the Congress.

The Congress shall have Power to dispose of and make all needful Rules and Regulations respecting the Territory or other Property belonging to the United States; and nothing in this Constitution shall be so construed as to Prejudice any Claims of the United States, or of any particular State.

Sandy's Note: Since the establishment of the United States in 1776 by the thirteen colonies, the number of states has expanded from thirteen to fifty. Each new state has been admitted on an equal status with the existing states. The amount of property and land the US owns and has the "power to dispose of" is quite difficult to ascertain, since the reports are hard to find. But according to OnlineMilitaryEducation.org, the property includes all US territories, plus more than 800 US foreign military bases spread across 70 nations![55] It has 163 embassies and 93 consulates spread all over the world.[56] The US also owns and leases over 363 million square feet of space in 8,397 buildings in more than 2,200 communities nationwide. It owns other properties that include land ports of entry, courthouses, laboratories, post offices, and data processing centers. Not all the lands owned or controlled by the US are states. Some lands are territories. Congress has the power to sell off or make rules and regulations regarding its property.[57]

Section. 4.

The United States shall guarantee to every State in this Union a Republican Form of Government, and shall protect each of them against Invasion; and on Application of the Legislature, or of the Executive (when the Legislature cannot be convened) against domestic Violence.

Sandy's Note: It is the United States' responsibility to guarantee that every state has a Republican form of government and protection against invasion and domestic violence. With the increase of the numbers of illegal aliens crossing the border every day, is the United States holding up its responsibility to "protect every State in this union ... against invasion and domestic violence"?

Article. V.

The Congress, whenever two thirds of both Houses shall deem it necessary, shall propose Amendments to this Constitution, or, on the Application of the Legislatures of two thirds of the several States, shall call a Convention for proposing Amendments, which, in either Case, shall be valid to all Intents and Purposes, as Part of this Constitution, when ratified by the Legislatures of three fourths of the several States, or by Conventions in three fourths thereof, as the one or the other Mode of Ratification may be proposed by the Congress; Provided that no Amendment which may be made prior to the Year One thousand eight hundred and eight shall in any Manner affect the first and fourth Clauses in the Ninth Section of the first Article; and that no State, without its Consent, shall be deprived of its equal Suffrage in the Senate.

Sandy's Note: Article V addresses the process to amend the Constitution. There are two ways to do it:

1. When two-thirds of both houses "deem it necessary," they can propose amendments to the Constitution.

2. When two-thirds of all fifty states call for a convention of states. This is Constitutional. It will take thirty-four states passing the resolution that calls for an Article V Convention of States before a convention can be called.

There is an effort by the Convention of States Action group in America today to call for an Article V convention of states to make proposals that would "limit the power and jurisdiction of the federal government, impose fiscal restraints, and place term limits on federal officials." To date there are nineteen states who have passed a resolution, seven who have passed it in one chamber but not in the other, and twenty-one who, as of 2024, were actively considering it.[58] I personally believe convening a Convention of States should be used *only* as a last resort.

Article. VI.

All Debts contracted and Engagements entered into, before the Adoption of this Constitution, shall be as valid against the United States under this Constitution, as under the Confederation.

This Constitution, and the Laws of the United States which shall be made in Pursuance thereof; and all Treaties made, or which shall be made, under the Authority of the United States, shall be the supreme Law of the Land; and the Judges in every State shall be bound thereby, any Thing in the Constitution or Laws of any State to the Contrary notwithstanding.

The Senators and Representatives before mentioned, and the Members of the several State Legislatures, and all executive and judicial Officers, both of the United States and of the several States, shall be bound by Oath or Affirmation, to support this Constitution; but no religious Test shall ever be required as a Qualification to any Office or public Trust under the United States.

Sandy's Note: The Constitution is the Supreme Law of the Land, and it supersedes all other constitutions in the land.

Article. VII.

The Ratification of the Conventions of nine States, shall be sufficient for the Establishment of this Constitution between the States so ratifying the Same.

Done in Convention by the Unanimous Consent of the States present the Seventeenth Day of September in the Year of our Lord one thousand seven hundred and Eighty seven and of the Independence of the United States of America the Twelfth In witness whereof We have hereunto subscribed our Names,

Delaware
Geo: Read
Gunning Bedford jun
John Dickinson
Richard Bassett
Jaco: Broom

Maryland
James McHenry
Dan of St Thos. Jenifer
Danl. Carroll

Virginia
John Blair
James Madison Jr.

North Carolina
Wm. Blount
Richd. Dobbs Spaight
Hu Williamson

South Carolina
J. Rutledge
Charles Cotesworth
    Pinckney
Charles Pinckney
Pierce Butler

Georgia
William Few
Abr Baldwin

New Hampshire
John Langdon
Nicholas Gilman

Massachusetts
Nathaniel Gorham
Rufus King

Connecticut
Wm. Saml. Johnson
Roger Sherman

New York
Alexander Hamilton

New Jersey
Wil: Livingston
David Brearley
Wm. Paterson
Jona: Dayton

Pennsylvania
B Franklin
Thomas Mifflin
Robt. Morris
Geo. Clymer
Thos. FitzSimons
Jared Ingersoll
James Wilson
Gouv Morris[59]

The Constitution would not be complete without the amendments or changes that have been made to it over time. Since our Nation's founding in 1776, there have been twenty-seven amendments, with the last one made in 1992. The National Constitution Center divides these amendments into four different periods:

The Founding Era 1791–1804

This period gave us our first twelve amendments, which include the Bill of Rights.

The Reconstruction Era 1865–1870

Some scholars call this period our nation's "Second Founding" because of the transformation brought by the 13th, 14th, and 15th amendments. (Note that there was a sixty-year gap between the 12th and 13th amendments.)

The Progressive Era 1913–1920

After another forty-plus-year gap, we were given the 16th, 17th, and 19th amendments.

The Modern Era 1933–1992

The remaining eight amendments (20th through 27th) were added over time, with the last one being added in 1992.[60]

The Bill of Rights (Ratified December 15, 1791)

Amendment I.

Congress shall make no law respecting an establishment of religion or prohibiting the free exercise thereof; Or abridging the freedom of speech, or of the press, or the right of the people peaceably to assemble, and to petition the government for a redress of grievances.

Sandy's Note: This amendment gave the American people freedom from a government-established religion, freedom to worship or not, and freedom to say or write what we choose without fear of being jailed, fined, or punished. It also gave us the right to assemble for whatever purpose we choose and the freedom to petition (make complaints against) the government when they do things we don't like.

Amendment II.

A well-regulated militia, being necessary to the security of a free state, the right of the people to keep and bear arms, shall not be infringed.

Sandy's Note: Eldridge Gerry was an American Founding Father, merchant, politician, and diplomat who served under President James Madison as the fifth Vice President of the United States. Gerry stated in a debate over the first militia bill in 1789, "Whenever governments mean to invade the rights and liberties of the people, they always attempt to destroy the militia." The right to bear arms is an individual right of the people who make up the militia. This is an individual right and "shall not be infringed" (*infringe* means "to limit or undermine").[61]

Amendment III.

No Soldier shall, in time of peace, be quartered in any house without the consent of the owner, nor in time of war, but any manner to be prescribed by law.

Sandy's Note: This amendment protects us from being forced by the government to house soldiers in our homes in times of peace and in times of war. The colonists saw these abuses from the British as tyrannical and viewed the Quartering Act of 1774 as an invasion of both the sanctity of private property and the home.

Amendment IV.

> The right of the people to be secure in their persons, houses, papers, and effects, against unreasonable searches and seizures, shall not be violated, and no warrant shall issue, but upon probable cause, supported by oath or affirmation in particularly describing the place to be searched and the persons or things to be seized.

Sandy's Note: What is protected in this amendment? Persons, houses, papers, and effects (or possessions). What are we protected against? We are protected against unreasonable searches and seizures by government officials. Before the government can search our homes or seize our property, it must follow very specific legal procedures to receive authority (a warrant) to do so. This is a core civil liberty.

Amendment V.

> No person shall be held to answer for a capital or otherwise Infamous crime, unless on a presentment or indictment of a grand jury, except in cases arising in the land or Naval forces, or in the militia, when in actual service in time of war or public danger; nor shall any person be subject for the same offense to be twice put in Jeopardy of life or limb, nor shall be compelled in any criminal case to be a witness against himself, nor be deprived of life, liberty, or property, without due process of law; nor shall private property be taken for public use without just compensation.

Sandy's Note: This amendment grants certain rights to criminal defendants: a person cannot be tried twice for the same offense, cannot be required to testify against themselves, has the right to a grand jury for capital crimes and a right to the due and fair process of law before the government may deprive them of life, liberty, or property. (When someone states "I plead the fifth," they are speaking of the right to remain silent, which is included in this amendment.) Finally, the

Takings Clause is connected to the Founders' commitment to property rights. If the government wants to take your personal property, it must be for public use, and they must pay you a fair price for it.

Amendment VI.

> In all Criminal prosecutions, the accused shall enjoy the right to a speedy and public trial, by an impartial jury of the state and District wherein the crime shall have been committed; which district shall have been previously ascertained by law, and to be informed of the nature and cause of the accusation; to be confronted with the witnesses against him; to have compulsory process for obtaining Witnesses in his favor, and to have the assistance of counsel for his defense.

Sandy's Note: The 6th Amendment grants even more rights to criminal defendants. These include the rights to a jury trial in criminal cases, counsel (a lawyer), a speedy and public trial, an impartial jury, being informed what crime he's being charged with, and the ability to cross-examine witnesses against you in person (known as the Confrontation Clause). It also grants to the court subpoena power, the power to order someone to appear in court as a witness for the defense. As I read what I just wrote, I wondered if our justice system consistently provides all citizens with these rights.

Amendment VII.

> In Suits at common law, where the value in controversy shall exceed twenty dollars, the right of trial by jury shall be preserved, and no fact tried by a jury shall be otherwise re-examined in any Court of the United States, then according to the rules of the common law.

Sandy's Note: The 7th Amendment came out of the concerns of the Anti-Federalists that in Article III the original Constitution protected the right to trial by jury in criminal cases only, not civil cases. This amendment protects the right to a jury trial in civil (noncriminal) cases. James Madison drafted the 7th Amendment because he feared that a second constitutional convention might be called if a right to civil jury trial were not included in a federal Bill of Rights.[62]

Amendment VIII.

Excessive bail shall not be required, nor excessive fines imposed, nor cruel and unusual punishments inflicted.

Sandy's Note: The 8th Amendment protects the right against cruel and unusual punishment, excessive bail, and excessive fines. This amendment reflected concerns of Anti-Federalists such as Patrick Henry, who worried that a new (and powerful) national government would simply invent new crimes to oppress the American people. As I think about the excessive fines of $435 million in former President Trump's 2024 case in New York, I must ask myself, did he receive fair treatment as stated in the Eighth Amendment?[63]

Amendment IX.

The enumeration in the constitution of certain rights shall not be construed to deny or disparage others retained by the people.

Sandy's Note: Most scholars believe that this is referring to the "natural rights" we already have. The ones listed in the Bill of Rights shall not deny us of all the other rights we have, which are not written clearly in the Constitution.

Amendment X.

The powers not delegated to the United States by the Constitution, nor prohibited by it to the states, are reserved to the States respectively or to the people.

Sandy's Note: This amendment was designed to protect the "reserved powers" of the states (powers the states held before the ratification of the Constitution) and remind the government that power originates with the American people, who are the "sovereignty."

Amendment XI. (Ratified February 7, 1795)

The judicial power of the United States shall not be construed to extend to any suit and law or equity, commenced or prosecuted against one of the United States by citizens of another state, or the citizens or subjects of any foreign state.

Sandy's Note: Four years after the ratification of the Bill of Rights, the American people ratified the 11th Amendment. This amendment bans the national courts from hearing certain lawsuits against states.

Under Article III in the original Constitution, the national courts were granted the power to decide cases "between" a state and citizens of another state or nation. The Federalists (who supported the Constitution) argued that the Constitution wouldn't allow this to happen unless the States gave their approval. The Anti-Federalists disagreed. In 1793, the US Supreme Court decided the case of *Chisholm v. Georgia*, in which a citizen of South Carolina sued the State of Georgia. Georgia argued that the national court didn't have the power to hear this lawsuit. But in a 4-1 vote, the US Supreme Court sided with Chisholm, arguing they *did* have the power to hear the case. The Anti-Federalists were right, and their fears had come true. Consequently, the Eleventh Amendment was proposed and ratified in less than one year.[64]

Amendment XII (Ratified June 15, 1804)

The Electors shall meet in their respective states and vote by ballot for President and Vice-President, one of whom, at least, shall not be an inhabitant of the same state with themselves; they shall name in their ballots the person voted for as President, and in distinct ballots the person voted for as Vice-President, and they shall make distinct lists of all persons voted for as President, and of all persons voted for as Vice-President, and of the number of votes for each, which lists they shall sign and certify, and transmit sealed to the seat of the government of the United States, directed to the President of the Senate;—the President of the Senate shall, in the presence of the Senate and House of Representatives, open all the certificates and the votes shall then be counted;—The person having the greatest number of votes for President, shall be the

President, if such number be a majority of the whole number of Electors appointed; and if no person have such majority, then from the persons having the highest numbers not exceeding three on the list of those voted for as President, the House of Representatives shall choose immediately, by ballot, the President. But in choosing the President, the votes shall be taken by states, the representation from each state having one vote; a quorum for this purpose shall consist of a member or members from two-thirds of the states, and a majority of all the states shall be necessary to a choice. [And if the House of Representatives shall not choose a President whenever the right of choice shall devolve upon them, before the fourth day of March next following, then the Vice-President shall act as President, as in case of the death or other constitutional disability of the President.—] The person having the greatest number of votes as Vice-President, shall be the Vice-President, if such number be a majority of the whole number of Electors appointed, and if no person have a majority, then from the two highest numbers on the list, the Senate shall choose the Vice-President; a quorum for the purpose shall consist of two-thirds of the whole number of Senators, and a majority of the whole number shall be necessary to a choice. But no person constitutionally ineligible to the office of President shall be eligible to that of Vice-President of the United States.

Sandy's Note: Under the original Constitution, electors cast ballots not for one presidential candidate, but for two of them, with the second-place winner becoming Vice President. This system turned into a serious political crisis when, in 1796, Vice President Adams faced off against former Secretary of State Thomas Jefferson. Adams was a Federalist and Jefferson was a Democratic-Republican. In the end Adams won seventy-one electoral votes and Thomas Jefferson won sixty-nine. In the second vote, none of the Federalist's candidates received more total votes than Jefferson, so he became Adams's (his opponent's) vice president. There are many more interesting details to this story that eventually led to the reforming of the Electoral College after the Election of 1800, which led to the 12th Amendment. This amendment ironed out some of the most glaring problems in the original system. With the new system, electors would still cast two votes, but one for president and the other for vice president.[65]

Amendment XIII. (Ratified December 6, 1865)

Section 1. Neither slavery nor involuntary servitude, except as a punishment for Crime whereof the party shall have been duly convicted, shall exist within United States, or any place subject to their jurisdiction.

Section 2. Congress shall have power to enforce this article by appropriate legislation.

Sandy's Note: This historic amendment abolished slavery in the United States!

Amendment XIV. (Ratified July 9, 1868)

Section 1. All persons born or naturalized in the United States, and subject to the jurisdiction thereof, are citizens of the United States and of the State wherein they reside. No State shall make or enforce any law which shall abridge the privileges or immunities of citizens of the United States; nor shall any State deprive any person of life, liberty, or property, without due process of law; nor deny to any person within its jurisdiction the equal protection of the laws.

Sandy's Note: Section 1 of the 14th Amendment specifically deals with the matter of citizenship.

Section 2. Representatives shall be apportioned among the several States according to their respective numbers, counting the whole number of persons in each State, excluding Indians not taxed. But when the right to vote at any election for the choice of electors for President and Vice-President of the United States, Representatives in Congress, the Executive and Judicial officers of a State, or the members of the Legislature thereof, is denied to any of the male inhabitants of such State, being twenty-one years of age, and citizens of the United States, or in any way abridged, except for participation in rebellion, or other crime, the basis of representation therein shall be reduced in the proportion which the number of such male citizens shall bear to the whole number of male citizens twenty-one years of age in such State.

Sandy's Note: Section 2 lists the voting rights of citizens, determines how the vote is balanced between the states, and eliminates the three-fifths rule.

Section 3. No person shall be a Senator or Representative in Congress, or elector of President and Vice-President, or hold any office, civil or military, under the United States, or under any State, who, having previously taken an oath, as a member of Congress, or as an officer of the United States, or as a member of any State legislature, or as an executive or judicial officer of any State, to support the Constitution of the United States, shall have engaged in insurrection or rebellion against the same, or given aid or comfort to the enemies thereof. But Congress may by a vote of two-thirds of each House, remove such disability.

Sandy's Note: Section 3 places restrictions on citizens who might run for public office.[66]

Section 4. The validity of the public debt of the United States, authorized by law, including debts incurred for payment of pensions and bounties for services in suppressing insurrection or rebellion, shall not be questioned. But neither the United States nor any State shall assume or pay any debt or obligation incurred in aid of insurrection or rebellion against the United States, or any claim for the loss or emancipation of any slave; but all such debts, obligations and claims shall be held illegal and void.

Sandy's Note: Section 4 validated the debt that had been incurred and passed it on to the citizens.[67]

Section 5. The Congress shall have power to enforce, by appropriate legislation, the provisions of this article.

Amendment XV. (Ratified February 3, 1870)

Section 1. The right of citizens of the United States to vote shall not be denied or Abridged by the United States or by any state on account of race color or previous condition of servitude.

Section 2. The Congress shall have power to enforce this article by appropriate legislation.

Sandy's Note: The 15th Amendment promised to end racial discrimination in voting. It did on the basis of race, but it left the door open for states to determine the specific qualifications for suffrage (the right to vote), such as literacy tests, poll taxes, etc., until President Lyndon Johnson signed into law the Voting Rights Act in 1965.[68]

Amendment XVI. (Ratified February 3, 1913)

The Congress shall have power to lay and collect taxes on incomes, from whatever Source derived, without apportionment among the several states, and without regard to any census or enumeration.

Sandy's Note: There had been decades of activism and legal action following the Supreme Court's decision in *Pollock v. Farmers' Loan & Trust Co.*, which limited Congress's power to pass an income tax. The 16th Amendment was ratified in 1913 and gave Congress the power to pass an income tax. We have had an income tax ever since.[69] Sometimes it feels like we are the ATM for the federal government. I don't mind paying taxes, but I'm not okay with being treated like an ATM for every whim and wish of the government!

Amendment XVII. (Ratified April 8, 1913)

The Senate of the United States shall be composed of two Senators from each State, elected by the people thereof, for six years; and each Senator shall have one vote. The electors in each State shall have the qualifications requisite for electors of the most numerous branch of the State legislatures.

When vacancies happen in the representation of any State in the Senate, the executive authority of such State shall issue writs of election to fill such vacancies: Provided, That the legislature of any State may empower the executive thereof to make temporary appointments until the people fill the vacancies by election as the legislature may direct.

This amendment shall not be so construed as to affect the election or term of any Senator chosen before it becomes valid as part of the Constitution.

Sandy's Note: While many constitutional amendments have enforced or added to the rights of Americans, changed the balance of power between the federal government and the states, or modified elections for the president, the structure of Congress, as written in the Constitution, has barely been touched since 1791. The 17th Amendment is the only amendment to do so in a significant way. It removed the power from the state legislatures to choose US Senators and gave that power to the voters in each state. James Madison believed that giving the power to the state legislature to choose gave them the advantage because it helped secure the legislature's authority. George Mason argued that the state legislative selection gave states the power of self-defense against the federal government. Dan Culp expressed the idea that the Senate was specifically set up to represent the states and not necessarily the people in those states: "Direct popular election frustrates or even destroys that role. . . . The Senate is still more removed from the passions of the moment than the House is, simply because their terms are longer. But its original purpose has been perverted in that it is now just a slower version of the people's house, rather than a house devoted to state interests as it was intended to be."[70]

Amendment XVIII. (Ratified on January 16, 1919; repealed by the 21st Amendment on December 5, 1933)

Section 1. After one year from the ratification of this article the manufacture, sale, or transportation of intoxicating Liquors within, the importation thereof into, or the exportation thereof from the United States and all territory subject to the jurisdiction thereof for beverage purposes is hereby prohibited.

Section 2. The Congress and the several States shall have concurrent power to enforce this article by appropriate legislation.

Section 3. This article shall be inoperative unless it shall have been ratified as an amendment to the Constitution by the legislators of the several states, as provided in the Constitution, within seven years from the date of the submission hereof to the States by the Congress.

Sandy's Note: The Prohibition amendment banned "the manufacture, sale, or transportation of intoxicating liquors." It remained a live part of the Constitution for thirteen years until it was repealed in the 21st Amendment.

Amendment XIX. (Ratified August 18, 1920)

Section 1. The right of citizens of the United States to vote shall not be denied or Abridged by the United States or by any state on account of sex.

Section 2. Congress shall have the power to enforce this article by appropriate legislation.

Sandy's Note: With the passing of the 19th Amendment, women were guaranteed the right to vote. This came after decades of advocacy by the suffragists, composed of a group of people who advocated that the right to vote be extended to more people, especially women. Many people think that when the 19th Amendment was ratified, women were allowed to vote, but that is not true. That is when they were guaranteed the right to vote. By the time the 19th Amendment was ratified in 1920, women in many states and territories already had the right to vote. Please see the list below, compiled by Center for American Women and Politics, Rutgers, The State University of New Jersey.

The case of New Jersey:

- 1797: New Jersey made history by recognizing the right of women to vote. New Jersey women voted in large numbers until 1807, when the Assembly passed a law limiting suffrage to free white males.

The following territories provided full voting rights to women before statehood:

- 1869: Wyoming
- 1870: Utah

- 1883: Washington
- 1887: Montana
- 1913: Alaska

The following states granted women the right to vote prior to the 19th Amendment:

- 1890: Wyoming
- 1893: Colorado
- 1896: Utah, Idaho
- 1910: Washington
- 1911: California
- 1912: Arizona, Kansas, Oregon
- 1914: Montana, Nevada
- 1917: New York
- 1918: Michigan, Oklahoma, South Dakota

In the following states, women could vote for President prior to the enactment of the 19th Amendment:

- 1913: Illinois
- 1917: Indiana, Nebraska, Ohio, North Dakota, Rhode Island
- 1919: Iowa, Maine, Minnesota, Missouri, Tennessee, Wisconsin

The following states allowed women's suffrage only after the passage of the 19th Amendment:

Alabama, Arkansas, Connecticut, Delaware, Florida, Georgia, Kentucky, Louisiana, Maryland, Massachusetts, Mississippi, New Hampshire, New Jersey, New Mexico, North Carolina, Pennsylvania, South Carolina, Texas, Vermont, Virginia, West Virginia.[71]

Amendment XX. (Ratified January 23, 1933)

Section 1. The terms of the President and the Vice President shall end at noon on the 20th day of January, and the terms of Senators and Representatives at noon on the 3d day of January, of the years in which such terms would have ended if this article had not been ratified; and the terms of their successors shall then begin.

Sandy's Note: The 20th Amendment reduced the length of time between national elections and when Congress and the President took office. Prior to the ratification of the 20th Amendment, a new President and Congress took office in March rather than in January, as we do today. This limited the length of time of what is known as the "lame duck" president or Congress.

Section 2. The Congress shall assemble at least once in every year, and such meeting shall begin at noon on the 3d day of January, unless they shall by law appoint a different day.

Sandy's Note: Congress meets on January 3rd, and that is usually when each member is sworn in to Congress.

Section 3. If, at the time fixed for the beginning of the term of the President, the President elect shall have died, the Vice President elect shall become President. If a President shall not have been chosen before the time fixed for the beginning of his term, or if the President elect shall have failed to qualify, then the Vice President elect shall act as President until a President shall have qualified; and the Congress may by law provide for the case wherein neither a President elect nor a Vice President elect shall have qualified, declaring who shall then act as President, or the manner in which one who is to act shall be selected, and such person shall act accordingly until a President or Vice President shall have qualified.

Sandy's Note: The 20th Amendment determined that if the president-elect dies or is otherwise incapacitated before they are inaugurated, the vice president-elect takes up the now vacant role and serves for the full four-year term. If there is no president-elect before Inauguration Day, this amendment allows the vice president-elect to act in that role until a new one can be appointed by Congress.[72]

Section 4. The Congress may by law provide for the case of the death of any of the persons from whom the House of Representatives may choose a President whenever the right of choice shall have devolved upon them, and for the case of the death of any of the persons from whom the Senate may choose a Vice President whenever the right of choice shall have devolved upon them.

Sandy's Note: Section 4 gives Congress the power to establish procedures for presidential or vice-presidential succession in the event of death of the president-elect or vice president-elect.

Section 5. Sections 1 and 2 shall take effect on the 15th day of October following the ratification of this article.

Section 6. This article shall be inoperative unless it shall have been ratified as an amendment to the Constitution by the legislatures of three-fourths of the several States within seven years from the date of its submission.

Amendment XXI. (Ratified on December 5, 1933)

Section 1. The 18th article of amendment to the Constitution of the United States is hereby repealed.

Sandy's Note: The 21st Amendment is the only example in American history where a constitutional amendment completely repealed another constitutional amendment: the 18th amendment, which established the prohibition of alcohol.

Section 2. The transportation or importation into any State, Territory, or possession of the United States for delivery or use therein of intoxicating liquors, in violation of the laws thereof, is hereby prohibited.

Sandy's Note: After the repeal of the prohibition of alcohol in Section 1, most of the authority of the sale, transportation, or importing of alcohol was given to the states in Section 2.

Section 3. This article shall be inoperative unless it shall have been ratified as an amendment to the Constitution by conventions in the several States, as provided in the Constitution, within seven years from the date of the submission hereof to the States by the Congress.

Amendment XXII. (Ratified on February 27, 1951)

Section 1. No person shall be elected to the Office of the President more than twice, and no person who has held the office of President, or acted as President, for more than two years of a term to which some other person was elected President shall be elected to the Office of the President more than once. But this Article shall not apply to any person holding the office of President when this Article was proposed by the Congress and shall not prevent any person who may be holding the office of President, or acting as President, during the term within which this article becomes operative from holding the office of President or acting as President during the remainder of such term.

Section 2. This article shall be inoperative unless it shall have been ratified as an amendment to the Constitution by the legislators of three-fourths of the several States within seven years from the date of its submission to the States by the Congress.

Sandy's Note: The 22nd Amendment limited a president to two terms in office. President George Washington set a precedent by serving only two terms before retiring from public life. This precedent was held for 150 years until President Franklin Delano Roosevelt was elected four times in a row. Roosevelt was last elected in 1944. Republicans began pushing back as early as 1941 for an amendment that would restore the Washington precedent. The 22nd Amendment was ratified in 1951 and written into the Constitution.

Amendment XXIII. (Ratified on March 29, 1961)

Section 1. The district constituting the seat of government of the United States shall appoint in such manner as the Congress May direct:

A number of electors of President and Vice President equal to the whole number of Senators and representatives in Congress to which the district would be entitled if it were a State, but in no event more than the least populous State; they shall be in addition to those appointed by the States, but they shall be considered, for the purposes of the election of President and Vice president, to be electors appointed by a State; and they shall meet in the District and perform such duties as provided by the twelfth article of amendment.

Section 2. The Congress shall have power to enforce this article by appropriate legislation.

Sandy's Note: The 23rd Amendment granted the District of Columbia three electoral votes, giving its voters a voice in choosing the president and vice president.

Amendment XXIV. (Ratified on January 23, 1964)

Section 1. The right of citizens of the United States to vote in any primary or other election for President or Vice President, for electors for President or Vice President or for Senator or Representative in Congress, shall not be denied or abridged by the United States or any State by reason of failure to pay any poll tax or other tax.

Section 2. The Congress shall have power to enforce this article by appropriate legislation.

Sandy's Note: The 24th Amendment made it illegal for states to charge a tax at the polls for federal elections. This meant that states could not charge voters any money to vote for the president, senators, or members of the House. When this amendment was ratified, five states still had poll taxes on the books.[73]

Amendment XXV. (Ratified February 10, 1967)

Section 1. In case of the removal of the President from office or of his death or resignation, the Vice President shall become President.

Sandy's Note: After President John F. Kennedy's assassination, the 25th Amendment emerged to help cover the issue of presidential succession in the event of the death or incapacity of the President. It also declares that the Vice President would become President in that event.

> **Section 2.** Whenever there is a vacancy in the office of the Vice President, the President shall nominate a Vice President who shall take office up on confirmation by a majority vote of both Houses of Congress.
>
> **Section 3.** Whenever the President transmits to the President pro tempore of the Senate and the Speaker of the House of Representatives his written declaration that he is unable to discharge the powers and do these of his office, and until he transmits to them a written declaration to the contrary, such powers and duties shall be discharged by the Vice President as Acting President.

Sandy's Note: The 25th Amendment also lays out the process for filling the open seat for Vice President and permits the President to temporarily transfer power by a written statement that he is "unable to discharge the powers and duties of this office," but he can resume his responsibility with a second written statement saying he is ready for duty. (President Ronald Reagan transferred his authority to Vice President George Bush for a few hours while he had a planned surgery.)

> **Section 4.** Whenever the Vice President and a majority of either the principal officers of the executive departments or of such other body as Congress may by law provide, transmit to the President pro tempore of the Senate and the Speaker of the House of Representatives their written declaration that the President is unable to discharge the powers and duties of his office, the Vice President shall immediately assume the powers and duties of the office as Acting President.
>
> Thereafter, when the President transmits to the President pro tempore of the Senate and the Speaker of the House of Representatives his written declaration that no inability exists, he shall resume the powers and duties of his office unless the Vice President and a majority of either the principal officers of the executive department

or of such other body as Congress may by law provide, transmit within four days to the President pro tempore of the Senate and the Speaker of the House of Representatives their written declaration that the President is unable to discharge the powers and duties of his office. Thereupon Congress shall decide the issue, assembling within forty-eight hours for that purpose if not in session. If the Congress, within twenty-one days after receipt of the latter written declaration, or, if Congress is not in session, within twenty-one days after Congress is required to assemble, determines by two-thirds vote of both Houses that the President is unable to discharge the powers and duties of his office, the Vice President shall continue to discharge the same as Acting President; otherwise, the President shall resume the powers and duties of his office.

Sandy's Note: Finally, Section 4 addresses the situation when the president refuses to transfer his duties and denies his inability to perform his duties. The vice president and a majority of other principal officers of the executive office may deem the president unable to fulfill his duties, and then the vice president would become president. If the president challenges the decision regarding his inability to fulfill his presidential duties, this section further describes the Congressional process and timeline for responding to the president's challenge.

Amendment XXVI. (Ratified July 1, 1971)

Section 1. The right of citizens of the United States, who are eighteen years of age or older, to vote shall not be denied or abridged by the United States or by any State on account of age.

Section 2. The Congress shall have power to enforce this article by appropriate legislation.

Sandy's Note: The 26th Amendment was ratified in 1971 and set a national voting age of eighteen. Prior to the existence of the 26th Amendment, most states still limited voting to those twenty-one or older. This amendment was, in part, a response to the Vietnam War; many young people who had been drafted were still unable to vote.[74]

Amendment XXVII. (Ratified on May 7, 1992)

> No law, varying the compensation for the services of the Senators and Representatives, shall take effect, until an election of Representatives shall have intervened.

Sandy's Note: The story of the 27th Amendment is a little weird. It was originally written by James Madison in 1789 to be part of the Bill of Rights, but was not taken to the finish line until more than two hundred years later by a passionate student angry about a bad grade he had received on his homework. This amendment prevents members of Congress from raising their own salaries until there has been a new election. Therefore, a pay increase doesn't take effect until the beginning of the new Congress. This amendment basically prevents Congress from giving itself a raise.

After many years of failure to get the amendment ratified, followed by more years of its sitting in the dust of history, University of Texas sophomore Gregory Watson was given a class assignment to write a paper on some sort of government process. Watson began his research and eventually found a book that listed amendments that had never been ratified. Now he had a topic for his paper! His premise was that the proposal had no timeline to it. Article V of the Constitution hadn't set any deadline on the process for getting proposed amendments ratified, so Watson reasoned that what we now know as the 27th Amendment could still be ratified two hundred years later. What a find by the student, right? Except his professor gave him a C, and Watson became angry. He appealed his grade, but his professor wouldn't budge. So, Watson appealed his case to his fellow citizens and legislators. Most of them ignored him, but one Senator, William Cohen, loved the idea of resurrecting action on the long-dormant proposed amendment. Cohen pushed for its ratification in Maine, and in 1983 he succeeded. This inspired Watson to keep pushing. From there his amendment push gained steam. He talked about the public's dissatisfaction with Congress and how the people he spoke to didn't believe Congress was doing enough to help the American people. In 1985 five more states came on board and ratified the amendment. Finally, in 1992, more than two centuries had passed since the first Congress proposed the amendment to the States. Three-quarters of the states (38 of 50) ratified it, and the 27th Amendment became part of the Constitution on May 7, 1992. It just took about 203 years to get it done![75]

I know that what you have just read (and I trust you truly read it) was somewhat tedious and maybe a little boring at times, but regardless, it is the most important document written by our Founding Fathers. It is the form or structure of government that our country was given, and how it has been amended over time. The Constitution has been the guide we have followed for nearly 250 years. As we've followed it, we've remained a free people.

But why did our Founding Fathers need to set up another government when they had just fled from one? Why did they believe that government was necessary? Larry P. Arnn, president of Hillsdale College, professor of politics and history, and author of *The Divine and Natural Connection Between the Declaration and the Constitution and What We Risk by Losing It*, states the following about why government is necessary:

> The founders believed that men are moral beings called to do right but sometimes fail. Government is necessary to restrain and correct man's moral failings. At the same time, those in charge of government are human, too, and subject to the same moral failings as other human beings. As a result, the government needs to be controlled by the governed to prevent those who rule from becoming tyrants.[76]

What are the main points we need to take away from the Constitution?

1. Our Founding Fathers understood the importance of individual rights. To have them, men need to be free, and to be free, there must be limits on those who govern.

2. The Constitution's most important words are "We the People." They declare that the Constitution derives its power not from a king or a Congress but from the people themselves.

3. The first three articles establish the three branches of government and their powers: Legislative (Congress), Executive (office of the president), and Judicial (federal court system). A system of checks and balances prevents any one of these separate powers from becoming dominant.

4. The powers not given to the government are reserved to the states and the people.

5. The Constitution can be amended, but as we have learned, it can sometimes be difficult to do when you must have either two-thirds of the House and Senate to ratify an amendment, or have two-thirds of the state legislatures call a Convention of States.

America has enjoyed more prosperity and freedom than any other nation in the world. People from around the world are leaving their own countries to come to the United States to escape persecution, poverty, and war and for a chance at a better life for their families. This has been going on as long as the United States has existed.

But there are those who have called for change and some that are now challenging the relevance of our Declaration of Independence and the Constitution. As early as 1911, President Woodrow Wilson gave a July Fourth speech in honor of the Declaration of Independence. He stated, "If you want to understand the real Declaration of Independence, do not repeat the Preface." Now, what does the Preface say? It talks about everyone's natural rights "endowed by our Creator" and mentions that "all men are created equal."

Frank Goodnow, an American educator, legal scholar, and former president of John Hopkins University, as well as a progressive, contrasted the theory of the Declaration of Independence with a new theory that progressives were adopting in Europe. He drew a comparison between Americans' belief in their rights coming from our Creator with his belief that our rights come from our society and that those rights are to be determined by the legislative authority in view of that society's needs. Goodnow believed that "social expediency" rather than natural rights, should determine "the sphere of individual freedom of action."[77] Think about that! Do you want the society we're living in today determining what freedoms you have? I don't!

There are others who often call our country a "democracy," but we are a constitutional republic. A *democracy* is a government that is ruled according to the will of the majority. A republic is a representative form of government that is ruled according to a charter, or constitution it; further, a republic is a limited democracy in which the power rests with the people through their representatives. It's a form of government where the people select their representatives by voting for them at the ballot box. This is why the integrity of our elections should be placed at the highest priority! If not, we the people will lose our ability to choose those who govern over us, and our sovereignty will be lost! [78]

The Declaration of Independence cautions, "Prudence, indeed, will dictate that Governments long established should not be changed for light and transient causes." We need to heed this advice. Many unconstitutional actions are being taken by our representatives, and "we the people" must hold our government accountable to preserve our freedom.

In conclusion, I would like to share a few statistics that show the strength and beauty of what our Founding Fathers gave us, as shared by Digital History:

> The US Constitution has the oldest written national framework of government in the world. At the end of the 20th century, there were about 159 other national constitutions, and 101 had been adopted since 1970. While a single framework of government has governed the United States for over two centuries, France, in contrast, has had 10 separate and distinct constitutional orders (including five republics, two empires, a monarchy, and two dictatorships). The country of El Salvador has had 36 constitutions since 1824.
>
> Nearly all of the national constitutions now in use bear the marks of the 55 men who met in Philadelphia in the summer of 1787 to create the framework of the United States government. Like the US Constitution, they are written constitutions. They also spell out human and civil rights similarly to those in the US document. A bill of rights is particularly common. The principles of American constitutionalism—the separation of powers, a bicameral legislature, and a presidential form of government—were followed by many nations. The Constitutional Convention of 1787 created a governmental framework that has lasted two centuries and served as a model for freedom-loving people worldwide.
>
> In almost every way imaginable, the United States has been radically transformed over the past two centuries. Its population has soared from

just 4 million to over 300 million. The federal budget has risen from $4 million in 1790 to over $1 trillion. Yet the basic framework of government has remained unchanged.[79]

What have we learned?

Summary of the Declaration of Independence and the Constitution:

1. Our ancestors were under a tyrannical ruler who restricted their ability to live free and independent lives due to King George III's desire to control them.
2. They declared their independence from Great Britian and the king and listed the abuses that caused them to do so.
3. Their independence was granted not just because they declared it in writing but because they fought for it!
4. Our Founding Fathers struggled as they set up our new form of government, beginning with the Articles of Confederation.
5. The Constitution is an amazing foundational framework, which, unlike the framework of any other civilization, provides us with individual freedom, the ability to prosper, and protection.
6. As we have followed the Constitution, it has provided stability and will continue to provide that stability if we follow it.

The Constitution was and still is a brilliant framework, but we must follow it to ensure that freedom will be there for our children, grandchildren, and beyond!

In the next chapter, we will explore what has changed over the years and how America has evolved from a limited government to the monstrosity it is today.

> **He is like a man building a house, who dug deep and laid the foundation on the rock. When the flood came, the river crashed against that house and couldn't shake it, because it was well built.**
>
> **Luke 6:48**

Chapter Three
Evolution from Limited Government to the Administrative State

An Elective Despotism was not the government we fought for; but one in which the powers of government should be divided and balanced among the several bodies of magistracy as that no one could transcend their legal limits without being effectively checked and restrained by the others.

James Madison, *Federalist* No. 58, February 1, 1788

Now that we have read and better understand the Declaration of Independence, the Constitution, and how our government and the rule of law are supposed to work, we need to ask a couple of questions: Is our government still working as it should today, or have there been significant changes over the years? If so, what are those changes, and how have they affected our country and individual freedoms?

While we will not cover all that has happened since our country declared its independence in 1776, I want to highlight a few things that have influenced the changes we see today.

First, let's recap three important principles we learned from the Constitution that the Founders put in place to give the "checks and balances" we need to protect the American people.

1. Article I of the Constitution gave all legislative powers to Congress, which consists of the House and Senate. In other words, Congress writes the laws of our country.

2. Article II of the Constitution gives executive power to the president of the United States, which means the president protects the people's rights of life, liberty, and property by ensuring the laws that Congress writes are executed properly. He can also veto those laws, but Congress can overturn his veto with a two-thirds vote.

3. Article III of the Constitution gives judicial power to the "Supreme Court and any such inferior courts," which means they interpret laws according to the Constitution, determining legal rights in prosecutions and lawsuits.

These powers were given to separate branches of government to avoid abuse and tyranny of the people. Now that we have reiterated the importance of the separation of powers, let's learn more about the changes our country has experienced and see if we still follow the Constitution as the Founders intended.

A Little Background

For those of you who are like I was before I started working for Congress and don't know much about executive or federal agencies, where they began, why they were created, what they do, how many there are, and how they affect you and me personally, let me give you a little background and bring you up to speed.

The title of this chapter is "The Evolution from Limited Government to the Administrative State," but what is "the Administrative State"? Before describing how the Administrative State developed, you need to understand what it is. Knowing that will help you see and understand how it has led us away from limited government.

What is the Administrative State?

The *Administrative State* is a term used to describe the power many government agencies have to write, execute, and judge their own laws.[80] The Administrative State is sometimes called the "Fourth Branch of Government" or "The Federal

Bureaucracy." According to Jonathan Turley, writing in the *Washington Post*, "It is called this because of how it has grown over the past one hundred years. In politics of the United States, 'fourth branch of government' is an unofficial term referring to groups or institutions perceived as influencing or acting in the stead of the three branches of the US federal government defined in the Constitution of the United States (legislative, executive, and judicial)."[81]

The Administrative State is, sadly, a return to the despotism from which our Founding Fathers declared their independence in 1776.

You might say, "Wow, what a strong statement to make! We're living in 2024, and no king is ruling over us." But *despotism*, as the *Oxford English Dictionary* describes it, is "a country or political system where the ruler holds absolute power."[82] *Merriam Webster* describes despotism as "oppressive absolute power and authority exerted by government."[83] King George III is not ruling over us today, but the Administrative State is.

Over the years, Congress has given great power to hundreds of agencies. These agencies were created to help solve various problems that developed due to our country's growth, expansion, and progress. It is not a problem that we have created structure to help things run smoothly, but there is a problem when all three powers—legislative, executive, and judicial—are given to these agencies to make the law, enforce the law, and interpret the law. This is unconstitutional and has effectively taken away our representative government and replaced it with an overbearing and abusive administrative one, which is now referred to as "the Administrative State." Let's learn more about where it all started.

The Early Years

According to most records, Congress created the first federal administrative agency, the Department of Foreign Affairs, on July 31, 1789, to "estimate duties payable on imports and to perform other related duties."[84] George Washington appointed the first executive department heads in 1789. They were the Attorney

General, Secretary of State, Secretary of Treasury, and Secretary of War. Executive agencies are created by and are under the authority of the President. An act of Congress establishes federal and independent agencies, and Congress is required oversee all agencies and their activities.

As the federal government's scope and functions grew, the number of executive departments increased. The heads of these departments all have the title of Secretary—except for the Attorney General of the US Department of Justice—and together they make up the core of the president's cabinet.

Growth in the country and increased governmental responsibilities led to the creation of the Department of Interior in 1849, the Department of Justice in 1870, and the Post Office Department in 1872.

Following are the executive cabinet departments, in the order they were established, as they exist today:

1. Department of Justice (1789)
2. Department of State (1789)
3. Department of the Treasury (1789)
4. Department of the Interior (1849)
5. Department of Agriculture (1889)
6. Department of Commerce (1903; originally included Labor)
7. Department of Labor (1913)
8. Department of Defense (1947)
9. Department of Health and Human Services (1953)
10. Department of Housing and Urban Development (1965)
11. Department of Transportation (1967)
12. Department of Energy (1977)
13. Department of Education (1979)
14. Office of Faith-Based and Community Initiatives (2001)
15. Department of Homeland Security (2002/2003)
16. USA Freedom Corps (2002)

The executive branch also includes independent agencies and other boards, commissions, and committees that fall under one of the above-listed "parent" agencies. It is hard to keep track of them since new subagencies and other entities are frequently added.

The Beginning of Independent Agencies
Economic Concerns

From 1865 through 1900, Congress created many independent regulatory commissions. They were created to supervise and "set standards in a specific field of activity, or operations, in the private sector of the economy and then to enforce those standards."[85]

Due to the complexity of society's issues, members of Congress believed more oversight was necessary. The existing executive agencies could not cover the oversight, and a simple law passed by Congress was insufficient to bring order, so the first of many regulatory agencies was created.

The first agency was the Interstate Commerce Commission. It was created in 1887 in response to exorbitant rates that farmers and merchants were being forced to pay railroads to ship their products to the market. The Interstate Commerce Act (ICC) of 1887, required that railroad rates be "just and reasonable."[86]

Reformers believed independent regulatory commissions would bring greater expertise, specialization, and continuity to economic problems. They also believed that Congress could and would operate in a dispassionate, nonpolitical environment. The problem with this was that many regulatory commissions had contradictory objectives. They were controlling and directing a specific industry and promoting that same industry.

Social and Public Health Concerns

In the same way that economic concerns led Congress to create independent regulatory commissions, social concerns, such as public health and safety (due to the unsanitary practices of the meat industry), soon joined them.

Congress tried unsuccessfully to solve the problem with several meat inspection laws. They finally figured out that the best solution was to create more comprehensive legislation and give broader authority to another administrative agency, which led to the Food and Drug Act of 1906. This act mandated public protection from the health hazards of mislabeled foods, drugs, cosmetics, and medical devices.[87]

But that wasn't the end of creating more agencies. It was just the beginning!

The New Deal (1933–1938)

Governmental concern with social issues grew exponentially during the Depression (1929– 1939) when President Franklin D. Roosevelt implemented the New Deal.[88] The New Deal was a series of programs, public work projects, financial reforms, and regulations that Roosevelt enacted in the United States between 1933 and 1938.

Roosevelt's New Deal platform created many federal agencies to implement new policies and regulations. Almost all these agencies had acronyms such as CCC, TVA, or HOLC. Therefore, they came to be known as FDR's "Alphabet Soup Agencies," or just "Alphabet Agencies."[89] These agencies brought a vast expansion in federal government programs and agencies as the nation struggled toward economic recovery.

Agencies that remain in effect today from the New Deal include"

- Federal Deposit Insurance Corporation (FDIC) in banking,
- Fannie Mae (FNMA) in mortgage lending,
- Securities and Exchange Commission (SEC),
- Federal Housing Administration (FHA),
- Farm Credit Administration (FCA).
- Federal Communications Commission (FCC),
- Soil Conservation Service (which remains today as the as the Natural Resources Conservation Service, or NRCS), and
- Perhaps the most notable New Deal program still in effect, Social Security Administration (SSA), which was created by the Social Security Act in 1935 to oversee the national old-age pension system.[90]

Congress created these administrative agencies through legislation that delegated authority to each agency by giving it specific directives.

Agencies were usually given broad powers to investigate, set standards, and enforce those standards on the American people, but there was no uniform administrative law governing the agencies. While there was much debate on the subject, many Americans resisted the creation of formal, uniform administrative law because they believed that it would enhance the government's ability to exercise power over the citizens and diminish individual rights.[91] But on June 11, 1946, Congress passed the Administrative Procedure Act into law as Public Law 404—79th Congress.

The passing of this act was and is a big deal because it gave permission and still permits most agencies created by Congress the authority to create laws, enforce the laws they create, and choose the penalty for anyone breaking those laws.

So, you're probably thinking, "Wait just a minute, did I read that right? Did our elected representatives give the federal agencies they created all three powers—legislative, executive, and judicial? I thought we just read that the Framers of the Constitution, to prevent abuse and tyranny, declared that this shouldn't be done."

Unfortunately, that is exactly what they did!

Just so you know that I'm not making this up, I have listed the permissions Congress gave the agencies, with the actual language and description used in the Administrative Procedures Act. I've compared it to the Constitution to show you how this act is absolutely unconstitutional! I have also included a picture of the APA document with the sections that include that language starting on the next page.

Breaking It Down

1. Rule and Rule Making: This refers to the agency process for formulating, amending, or repealing a rule.

Formulation means "to create." (Legislative)

Amend means "to change." (Legislative)

Repeal means "to remove or do away with." (Legislative)

Rule means "an instruction that states the way you are allowed or not allowed to do something." (Legislative)

ADMINISTRATIVE PROCEDURE ACT

[Public Law 404—79th Congress]

[Chapter 324—2d Session]

[S. 7]

AN ACT To improve the administration of justice by prescribing fair administrative procedure

Be it enacted by the Senate and House of Representatives of the United States of America in Congress assembled,

TITLE

Section 1. This Act may be cited as the "Administrative Procedure Act".

Definitions

Sec. 2. As used in this Act—

(a) Agency.—"Agency" means each authority (whether or not within or subject to review by another agency) of the Government of the United States other than Congress, the courts, or the governments of the possessions, Territories, or the District of Columbia. Nothing in this Act shall be construed to repeal delegations of authority as provided by law. Except as to the requirements of section 3, there shall be excluded from the operation of this Act (1) agencies composed of representatives of the parties or of representatives of organizations of the parties to the disputes determined by them, (2) courts martial and military commissions, (3) military or naval authority exercised in the field in time of war or in occupied territory, or (4) functions which by law expire on the termination of present hostilities, within any fixed period thereafter, or before July 1, 1947, and the functions conferred by the following statutes: Selective Training and Service Act of 1940; Contract Settlement Act of 1944; Surplus Property Act of 1944.

(b) Person and party.—"Person" includes individuals, partnerships, corporations, associations, or public or private organizations of any character other than agencies. "Party" includes any person or agency named or admitted as a party, or properly seeking and entitled as of right to be admitted as a party, in any agency proceeding; but nothing herein shall be construed to prevent an agency from admitting any person or agency as a party for limited purposes.

(c) Rule and rule making.—"Rule" means the whole or any part of any agency statement of general or particular applicability

1

and future effect designed to implement, interpret, or prescribe law or policy or to describe the organization, procedure, or practice requirements of any agency and includes the approval or prescription for the future of rates, wages, corporate or financial structures or reorganizations thereof, prices, facilities, appliances, services or allowances therefor or of valuations, costs, or accounting, or practices bearing upon any of the foregoing. "Rule making" means agency process for the formulation, amendment, or repeal of a rule.

(d) ORDER AND ADJUDICATION.—"Order" means the whole, or any part of the final disposition (whether affirmative, negative, injunctive, or declaratory in form) of any agency in any matter other than rule making but including licensing. "Adjudication" means agency process for the formulation of an order.

(e) LICENSE AND LICENSING.—"License" includes the whole or part of any agency permit, certificate, approval, registration, charter, membership, statutory exemption or other form of permission. "Licensing" includes agency process respecting the grant, renewal, denial, revocation, suspension, annulment, withdrawal, limitation amendment, modification, or conditioning of a license.

(f) SANCTION AND RELIEF.—"Sanction" includes the whole or part of any agency (1) prohibition, requirement, limitation, or other condition affecting the freedom of any person; (2) withholding of relief; (3) imposition of any form of penalty or fine; (4) destruction, taking, seizure, or withholding of property; (5) assessment of damages, reimbursement, restitution, compensation, costs, charges, or fees; (6) requirement, revocation, or suspension of a license; or (7) taking of other compulsory or restrictive action. "Relief" includes the whole or part of any agency (1) grant of money, assistance, license, authority, exemption, exception, privilege, or remedy; (2) recognition of any claim, right, immunity, privilege, exemption, or exception; or (3) taking of any other action upon the application or petition of, and beneficial to, any person.

(g) AGENCY PROCEEDING AND ACTION.—"Agency proceeding" means any agency process as defined in subsections (c), (d), and (e) of this section. "Agency action" includes the whole or part of every agency rule, order, license, sanction, relief, or the equivalent or denial thereof, or failure to act.

PUBLIC INFORMATION

SEC. 3. Except to the extent that there is involved (1) any function of the United States requiring secrecy in the public interest or (2) any matter relating solely to the internal management of any agency—

(a) RULES.—Every agency shall separately state and currently publish in the Federal Register (1) descriptions of its central and field organization including delegations by the agency of final authority and the established places at which, and methods whereby, the public may secure information or make submittals or requests; (2) statements of the general course and method by which its functions are channeled and determined, including the nature and requirements of all formal or informal procedures available as well as forms and instructions as to the scope and contents of all papers, reports, or examinations; and (3) substantive rules adopted as authorized by law and statements of general policy or interpretations formulated to the extent that the facts are subject to trial de novo by the reviewing court. In making the foregoing determinations the court shall review the whole record or such portions thereof as may be cited by any party, and due account shall be taken of the rule of prejudicial error.

EXAMINERS

SEC. 11. Subject to the civil-service and other laws to the extent not inconsistent with this Act, there shall be appointed by and for each agency as many qualified and competent examiners as may be necessary for proceedings pursuant to sections 7 and 8, who shall be assigned to cases in rotation so far as practicable and shall perform no duties inconsistent with their duties and responsibilities as examiners. Examiners shall be removable by the agency in which they are employed only for good cause established and determined by the Civil Service Commission (hereinafter called the Commission) after opportunity for hearing and upon the record thereof. Examiners shall receive compensation prescribed by the Commission independently of agency recommendations or ratings and in accordance with the Classification Act of 1923, as amended, except that the provisions of paragraphs (2) and (3) of subsection (b) of section 7 of said Act, as amended, and the provisions of section 9 of said Act, as amended, shall not be applicable. Agencies occasionally or temporarily insufficiently staffed may utilize examiners selected by the Commission from and with the consent of other agencies. For the purposes of this section, the Commission is authorized to make investigations, require reports by agencies, issue reports, including an annual report to the Congress, promulgate rules, appoint such advisory committees as may be deemed necessary, recommend legislation, subpena witnesses or records, and pay witness fees as established for the United States courts.

CONSTRUCTION AND EFFECT

SEC. 12. Nothing in this Act shall be held to diminish the constitutional rights of any person or to limit or repeal additional requirements imposed by statute or otherwise recognized by law. Except as otherwise required by law, all requirements or privileges relating to evidence or procedure shall apply equally to agencies and persons. If any provision of this Act or the application thereof is held invalid, the remainder of this Act or other applications of such provision shall not be affected. Every agency is granted all authority necessary to comply with the requirements of this Act through the issuance of rules or otherwise. No subsequent legislation shall be held to supersede or modify the provisions of this Act except to the extent that such legislation shall do so expressly. This Act shall take effect three months after its approval except that sections 7 and 8 shall take effect six months after such approval, the requirement of the selection of examiners pursuant to section 11 shall not become effective until one year after such approval, and no procedural requirement shall be mandatory as to any agency proceeding initiated prior to the effective date of such requirement.

Approved June 11, 1946.

Article I of the Constitution gave Congress the legislative power to write law, but it did *not* give that power to unelected bureaucratic agencies.

2. Order and Adjudication: This means the agency process for formulating an order.

Order means something that must be obeyed. (Legislative)

Article I gave Congress the authority to legislate.

Adjudication means resolving the differences between two parties. (Judicial)

Article III gave the power to adjudicate , i.e., to interpret laws according to the Constitution, to the judicial branch, which determines the legal rights of individuals in prosecutions and lawsuits. These powers were *not* given to unelected bureaucrats in federal agencies.

3. License and Licensing: Includes agency process respecting the grant, renewal, denial, revocation, suspension, annulment, withdrawal, limitation amendment, modification, or conditioning of a license.

License is a permit from an authority to own or use something, do a particular thing, or carry on a trade. (Judicial)

Licensing is governmental permission to perform a particular act (like getting married), conduct a particular business or occupation, operate machinery or vehicles after proving the ability to do so safely, or use property for a certain purpose. (Judicial)

The 10th Amendment of the Constitution clearly states, "The powers not delegated to the United States by the Constitution, nor prohibited by it to the States, are reserved to the States respectively or to the people."

Many federal agencies are getting involved in business that should be left to the states or the people.

4. Sanction and Relief : *Sanction* means

1. Prohibiting, requiring, limiting, or using other conditions to affect the *freedom of any person* (Judicial),
2. Withholding of relief (Judicial),
3. Imposition of penalty or fine (Judicial),
4. Destruction, taking, seizure, or withholding of property (Judicial),
5. Assessment of damages, reimbursement, restitution, compensation, cost, charges, or fees (Judicial),
6. Requirement, revocation, or suspension of a license (Judicial), or
7. Taking of other compulsory or restrictive action (Judicial).

The 4th Amendment states, "The right of the people to be secure in their persons, papers, and effects, against unreasonable searches and seizures, shall not be violated, and no Warrants shall issue, but upon probable cause, supported by Oath or affirmation, and particularly describing the place to be searched, and the persons or things to be seized."

The 5th Amendment of the Constitution states, "No Person shall be . . . deprived of life, *liberty*, or property, without due process of law."

The Administrative Procedures Act gives these agencies permission to deprive American citizens of all three of these rights—life, liberty, and property—but that act does *not* trump the Constitution!

The 8th Amendment clearly states, "Excessive bail shall not be required, nor excessive *fines* imposed, nor cruel and unusual punishment inflicted."

Article III gave the power to give a fine or penalty to any entity or person who broke the law to the judicial branch, and it is supposed to interpret laws according to the Constitution, which determines the legal rights of individuals in prosecutions and lawsuits. This power was *not* given to unelected bureaucratic agencies but to the judicial branch—and yet, here we are again with unelected bureaucrats punishing American citizens as if they are the judicial branch!

The 7th Amendment states, "In Suits at common law, where the value in controversy shall exceed twenty dollars, the right of trial by jury shall be preserved, and no fact tried by a jury shall be otherwise re-examined in any Court of the United States, than according to the rules of the common law."

These independent agencies have been given power to assess damages, how much you need to reimburse, what restitution you need to pay, compensation that may need to be given, and charges or fees.

I can guarantee you from my experience in working with these agencies that not only are their fines or judgments always more than twenty dollars, but they are also acting as the judge, jury, *and* executioner! This is unconstitutional!

Relief means

1. Grant of money, assistance, license, authority, exemption, exception, privilege, or remedy (Executive/Administrative);
2. Recognition of any claim, right, immunity, privilege, exemption, or exception (Executive/Administrative); or
3. Taking of any other action upon the application or petition of, and beneficial to any person (Executive/Administrative).

Many times, in the cases we handle in my Congressional office, the agency with whom the constituent is having the problem will say they do not have the ability or authority to exempt a constituent from punishment (even when it was the agency that made the mistake) or to remedy their problem. Yet the law described above states very clearly that in the matter of "remedy, exception, privilege," or even "taking of any other action up on the application or petition of, and beneficial to any person," these agencies *can* provide relief!

Early on in my work in Congress, we received a call from a man who had been fined tens of thousands of dollars for a mistake the Department of Labor (DOL) made. They even admitted that they had made the mistake in a letter they had sent to him. When he called though, no one would answer his phone calls or respond to his emails to hear his pleas for relief. Our office was finally able to reach someone in a position of management at the DOL who told us that they had no power to give any relief or exemption from the fine they were imposing on our constituent. I was not aware of the Administration Procedures Act at the time, but if so, I would have pointed out that while they seem to have no problem imposing laws and punishments, they seem determined to overlook the part of the APA that allows them to provide relief. While they shouldn't be making these decisions anyway, constitutionally (the judicial branch should be), the agencies of the Administrative State are making those decisions for all Americans now! Congress has largely abdicated its responsibility to represent and protect the American people.

The Administrative Procedure Act was passed on June 11, 1946, by Congress and signed into law by President Harry S. Truman.[92] It gave many independent agencies power to rule over us without input and oversight from our representatives in Congress. This effectively removed our representative government and left us with a modern-day "King George III" ruler, a.k.a., the Administrative State, which continued to grow under the Johnson Administration in the 1960s.

The Great Society (1964–1965)

The period known as the Great Society, simply put, was a robust time of policy initiatives, legislation, and programs spearheaded by President Johnson in hopes of ending poverty, reducing crime, abolishing inequality, and improving the environment. In May 1964 he laid out his agenda for a "Great Society" during a speech at the University of Michigan. He introduced the largest social reform plan in modern history.[93]

During Lyndon Johnson's presidency, he enacted two hundred laws and programs that impacted education, healthcare, public housing, transportation, and civil liberties. Some of those agencies and programs that still exist today include

- Medicare,
- Medicaid,
- The Food Stamp Act,
- The National Endowment for the Arts, and
- Upward Bound (a program that helps disadvantaged high school students get into college).

By the 1960s and 1970s, we had moved a long way from our limited government. It is easy to understand that law and order are important in a growing population and ever-expanding country, and it would take an organization to run it efficiently. Unfortunately, along the way, our freedoms were sacrificed and placed in the hands of the ever-expanding Administrative State.

According to the Center for Effective Government,

> With the creation of these regulatory agencies came an acceleration of regulatory activity. However, by the late 1970s, this trend had slowed. "Excessive" regulation began being blamed for everything from raising interest rates to forcing small businesses into bankruptcy and making US businesses uncompetitive in world markets.
>
> The regulatory process itself came under sharp attack. Complaints became commonplace about "interference in the marketplace," "red tape," "big government," and "faceless, nameless bureaucrats." The sheer volume of federal rules and regulations, complexity, costs, and delays led to public and business-sector frustration and impatience with the federal government.
>
> It was becoming increasingly clear that power in federal decision-making was shifting away from elected officials and toward government agencies.[94]

Congress recognized this problem and passed several laws to try to exert control over federal agencies. These laws included the Unfunded Mandates Reform Act, the Congressional Review Act, and the Paperwork Reduction Act. The White House led the charge in attempting to create a system where agencies operate under the scrutiny and control of elected officials. This was often done through executive orders (EOs) issued by the President.

Here are some examples:

- In 1971, President Richard Nixon proposed the idea of a White House regulatory review process.

- In 1974, President Gerald Ford proposed cost-benefit analysis as a tool that agency officials would be required to use in developing significant regulations.

- In 1978, President Jimmy Carter worked to strengthen aspects of White House regulatory review and further defined certain issues relevant to the process.

- President Ronald Reagan went further than any other president in exerting White House control over the rulemaking process. He not only tightened White House control and added additional requirements for agencies, but he also signed Executive Order 12291, stating its intent was "to reduce the burdens of existing and future regulations." In 1985, Reagan issued Executive Order 12498, requiring agencies to develop a detailed regulatory plan to assure the Office of Management and Budget (OMB) that their forthcoming regulations were consistent with White House priorities.

- In 1993, President Bill Clinton combined and revised the two Reagan executive orders to be consistent with the regulatory reviews of the Clinton Administration when he issued Executive Order 12866.

- In 2007, President George W. Bush issued Executive Order 13422 in which he made significant amendments to President Clinton's EO 12866. The amendments allowed the White House to further manage the activities of federal agencies by including agency guidance, documents, interpretive memos, guidelines, policy statements, etc., into the regulatory review process and installing presidentially appointed regulatory policy officers in the agencies themselves."[95]

Our government realized the monster they created early on, but do you think that stopped them from making it bigger and adding more agencies and bureaucratic "red tape"? No, it did not!

Many people have argued over the years that the agencies are undermining the separation of powers, and they are, but very little has been done about it.

The Judicial Branch Weighs In

In 1977, "Congress amended the Clean Air Act to impose certain requirements on states that had not attained the national air quality standards previously established by the Environmental Protection Agency (EPA). One of these requirements was that these 'non-attainment' states set up a permit program regulating 'new or modified major stationary sources' of air pollution."[96] Chevron USA challenged the precedent that was established in the courts.

In 1984, the US Supreme Court issued a landmark decision against Chevron. This decision (*Chevron USA, Inc v. Natural Resources Defense Council, Inc.*, 468 U.S. 837 1984), established a precedent that courts defer to agency interpretations so long as Congress has not spoken directly to the precise issue in question.[97] This ruling solidified, empowered, and emboldened agencies.

Peter J. Wallison, president emeritus of American Enterprise Institute, states in his book, *Judicial Fortitude: The Last Chance to Rein in the Administrative State*, that "the judicial branch has failed to ensure that the laws binding on the American people will be made in the future by Congress and not by unelected officials in the federal government's administrative agencies."[98] He also wrote an article titled "Justice Kavanaugh and the Administrative State," published in 2018 by the American Enterprise Institute, in which he shared that

> Although administrative agencies are theoretically part of the executive branch, presidents cannot effectively control them. . . .

Congress also seems powerless to control the growth of administrative power. Many legislative efforts to rein in the ability of agencies to create new rules have failed to pass Congress.

In effect, then, the administrative agencies of the executive branch—uncontrolled by the president, Congress, or the courts—have become the US government's most important lawgivers. This nullifies the separation of powers by combining legislation and administration in the executive branch.[99]

Before the Administrative State with all its agencies existed, James Madison described it perfectly in Federalist Paper No. 47, when he wrote, "The accumulation of all powers, legislative, executive, and judiciary, in the same hands, whether of one, a few, or many, and whether hereditary, self-appointed or elective, may justly be pronounced the very definition of tyranny."[100]

For the past several months, two members of my staff have been working with the Social Security Administration trying to get problems resolved for multiple constituents. These constituents had been trying to reach the SSA long before they came to us in desperation.

One SSA official refuses to answer any of our emails in writing, most likely so as not to leave a record of what she is doing or saying to us. Her reason, we speculate, is she has already cost one of our constituents nearly $47,000 in penalties because of bad advice she gave the constituent. The SSA caught the agent's mistake due to emails she sent to us and our constituent. Instead of being fired, she was promoted to a different office as manager and continues to make poor decisions for our constituents.

We have complained to higher-level managers that oversee that office from a different state. In response, they defend her or make excuses for her and the other agents who have a similar work ethic and deficiency! This agency is one of hundreds of agencies that can exercise all three powers: legislative, executive and judicial. Sometimes it feels like we are fighting with our hands and our feet tied, and there is nothing we can do. Their word is law, their regulations rule, and their punishments are final.

We have a running workload of more than six hundred constituent cases every day needing help from the Internal Revenue Service (IRS), Social Security Administration (SSA), Department of Labor (DOL), United States Customs and Immigration Services (USCIS), Office of Personnel Management (OPM), Small Business Administration (SBA), Veterans Administration (VA), Department of Transportation (DOT), United States Postal Service (USPS), Housing and Urban Development (HUD), United States Department of Agriculture (USDA), United States Department of Forestry (USFS), Department of State (DOS), National Visa Center (NVC), Securities and Exchange Commission (SEC), and the list goes on. This is the tyranny that James Madison was referring to.

In 1940, President Roosevelt vetoed the Walter-Logan bill, which would have placed administrative agencies directly under the courts and allowed for judicial review of all agency decisions. In his veto message, he indicated that a report would soon address comprehensive reform of federal administrative processes, but that didn't happen.

Our government has created an absolute *behemoth*, and it has slowly but surely replaced our representative government. Our voice doesn't matter much today. If we want to regain our voice and remain a free people, we must return to the fundamental purposes and guiding principles of our Constitution, which begins with the words "We the People." We, the people, must hold our representatives accountable to the Constitution. To do that, we must know what it says!

There have been many books written about the growth and expansion of government, but let's fast forward to 2024 and examine the Administrative State as it exists today. Please join me in the next chapter for a peek at the behemoth our elected representatives and unelected bureaucrats have forced upon us.

> **Haven't I commanded you: be strong and courageous? Do not be afraid or discouraged, for the Lord your God is with you wherever you go.**
>
> **Joshua 1:9**

Chapter Four
The Behemoth

I hope we once again have reminded people that man is not free unless government is limited. There's a clear cause and effect here that is as neat and predictable as a law of physics: As government expands, liberty contracts.

President Ronald Reagan, in his farewell address, January 11, 1989

Over the past year or so, I have researched as much as possible to understand the size and expansion of the federal government since its founding. It has been mind-boggling (to say the least) and astonishing to learn about the kinds of agencies created not just by presidents and Congress, but also by the agencies themselves. I am compelled to share with my fellow Americans what I found so they can understand how out of control the growth of government really is.

After you see the size of our government, you will understand why our national debt as of August 2024 was nearly $35 trillion, why your taxes are so high, and why most Americans are struggling to make ends meet. Our own government is robbing us to pay for things we often don't agree with, things the government has no business being involved with, and things it doesn't do well.

I hope you will appreciate what you learn here. You will find months of research into how many agencies have been created since the first one in 1789.

To the best of my ability, I have also tried to provide the following information for each agency:

1. The name of the agency,
2. The parent agency it falls under,
3. The year it was founded,
4. The founder of the agency,
5. The mission or vision of the agency,
6. The number of employees,
7. The annual budget,
8. The subagencies that have been created underneath it,
9. My take on some of the agencies listed, and
10. The sources from which I obtained this information.

Through my research, I have gathered hundreds of pages of information covering nearly five hundred agencies that I've been able to identify, often including subagencies, boards, commissions, or committees that might fall under them. That would make a daunting read if I shared it all in this book, so I will only give you a sampling of several dozen of those federal agencies, many of which you will recognize. However, I have created a website listing all the agencies I found. You can access it through the QR code shown on this page or visit GovernmentServantOrMaster.com to better visualize and grasp the immense size of the government today. Note that much of the history, mission, and vision verbiage included in each agency's summary is based, in large part, on how the information is presented in the sources used to research each agency. That is, much of it will read like promotional material, but that doesn't come from me. My own comments in "Sandy's Take" will be more objective and opinionated, and based on personal experience.

Agency: US Department of Agriculture (USDA)

Umbrella Agency: Executive Department.

Year Founded/Founder: Founded in 1862 when President Abraham Lincoln signed into law an act of Congress establishing the United States Department of Agriculture.

Mission: "To serve all Americans by providing effective, innovative, science-based public policy leadership in agriculture, food and nutrition, natural resource protection and management, rural development, and related issues with a commitment to delivering equitable and climate-smart opportunities that inspire and help America thrive."

Vision: "An equitable and climate-smart food and agriculture economy that protects and improves the health, nutrition, and quality of life of all Americans, yields healthy land, forests, and clean water, helps rural America thrive, and feeds the world."

Number of Employees: The US Department of Agriculture (USDA) consists of 29 agencies and offices, with nearly 100,000 employees who serve the American people at more than 4,500 locations across the country and abroad.

Annual Budget: $195.5 billion. The 2023 request for mandatory programs was $164.8 billion. USDA's total outlays for 2023 were estimated at $209.3 billion.

Subagencies: Agricultural Marketing Service (AMS), Agricultural Research Service (ARS), Animal and Plant Health Inspection Service (APHIS), Economic Research Service (ERS), Farm Service Agency (FSA), Food and Nutrition Service (FNS), Food Safety and Inspection Service (FSIS), Foreign Agricultural Service (FAS), Forest Service (FS), FPAC Business Center, National Agricultural Statistics Service (NASS), National Institute of Food and Agriculture (NIFA), Natural Resources Conservation Service (NRCS), Risk Management Agency (RMA), Rural Development (RD), Rural Utilities Service (RUS), Rural Housing Service (RHS), Rural Business-Cooperative Service (RBS), National Agricultural Library (NAL).

Staff Offices: Departmental Administration (DA), Office of Partnerships and Public Engagement (OPPE), Office of Budget & Program Analysis (OBPA), Office of the Chief Economist (OCE), Office of the Chief Financial Officer (OCFO),

Office of the Chief Scientist (OCS), Office of Communications (OC), Office of Congressional Relations (OCR), Office of the Executive Secretariat (OES), Office of Hearings and Appeals (OHA), Office of Inspector General (OIG), Office of Tribal Relations (OTR).

Sandy's Take: Over the course of the past three and a half years, the Congressman and I and members of our staff, have visited with many farmers across our district. We've heard concerns about the increasing regulations and the difficulty hiring good workers. Many rely on the H2A program that allows them to bring "nonimmigrant" workers from certain countries to fill temporary agricultural jobs. These nonimmigrant workers make up approximately 10 percent of the agricultural laborers.

Sources: "USDA Celebrates 150 Years," "Offices," "Agricultural Marketing Service (AMS)," US Department of Agriculture, www.usda.gov; "United States Department of Agriculture US Department of Agriculture, FY 2023 Budget Summary," www.usda.gov; "Department of Agriculture (1862–)," National Archives Catalog, catalog.archives.com.

Agency: US Department of Defense (DOD)

Umbrella Agency: Executive Department.

Year Founded/Founder: The Continental Congress authorized the creation of the Continental Army on June 14, 1775, but the Department of Defense was not officially formed until July 26, 1947, when the National Security Act was passed and merged the Navy and War Departments and the newly independent Air Force into a single organization called the National Military Establishment led by a civilian secretary of defense. The National Security Act was amended on August 10, 1949, renaming the National Military Establishment the Department of Defense.

Mission/Vision Statement: "The Department of Defense is America's largest government agency. Our military's roots date back to pre-Revolutionary times, and the department has grown and evolved with our nation. Our mission is to provide the military forces needed to deter war and ensure our nation's security."[101]

Number of Employees: 3.4 million.

Annual Budget: $841.4 billion.

Subagencies: The United States Armed Forces are composed of the Army, Marine Corps, Navy, Air Force, Space Force, and Coast Guard. The Army National Guard and the Air National Guard are reserve components of their services and operate partly under state authority.

Source: "We Are Your Defense," US Department of Defense, www.defense.gov.

Agency: Bureau of Engraving and Printing (BEP)

Umbrella Agency: US Department of the Treasury (USDT).

Year Founded/Founder: The Bureau of Engraving and Printing had its foundations in 1862, with workers signing, separating, and trimming sheets of demand notes in the Treasury building. Gradually, more and more work, including engraving and printing, was entrusted to the organization. Within a few years, BEP produced Fractional Currency, revenue stamps, government obligations, and other security documents for many federal agencies. In 1877, BEP became the sole producer of all United States currency.

Mission: To develop and produce United States currency notes that are trusted worldwide.

Vision: To set the world standard for banknotes and document security through excellence in manufacturing and innovation.

Number of Employees: 1,957.

Annual Budget: $240 million.

Sources: "History," The Bureau of Engraving and Printing, www.bep.gov; "Records of the Bureau of Engraving and Printing," National Archives, www.archives.org; "Open Government: Data," opm.gov; "Department of the Treasury," www.whitehouse.gov.

Agency: Bureau of Indian Affairs (BIA)

Umbrella Agency: US Department of the Interior (DOI).

Year Founded/Founder: Since its inception in 1824, the Bureau of Indian Affairs has been a witness to and a principal player in the relationship between the federal government and Indian tribes and Alaska Native villages. The BIA has changed dramatically over the past 200 years, evolving as federal policies designed to subjugate and assimilate American Indians and Alaska Natives have changed to policies that promote Indian self-determination.

In the early years of the United States, Indian affairs were governed by the Continental Congress, which in 1775 created a Committee on Indian Affairs headed by Benjamin Franklin. Article I, Section 8 of the US Constitution describes Congress's powers over Indian affairs: "To regulate commerce with foreign nations, and among the several States, and with the Indian tribes." The BIA, one of the oldest bureaus in the federal government, was administratively established by then-Secretary of War John C. Calhoun, on March 11, 1824, to oversee and carry out the federal government's trade and treaty relations with the tribes. Congress gave the BIA statutory authority by the act of July 9, 1832 (4 Stat. 564, chap. 174). In 1849, the BIA was transferred to the newly created US Department of the Interior. For years thereafter, the Bureau was known variously as the Indian office, the Indian bureau, the Indian department, and the Indian Service. The Interior Department formally adopted the name "Bureau of Indian Affairs" for the agency on September 17, 1947.

Mission/Vision Statement: The Bureau of Indian Affairs' mission is to enhance the quality of life, to promote economic opportunity, and carry out the responsibility to protect and improve the trust assets of American Indians, Indian tribes, and Alaska Natives.

Number of Employees: 9,231.

Annual Budget: $4.5 billion.

Subagencies/Offices: Coeur d'Alene, Colville, Flathead, Fort Hall, Metlakatla, Northern Idaho, Olympic Peninsula, Puget Sound, Spokane, Taholah, Umatilla, Wapato Irrigation Project, Warm Springs, and Yakama.

Sources: "Bureau of Indian Affairs" US Department of the Interior, www.bia.gov; "Open Government: Data," opm.gov; " and "President Biden's Fiscal Year 2023 Budget Makes Significant Investments in Indian Affairs Programs,"

Agency: Bureau of Land Management (BLM)

Umbrella Agency: US Department of Homeland Security (DHS).

Year Founded/Founder: The roots of the Bureau of Land Management go back to the years after America's independence, when the young nation began acquiring additional lands. At first, these lands were used to encourage homesteading and westward migration. The General Land Office was created in 1812 to support this national goal. President Truman merged the General Land Office and the Grazing Service to create the Bureau of Land Management in 1947.

Mission/Vision Statement: The Bureau of Land Management's mission is to sustain the health, diversity, and productivity of public lands for the use and enjoyment of present and future generations.

Number of Employees: 10,320.

Annual Budget: $1.6 billion.

Subagencies: Energy and Minerals; Planning and NEPA; National Conservation Lands; Recreation and Visitor Services; Wild Horse and Burro; Lands; Realty & Cadastral Survey; Law Enforcement; Fire; Cultural Heritage; Paleontology; Plants and Seeds; Air Resources; Forests & Woodlands; Rangelands and Grazing; Weeds and Invasives; Wildlife Conservation; Aquatic Resources; AML & Environmental Cleanup; Subsistence; Land and Water Conservation Fund.

Sources: "Celebrating 75 Years of the Bureau of Land Management," "Our Mission," and BLM Budget, Bureau of Land Management, www.blm.gov;."Open Government: Data," www.opm.gov; "BLM Budget,"

Agency: US Citizenship and Immigration Services (USCIS)

Umbrella Agency: Department of Homeland Security (DHS).

Year Founded/Founder: The United States Citizenship and Immigration Services (USCIS) has a legacy of more than one hundred years of federal immigration and naturalization administration. The Immigration Act was introduced in the House as H.R. 13586, signed into law by President Benjamin Harrison on March 3, 1891. It gave the federal government direct control over inspecting, admitting, rejecting, and processing all immigrants seeking admission to the United States. The 1891 Act also expanded the list of excludable classes, barring the immigration of polygamists, persons convicted of crimes of moral turpitude, and those suffering from loathsome or contagious diseases.

Federal oversight of immigration began in 1891 when Congress created the first Office of Immigration in the Treasury Department. As immigration grew over the following decades, so did the duties of federal immigration employees. By 1906, lawmakers voted to reform the nation's pathway to citizenship, and the Bureau of Immigration added oversight of naturalization to its responsibilities.

Mission/Vision Statement: USCIS upholds America's promise as a nation of welcome and possibility with fairness, integrity, and respect for all we serve.

Number of Employees: 19,000.

Annual Budget: $913.6 Million

Sandy's Take: The United States Citizenship and Immigration Service is an agency created to manage lawful immigration into the US. Its mission is to uphold "America's promise as a nation of welcome and possibility with fairness, integrity, and respect for all." How I wish the intended role for this agency of the government were its function now! The operative word for USCIS is "lawful," and over the past three years the current administration has allowed into our country more than twelve million unlawful aliens! The very rules and regulations established by USCIS are being used against the United States' own citizens to benefit those who have entered this land of opportunity illegally. It is a shame that those who are standing (or have stood) in line for many years are punished for being law-abiding people wanting to assimilate into a place of individual liberty and the American way of life.

Sources: "Our History" and "Mission and Core Values," US Citizenship and Immigration Services (USCIS), www.uscis.gov; "Citizenship and Immigration Services Overview," Homeland Security, www.dhs.gov; "Department of Homeland Security," www.whitehouse.gov.

Agency: Centers for Disease Control and Prevention (CDC)

Umbrella Agency: US Department of Health and Human Services (HHS).

Year Founded/Founder: On July 1, 1946, the Communicable Disease Center (CDC) opened its doors and occupied one floor of a small building in Atlanta. Its primary mission was simple: to prevent malaria from spreading nationwide. Armed with a budget of only $10 million and fewer than four hundred employees, the agency's early challenges included obtaining enough trucks, sprayers, and shovels to wage war on mosquitoes. As the organization took root deep in the South, once known as the heart of the malaria zone, CDC Founder Dr. Joseph Mountin continued to advocate for public health issues and push the CDC to extend its responsibilities to other communicable diseases. He was a visionary public health leader with high hopes for this small and, at that time, relatively insignificant branch of the Public Health Service. In 1947, the CDC made a token payment of $10 to Emory University for fifteen acres of land on Clifton Road in Atlanta, which now serves as the headquarters of the CDC. The new institution expanded its focus to include all communicable diseases and to provide practical help to state health departments when requested.

Mission: The CDC works 24/7 to protect America from health, safety, and security threats, both foreign and in the US. Whether diseases start at home or abroad, are chronic or acute, curable or preventable, human error or deliberate attack, the CDC fights disease and supports communities and citizens to do the same. The CDC increases the health security of our nation. As the nation's health protection agency, CDC saves lives and protects people from health threats. To accomplish its mission, the CDC conducts critical science, provides health information that protects our nation against expensive and dangerous health threats, and responds when these arise.

Vision: Equitably protecting health, safety & security.

Number of Employees: 9,417.

Annual Budget: $10.675 billion.

Sandy's Take: I started working for Congress while COVID was happening, and after watching the debacle that took place across America and in our district,

I have questioned the wisdom and "mission" of the CDC. As with most federal agencies, they start with the most noble of intentions, but many times their involvement leads to an abuse of power and control. This was demonstrated when the government shut down businesses, schools, and churches and forced vaccine and mask mandates.

Sources: "Our History, Our Story," Centers for Disease Control and Prevention, www.cdc.gov; "Open Government, Data," www.opm.gov; "Fiscal Year 2023 (CDC) Justification of Estimates for Appropriation Committees," Department of Health and Human Services, www.cdc.gov.

Agency: Central Intelligence Agency (CIA)

Umbrella Agency: Independent Agency.

Year Founded/Founder: The Central Intelligence Agency (CIA) is built on the creativity and agility of intelligence officers dedicated to safeguarding our Nation. The Office of Strategic Services (OSS), the Agency's forerunner, was created during World War II and was America's first global intelligence organization. OSS was capable of coordinated espionage, covert action, and counterintelligence—all of which are pieces of today's CIA. As the war ended, OSS's success proved that strategic intelligence had its place in war and peace. President Truman signed the National Security Act of 1947. This established the CIA.

Mission: To preempt threats and further US national security objectives by collecting foreign intelligence that matters, producing objective all-source analysis, conducting effective covert action as directed by the president, and safeguarding the secrets that help keep our nation safe.

Vision: For the CIA's information, insights, and actions to consistently provide tactical and strategic advantage for the United States.

Number of Employees: Approximately 17,000.

Annual Budget: $3.1-3.2 Billion. Some of the funding is undisclosed for security purposes.

Sources: "Legacy" and "Mission and Vision," Central Intelligence Agency, www.cia.gov; "Other Independent Agencies," www.whitehouse.gov; "FY 2023 Budget Request Figure for the National Intelligence Program," Intelligence Resource Program.

Agency: US Courts of Appeals

Umbrella Agency: The United States Courts of Appeals are the intermediate appellate courts of the United States Federal Judiciary. They hear appeals of cases from the United States district courts and some US administrative agencies, and their decisions can be appealed to the Supreme Court of the United States.

Year Founded/Founder: Congress, in the Judiciary Act of 1891, commonly known as the Evarts Act, established nine courts of appeals, one for each judicial circuit at the time. The Act created another judge position for each circuit, identified in the legislation as the circuit justice. Three-judge panels made up of the circuit justice, a court of appeals judge, and a district court judge heard appeals from trial court decisions. The Act recognized nine circuits. Today, twelve circuits hear appeals.

Mission/Vision Statement: The United States Courts are an independent, national judiciary providing fair and impartial justice within the jurisdiction conferred by the Constitution and Congress. As an equal branch of government, the federal judiciary preserves and enhances its core values as the courts meet changing national and local needs.

Number of Employees: 30,000.

Annual Budget: $808 million.

Sources: "The Evarts Act: Creating the Modern Appellate Courts," United States Courts, www.uscourts.gov; "US Courts of Appeals," and "United States Courts," www.linkedin.com.

Agency: US Department of Commerce (DOC)

Umbrella Agency: Executive Department.

Year Founded/Founder: On March 4, 1913, nearly 125 years after the Constitution established the promotion of the "general welfare" as one of the great goals of government, President William Taft signed legislation creating the Department of Commerce.

Mission/Vision Statement: The Department of Commerce's mission is to create the conditions for economic growth and opportunity for all communities.

Number of Employees: 50,846.

Annual Budget: $11.7 billion.

Subagencies: Enterprise Services (ES), Office of Public Engagement (OPE), Office of Executive Secretariat, Office of Faith Based and Neighborhood Partnerships (OFBNP), Office of Inspector General (OIG), Office of Legislative and Governmental Affairs (OLIA), Office of Native Affairs and Economic Development (ONAED), Office of Policy and Strategic Planning (OPSP), Office of Price Administration (OPA), National Institute of Standards and Technology (NIST), National Oceanic and Atmospheric Administration (NOAA), National Technical Information Service (NTIS), National Telecommunications and Information Administration (NTIA), United States Patent and Trademark Office (USPTO), Office of the Secretary (OS), Chief Financial Officer and Assistant Secretary for Administration (CFO/ASA), Office of Small and Disadvantaged Business Utilization (OSDBU), Overseas Criminal Investigations Divisions (OCIO), Office of Community Services (OCS), Office of the Deputy Secretary (ODS), Office of the General Council (OGC), Office of the White House (OWHL), The White House Initiative on Asian Americans and Pacific Islanders (WHIAAPI).

Source: "Origins: 1776–1913," "About Commerce," "Budget and Performance," and "Bureaus and Offices," US Department of Commerce, www.commerce.gov.

Agency: US Commission on International Religious Freedom (USCIRF)

Umbrella Agency: Executive Department.

Year Founded/Founder: The United States Commission on International Religious Freedom (USCIRF) is an independent, bipartisan US Federal

Government agency created by the 1998 International Religious Freedom Act (IRFA), sponsored by Rep. Frank R. Wolf, a Republican from Virginia.

Mission/Vision Statement: To advance international freedom of religion or belief by independently assessing and unflinchingly confronting threats to this fundamental right.

Number of Employees: 24.

Annual Budget: $3.5 million.

Sources: "United States Commission on International Religious Freedom," www.uscirf.gov; "Open Government, Data," opm.gov; "S. 3895; United States Commission on International Religious Freedom Reauthorization Act of 2022," Congressional Budget Office, www.cbo.gov.

Agency: Commission on Security and Cooperation in Europe (CSCE) (US Helsinki Commission)

Umbrella Agency: Independent.

Year Founded/Founder: In 1975, members of the US Congress created the Helsinki Commission to monitor and encourage compliance with the Helsinki Final Act Public Law 94-304. This was a new opportunity to press governments to improve their human rights records and allow expanded contact between people despite Europe's division. The Helsinki Final Act was an agreement signed by thirty-five nations that concluded the Conference on Security and Cooperation in Europe held in Helsinki, Finland. The multifaceted Act addressed many prominent global issues and had a far-reaching effect on the Cold War and US–Soviet relations.

Mission/Vision Statement: This agency describes itself as a US government commission that promotes human rights, military security, and economic cooperation in fifty-seven countries in Europe, Eurasia, and North America. Nine commissioners are members of the Senate, nine are members of the House of Representatives, and three are executive branch officials.

Number of Employees: 21.

Annual Budget: The draft budget for 2023 sets appropriations of €185.6 billion in commitments and €166.3 billion in payments.

Sandy's Take: What are these billions of dollars being used for in these foreign countries? Where is the accountability? How is it benefitting the US? Pay heed to the makeup of its twenty-one employees: nine Senators, nine Representatives, and three executive branch officials.

Sources: "Our History," "Join Our Team," and "Public Law Establishing the Commission," Commission on Security and Cooperation in Europe, www.csce.gov; "Helsinki Final Act, 1975," Office of the Historian, US Department of State, history.state.gov.

Agency: US Customs and Border Protection (CBP)

Umbrella Agency: US Department of Homeland Security (DHS).

Year Founded/Founder: The US Customs Service, the legacy agency of our current US Customs and Border Protection agency, was established on July 31, 1789, by President George Washington. The US Customs Service holds an important place in our nation's history. For its first one hundred years, it was the primary source of funds for the growing US government.

The US Customs Service closed when the US Customs and Border Protection (CBP) agency was established in 2003 as the nation's first comprehensive border security agency. The commissioner and the majority of the Customs Service staff joined CBP then. CBP continues to honor the rich legacy of the US Customs Service by maintaining the integrity of our nation's ports and borders.

Mission: Protect the American people, safeguard our borders, and enhance the nation's economic prosperity.

Vision: Enhancing the nation's security through innovation, intelligence, collaboration, and trust.

Number of Employees: 58,027.

Annual Budget: $14.46 billion.

Subagencies: Air and Marine Operations (AMO), Office of Field Operations (OFO), United States Border Patrol (USBP), Office of Trade, Enterprise Services (ESM), Acquisition, Finance, Human Resources Management (HRM), Training and Development, Information and Technology, Operations Support (OS), Laboratories and Scientific Services (LSS), International Affairs (IA), Chief Counsel, Congressional Affairs (CA), Intergovernmental Liaison (IAPL), Privacy and Diversity, Professional Responsibility, Public Affairs (PA), Trade Relations (TR).

Sandy's Take: Americans are being murdered by illegals crossing our border. Our tax dollars are paying for the millions of people that are crossing our border. I received an email today regarding US Customs and Border Patrols actual numbers of Nationwide Encounters of migrants crossing our borders since Joe Biden and Kamala Harris took office. I have included the graphs below so you can actually see what CBP's reported numbers are. It is alarming and causes me to ask the question: Is this agency fulfilling its stated mission to "Protect the American people, safeguard our borders, and enhance the nation's economic prosperity?"

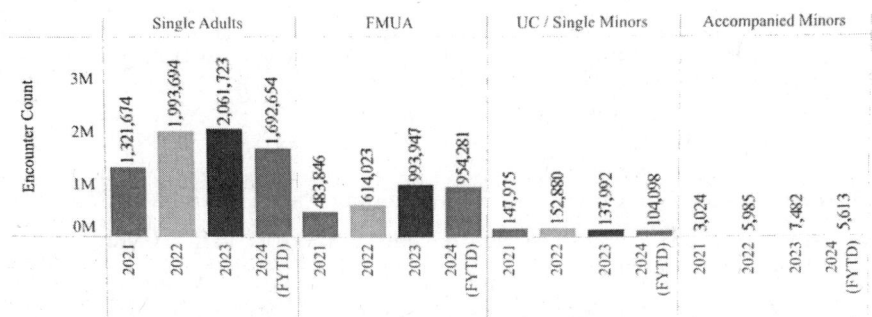

Sources: "Celebrating 227 Years of the US Customs Service, Homeland Security," www.dhs.gov; "About CBP," US Customs and Border Protection, www.cbp.gov; "Open Government, Data," www.opm.gov; "Department of Homeland Security," www.whitehouse.gov.

Agency: Cybersecurity and Infrastructure Security Agency (CISA)

Umbrella Agency: US Department of Homeland Security (DHS)

Year Founded/Founder: President Trump issued Executive Order 13800, "Strengthening the Cybersecurity of Federal Networks and Critical Infrastructure," on May 11, 2017. This was done to improve the nation's cyber posture and capabilities in the face of intensifying cybersecurity threats.

Mission: It leads the national effort to understand, manage, and reduce risk to our cyber and physical infrastructure.

Vision: A secure and resilient critical infrastructure for the American people.

Number of Employees: 2,400.

Annual Budget: $1.96 billion.

Sandy's Take: Since working for the federal government, I have learned through mandatory cybersecurity training that there are an average of 1.1 million cyberattacks each month that must be averted. I have also learned that CISA granted an Information Sharing and Analysis Center (ISAC) contract to Center for Internet Security (CIS), which is a nongovernmental organization that now has access to near real-time access to *all* election records in all fifty states with *zero* public oversight. Since CIS is a nongovernmental organization, it cannot be liable to a Freedom of Information Act (FOIA) request! Suspicious, at best! It is also interesting that our voting systems, "allegedly" not connected to the internet, need to be protected by an organization called "Center for Internet Security."

Sources: "Executive Order on Strengthening the Cybersecurity of Federal Networks and Critical Infrastructure" and "About CISA," Cybersecurity & Infrastructure Security Agency, www.cisa.org; "Cybersecurity and Infrastructure Security Agency Salary Statistics for 2022," www.federalpay.org; "Appendix: Budget of the U.S. Government Fiscal Year 2023," www.whitehouse.gov.

Agency: Defense Advanced Research Projects Agency (DARPA)

Umbrella Agency: US Department of Defense (DOD).

Year Founded/Founder: DARPA owes its creation to the October 1957 launch of Sputnik by the Soviet Union, which many Americans viewed as a technological achievement as unexpected and challenging as Japan's attack on Pearl Harbor.

President Dwight D. Eisenhower created DARPA, among other countermeasures, to sort out and organize competing American missile and space projects, and to delineate boundaries separating the military from civilian space research.

On October 4, 1957, the Soviet Union (USSR) launched the first satellite ever, triggering events that led to the creation of the Advanced Research Projects Agency (ARPA) on February 7, 1958. Although it was well known that both the USSR and the United States were working on satellites for the international scientific collaboration known as the International Geophysical Year (an 18-month "year" from July 1, 1957, to December 31, 1958, and designed to coincide with a peak phase of the solar cycle), many in the United States never fathomed that the USSR would be the first into space. "Now, somehow, in some way, the sky seemed almost alien," then-Senate Majority Leader Lyndon B. Johnson recalled feeling on that night, adding that he remembered "the profound shock of realizing that it might be possible for another nation to achieve technological superiority over this great country of ours." Since its establishment on February 7, 1958, ARPA—which later added the D for "Defense" at the front of its name—has been striving to keep that technological superiority in the hands of the United States.

Mission/Vision Statement: DARPA has held to a singular and enduring mission: to make pivotal investments in breakthrough technologies for national security.

Number of Employees: 220.

Annual Budget: $4.12 billion.

Subagencies: Biological Technologies Offices, Defense Sciences Office, Information Innovations Office, Microsystems Technologies Office, Strategic Technologies Offices, Tactical Technologies Offices.

Sources: "Defense Advanced Research Projects Agency," Britannica, www.britannica.com; "The Sputnik Surprise" and "About DARPA," Defense Advanced Research Projects Agency, www.darpa.mil.

Agency: Department of Education (ED)

Umbrella Agency: Executive Department.

Year Founded/Founder: Although the ED is a relative newcomer among cabinet-level agencies, its origins go back to 1867, when President Andrew Johnson signed legislation creating the first Department of Education. Its main purpose was to collect information and statistics about the nation's schools. However, due to concern that the department would exercise too much control over local schools, the new Department was demoted to an Office of Education in 1868.

Over the years, the office remained relatively small, operating under different titles and housed in various agencies, including the US Department of the Interior and the former US Department of Health Education and Welfare (now Health and Human Services).

Beginning in the 1950s, political and social changes resulted in expanded federal funding for education. The successful launch of the Soviet Union's Sputnik in 1957 spurred nationwide concern that led to increased aid for science education programs. The 1960s saw even more expansion of federal education funding: President Lyndon Johnson's War on Poverty called for the creation of many programs to improve education for poor students at all levels—early childhood through postsecondary. This expansion continued in the 1970s with national efforts to help racial minorities, women, people with disabilities, and non-English-speaking students gain equal access to education. In October 1979, Congress passed the Department of Education Organization Act (Public Law 96–88). Created by combining offices from several federal agencies, the Department began operations in May 1980.

In the 1860s, a budget of $15,000 and four employees handled education fact-finding. By 1965, the Office of Education had more than 2,100 employees and a budget of $1.5 billion. As of mid-2010, the Department had nearly 4,300 employees and a budget of about $60 billion. By fiscal year 2022, the Department's discretionary and mandatory appropriation topped $80 billion, not including student loan outlays. Each of its programs has federal strings and red tape attached. In addition, in 2020, $20–190 billion came through the pandemic's Elementary and Secondary School Emergency Relief Funds (ESSER). That same year, the ED provided $22.5 billion in Pell Grants and oversaw outlays of nearly $100 billion in direct student loans.

Mission/Vision Statement: The ED's mission is to promote student achievement and preparation for global competitiveness by fostering educational excellence and ensuring equal access.

Number of Employees: 4,400.

Annual Budget: $88.3 billion.

Subagencies: Federal Student Aid, Office for Civil Rights, Office of Finance and Operations, Office of Elementary and Secondary Education, Office of Inspector General (ED), Office of Postsecondary Education, Office of Special Education and Rehabilitative Services, Institute of Education Sciences, Office of Planning Evaluation and Policy Development, Office of the General Counsel (ED), Office of Communication and Outreach, Immediate Office of the Secretary of Education, Office of the Chief Information Officer (ED), National Assessment Governing Board, Office of Legislation and Congressional Affairs, Office of the Under Secretary (ED), Office of English Language Acquisition, Office of Career, Technical, and Adult Education.

Sandy's Take: Constitutionally, education is a responsibility of the states. The federal Department of Education is primarily a data-gathering agency that gives mandates to the States to facilitate its objectives. Since the founding of the federal Department of Education, the cost to the States and the taxpayers for education has continually increased, largely because of the number of administrators they are hiring to meet the reporting requirements of the federal government. At the same time, testing scores and student performance continue to decline.

Sources: "An Overview of the US Department of Education," "About ED: Overview and Mission," "Statement by Miguel Cardona Secretary of Education on the US Department of Education," and "Department of Education Funding Levels," US Department of Education, www.ed.gov; Paul Dans and Steve Groves, eds., *Mandate for Leadership 2025*, The Heritage Foundation (2023), 320–321.

Agency: Department of Energy (DOE)

Umbrella Agency: Executive Department.

Year Founded/Founder: President Carter signed the Department of Energy Organization Act on August 4, 1977. The Federal Energy Administration and Energy Research and Development Administration were abolished. This created one of the most interesting and diverse agencies in the federal government. Activated on October 1, 1977, the twelfth cabinet-level department brought together for the first time within one agency two programmatic traditions that had long coexisted within the federal establishment: (1) defense responsibilities, including the design, construction, and testing of nuclear weapons dating back to the Manhattan Project effort to build the atomic bomb; and (2) a loosely knit amalgamation of energy-related programs scattered throughout the Federal government.

Mission/Vision Statement: The mission of the Energy Department is to ensure America's security and prosperity by addressing its energy, environmental, and nuclear challenges through transformative science and technology solutions.

Number of Employees: 14,000 federal employees and more than 95,000 management and operating contractors.

Annual Budget: $48.2 billion.

Subagencies: Office of Electricity, Energy Policy & Programs, Advanced Research Projects Agency, Program Offices (17 offices), Staff Offices (20 offices), Labs and Technology Centers (21 Offices), Power Marketing Administration (4 offices), Operations Offices (11 offices), Energy Information Administration, National Nuclear Security Administration.

Sources: "August 4, 1977: President Carter signs the Department of Energy Organization Act," "A Brief History of the Department of Energy," and "Mission," Department of Energy, www.energy.gov; "Department of Energy," "Offices," trumpadministration.archives.performance.gov.

Agency: Department of Homeland Security (DHS)

Umbrella Agency: Executive Department.

Year Founded/Founder: After September 11, 2001, President George W. Bush took decisive steps to protect America. These ranged from hardening cockpits and stockpiling vaccines to tightening our borders. The President used his maximum legal authority to establish the White House Office of Homeland Security and the Homeland Security Council to ensure that our federal response and protection efforts were coordinated and effective. The President also directed Tom Ridge, our first Homeland Security Advisor, to study the federal government as a whole to determine if the current structure allowed us to meet the threats of today while anticipating the unknown threats of tomorrow. After careful study of the current structure—coupled with the experience gained after September 11 and new information we have learned about our enemies while fighting a war—the President concluded that our nation needed a more unified homeland security structure. In designing the new department, the Administration considered several homeland security organizational proposals that have emerged from outside studies, commissions, and members of Congress.

Mission/Vision Statement: The Department of Homeland Security has a vital mission: to secure the nation from the many threats we face.

Number of Employees: 229,000.

Annual Budget: $85.6 billion.

Subagencies: United States Citizenship and Immigration Services (USCIS), United States Coast Guard (USCG), United States Customs and Border Patrol (CBP), Cybersecurity & Infrastructure Security Agency (CISA), Federal Emergency Management Agency (FEMA), Federal Law Enforcement Training Center (FLETC), United States Immigration and Customs Enforcement (ICE), United States Secret Service (USSS), Transportation Security Administration (TSA), Management Directorate (MGMT), Science and Technology Directorate (S&T), Countering Weapons of Mass Destruction Office (CWMD), Office of Intelligence & Analysis (I&A), Office of the Secretary and Administration (OSA), Office of Homeland Security (OHS), Office of the Immigration Detention Ombudsman (OIDO), and 4 organizational offices.

Sources: "The Department of Homeland Security," "Mission," and "Secretary of Homeland Security," www.dhs.gov; "Appropriations Committee Releases Fiscal Year 2023 Homeland Security Funding Bill," appropriations.house.gov.

Agency: US Department of Health and Human Services (HHS)

Umbrella Agency: Executive Department.

Year Founded/Founder: President Eisenhower created the cabinet-level Department of Health, Education, and Welfare (HEW), which officially came into existence on April 11, 1953. In 1979, the Department of Education Organization Act was signed into law, providing for a separate Department of Education. HEW became the Department of Health and Human Services, which officially came into existence on May 4, 1980.

Mission/Vision Statement: The mission of the US Department of Health and Human Services (HHS) is to enhance the health and well-being of all Americans by providing effective health and human services and by fostering sound, sustained advances in the sciences underlying medicine, public health, and social services.

Number of Employees: 80,000.

Annual Budget: $127.3 billion in discretionary; $1.7 trillion in mandatory budget authority for FY 2023.

Subagencies: Administration for Children and Families (ACF), Advance Research Projects Agency for Health (ARPA-H), Administration for Strategic Preparedness and Response (ASPR), Agency for Healthcare Research and Quality (AHRQ), Agency for Toxic Substances and Disease Registry (ATSDR), Assistant Secretary for Administration (ASA), Assistant Secretary for Financial Resources (ASFR), Office of the Assistant Secretary for Health (OASH), Office of Assistant Secretary for Legislation (OASL), Office of the Assistant Secretary for Planning and Evaluation (ASPE), Office of Assistant Secretary for Public Affairs (ASPA), Center for Faithbased and Neighborhood Partnerships (CFBNP), Centers for Disease Control and Prevention (CDC), Centers for Medicare and Medicaid services (CMS), Department Appeals Board (DAB), Food and Drug Administration (FDA), Health Resources and Services Administration (HRSA), Immediate Office of the Secretary (IOS), Indian Health Service (IHS), National Institutes of Health (NIH), Office for Civil Rights (OCR), Office of Global Affairs (OGA), Office of Inspector General (OIG), Intergovernmental and External Affairs (IEA), Office of Medicare Hearing and Appeals (OMHA), Office of General Council (OGC), Office of the National Coordinator for Health Information Technology (ONC), and Substance Abuse and Mental Health Services Administration (SAMHSA).

Sandy's Take: HHS is the largest grant-making agency in the US, giving away tens of thousands of grants each year. Most HHS grants are provided directly to states, territories, tribes, and educational and community organizations, then given to people and organizations who are eligible to receive funding. Please note the tables below of those who are to receive grant funding in 2024. I am scratching my head and wondering how we can do this when we have nearly $35 trillion in debt! Our country is falling off the fiscal cliff, and we're giving billions of dollars away! We're not giving this money to Americans only, but to other countries as well. Read the numbers for yourself and see if you can figure it out. The first table is only one of thirteen pages. Where do you think the government gets their money? They get money from "we, the people" by taxing us to death!

Grants by World Region

FY	OPDIV	Region	Award Row Count	Award Amount
2024	ALL	NA - North America	104,026	$597,798,631,453
2024	ALL	AF - Africa	612	$564,202,806
2024	ALL	EU - Europe	131	$31,676,460
2024	ALL	CA - Central America	47	$26,102,977
2024	ALL	AS - Asia	93	$17,410,011
2024	ALL	SA - South America	52	$10,265,686
2024	ALL	OC - Oceania	24	$5,981,505
2024	ALL	ME - Middle East	23	$2,637,324
			105,008	$598,456,908,221

Grant Awards by US State and Territory

FY	OPDIV	State	Award Row Count	Award Amount
2024	ALL	CA	11,807	$91,429,460,516
2024	ALL	NY	8,151	$61,462,503,922
2024	ALL	TX	5,125	$31,594,977,411
2024	ALL	PA	5,164	$24,349,581,710
2024	ALL	OH	3,002	$23,179,454,980
2024	ALL	FL	2,791	$21,171,739,299
2024	ALL	IL	3,327	$18,756,788,010
2024	ALL	NC	3,675	$18,041,817,191
2024	ALL	MI	3,184	$17,493,636,836
2024	ALL	VA	1,773	$16,641,680,052
2024	ALL	IN	1,416	$15,808,030,947

Sources: "HHS Historical Highlights," "The Mission of HHS," "HHS Agencies and Roles," and "HHS FY 2023 Budget in Brief," US Department of Health and Human Services, www.hhs.gov.

Agency: Department of Housing and Urban Development (HUD)

Umbrella Agency: Executive Department.

Year Founded/Founder: Created as part of President Lyndon B. Johnson's War on Poverty, the Department of Housing and Urban Development (HUD) was established as a cabinet department by the Department of Housing and Urban Development Act (42 U.S.C. 3532–3537), effective November 9, 1965. It consolidated a number of other older federal agencies.

Mission/Vision Statement: HUD's mission is to create strong, sustainable, inclusive communities and quality affordable homes for all.

Number of Employees: 9,600.

Annual Budget: $71.9 billion.

Subagencies: Federal Housing Administration (FHA), GINNIE MAE, Public Indian Housing (PIH), Office of Community Planning and Development (CPD), Office of Fair Housing and Equal Opportunity (FHEO), Office of Lead Hazard Control and Healthy Homes (OLHCHH), Center for Faithbased and Neighborhood Partnerships (CFBNP), Office of Policy and Research (PDR), Office of Sustainable Housing and Communities (OSHC) , Office of Strategic Planning and Management (OSPM), Planning and Management Office of Chief Operating Officer.

Sandy's Take: Our congressional office has received many complaints from constituents who live in local housing that falls under HUD's jurisdiction. In each case the quality of living has been subpar, and thy cannot even get basic help with simple things such as a stove that is not working, an infestation of roaches or rats, or water damage with no repairs after two years, even when money was provided by HUD to do the repairs. The tenants' questions go unanswered about rent, and the service from these public housing organizations is poor and uncaring. HUD needs to improve their management of its subcontractors and fulfill their mission as stated.

Sources: "Questions and Answers about HUD," "Mission," "Introduction," and "2023 Budget in Brief," US Department of Housing and Urban Development (HUD), www.hud.gov; "US Department of Housing and Urban Development HUD," www.usa.gov.

Agency: Department of Justice (DOJ)

Umbrella Agency: Executive Department.

Year Founded/Founder: The Office of the Attorney General was created by the Judiciary Act of 1789, officially titled "An Act to Establish the Judicial Courts of the United States," which President George Washington signed into law on September 24, 1789.

The Office of the Attorney General was a one-person, part-time position. The Act specified that the Attorney General was to be "learned in the law," with the duty "to prosecute and conduct all suits in the Supreme Court in which the United States shall be concerned, and to give his advice and opinion upon questions of law when required by the President of the United States, or when requested by the heads of any of the departments, touching any matters that may concern their departments."

However, the workload quickly became too much for one person, necessitating the hiring of several assistants for the Attorney General. As the work steadily increased along with the size of the new nation, private attorneys were retained to work on cases.

By 1870, after the end of the Civil War, the increase in litigation involving the United States required the very expensive retention of a large number of private attorneys to handle the workload. A concerned Congress passed the Act to establish the Department of Justice (ch. 150, 16 Stat. 162), creating "an executive department of the government of the United States" with the Attorney General as its head.

Officially established on July 1, 1870, the Department of Justice was empowered to handle all criminal prosecutions and civil suits in which the United States had an interest. To assist the Attorney General, the 1870 act also created the Office of the Solicitor General, representing the interests of the United States before the US Supreme Court.

The 1870 Act remains the foundation for the Department's authority, but its structure has changed over the years, with the addition of the offices of Deputy Attorney General and Associate Attorney General and the formation of various components, offices, boards, and divisions. From its beginning as a one-man, part-time position, the Department of Justice has evolved into the world's largest law office and the chief enforcer of federal laws.

Mission/Vision Statement: The mission of the Department of Justice (DOJ) is to uphold the rule of law, to keep our country safe, and to protect civil rights.

Number of Employees: 115,000.

Annual Budget: $37.7 billion.

Subagencies: Leadership Offices (4), Litigating Offices (9), Law Enforcement Offices (5), Corrections Offices (4), Grant Offices (9), Media and Community

Outreach Offices (4), Victim Services Offices (6), Management and Administration Offices (11), Oversight Offices (6), and Initiatives Projects and Task Forces (14).

Sandy's Take: The DOJ is an agency with a lot of power. I have received calls from constituents and employees who wanted to blow the whistle on this agency but were afraid of the repercussions. Two expressed fear of losing their lives. The Department's mission is to uphold the rule of law, to keep our country safe, and to protect civil rights. Is justice blind in America today?

Sources: "Judiciary Act of 1789: Primary Documents in American History" (Virtual Programs & Services), Library of Congress, guides.loc.gov; "About DOJ," "Why Justice" and "Agencies," and "US Department of Justice FY 2023 Budget Summary," US Department of Justice, www.justice.gov.

Agency: Department of Labor (DOL)

Umbrella Agency: Executive Department.

Year Founded/Founder: The law creating the US Department of Labor, signed by President William H. Taft on March 4, 1913, was virtually overlooked among the historic events of that day. The city of Washington was bursting with goings-on of all kinds. It was Inauguration Day for Woodrow Wilson, and the usual social whirl accompanied such an event. In addition, the 62nd Congress was still in session on Inauguration morning. The retiring president had a pile of bills upon which to act, one of them being the Sulzer Bill to create a Department of Labor headed by a cabinet officer.

Taft had mixed feelings about the bill and faced a difficult choice: he could sign it into law, even though he was not pleased with it; he could veto it outright, even though his objection to the bill might be misinterpreted; or, by taking no action, he could let the bill die when his term of office ran out—the so-called "pocket veto." That morning, the *New York Times* reported that the outgoing president might veto the bill, send his reasons to Congress, and give the measure's advocates a chance to override his veto if they could.

After an early breakfast, only a few hours before Woodrow Wilson took office, President Taft went to the executive office in the Senate. The Department of Labor bill was still unsigned. Following tradition, the president-elect arrived at the office before being received in the Senate. He could see the rotund figure of Taft at work in the next room, signing bills. During these closing hours of his administration, President Taft signed into law the act giving birth to the Department of Labor.

Mission/Vision Statement: To foster, promote, and develop the welfare of the wage earners, job seekers, and retirees of the United States, improve working conditions, advance opportunities for profitable employment, and assure work-related benefits and rights.

Number of Employees: 16,246.

Annual Budget: $14.6 billion.

Subagencies: Bureau of International Labor Affairs (ILAB), Bureau of Labor Statistics (BLS), Employee Benefits Security Administration (EBSA), Employment Training Administration (ETA), Mine Safety and Health Administration (MSHA), Occupational Safety and Health Administration (OSHA), Office of Congressional and Intergovernmental Affairs (OCIA), Office of the Assistant Secretary for Administration and Management (OASAM), Office of the Assistant Secretary for Policy (OASP), Office of the Chief Financial Officer (OCFO), Office of Disability Employment Policy (ODEP), Office of Federal Contract Compliance Programs (OFCCP), Office of Inspector General (OIG), Office of Labor Management and Standards (OLMS), Office of the Solicitor (SOL).

Sandy's Take: The DOL is a powerful agency that controls the benefits of many Americans. In my opinion, it is one of the most abusive agencies. It uses all three powers it has been given by the APA on a regular basis. It is an agency that often passes the buck to the constituent when they've made a mistake rather than taking responsibility for it.

Sources: "The Origin of the US Department of Labor," "Agencies," "About Us," and "FY 2023 Department of Labor Budget in Brief," US Department of Labor, www.dol.gov; "Open Government, Data," www.opm.gov.

Agency: Department of State (DOS)

Umbrella Agency: Executive Department.

Year Founded/Founder: The Constitution of the United States, drafted in Philadelphia in the summer of 1787 and ratified by the States the following year, gave the president responsibility for the conduct of the nation's foreign relations. It soon became clear, however, that an executive branch was necessary to support President Washington in the affairs of the new federal government.

The House and Senate approved legislation establishing a Department of Foreign Affairs on July 21, 1789. President Washington signed it into law on July 27, making the Department of Foreign Affairs the first federal agency to be created under the new Constitution. This legislation remains the basic law of the Department of State. In September 1789, additional legislation changed the agency's name to the Department of State and assigned it a variety of domestic duties.

Mission/Vision Statement: To protect and promote US security, prosperity, and democratic values, and to shape an international environment where all Americans can thrive.

Number of Employees: 69,000.

Annual Budget: $60.4 billion.

Subagencies: 68 subagencies. Check through the sources listed below to see an organizational chart.

Sandy's Take: This agency is one that congressional offices work with daily regarding passports, visas, embassies, and other issues. It is like a slow-moving machine that gets nowhere fast. Passport processing has improved, but my colleagues and I sometimes wonder if anyone is working.

Sources: "A History of the United States Department of State, 1789–1996," Department of State, 1997–2001," "About the US Department of State," "US Department of State and US Agency for International Development FY 2023 Budget Request," www.state.gov; "US Department of State (DOS)," www.usa.gov.

Agency: US Department of the Treasury (TREAS)

Umbrella Agency: Executive Department.

Year Founded/Founder: The Department of the Treasury is a cabinet department of the United States executive branch. It is managed by a secretary that the president appoints. The Department of the Treasury was officially formed by the Treasury Bill (HR-9) passed on July 2, 1789. President George Washington signed the bill into law on September 2, 1789.

Mission/Vision Statement: The department's original mission was to improve, regulate, and provide reports to Congress on the United States' revenue, expenditures, and public credit.

The mission of the Department of the Treasury now is to formulate and recommend economic, fiscal, and tax policies, serve as the government's financial agent, enforce the law, protect the president and other officials, and manufacture coins and currency.

Number of Employees: Over 100,000.

Annual Budget: $15.6 billion.

Subagencies: Alcohol and Tobacco Tax and Trade Bureau (TTB), Bureau of Engraving & Printing (BEP), Bureau of the Fiscal Service, The Financial Crimes Enforcement Network (FinCEN), The Inspector General (IG), Treasury Inspector General for Tax Administration (TIGTA), Internal Revenue Service (IRS), The Office of the Comptroller of the Currency (OCC), The U.S. Mint.

Sandy's Take: America needs the Treasury Department to keep our books in order and provide reports to Congress. It is a necessary agency, but recently my office has been made aware that, due to the passage of the Corporate Transparency Act, the Treasury is requiring all companies created in the US to complete a new form with the Treasury Department's Financial Crimes Enforcement Network (FinCEN). If companies fail to comply, they could receive a penalty of up to $591 per day, two years in prison, and a fine up to $10,000. We have had several constituents receive the letter that they needed to comply. Supposedly the goal is to "safeguard the financial system from illicit activity, counter money laundering . . . and promote national security through strategic use of financial authorities and the collection, analysis, and dissemination of financial intelligence."[102] This is an overreach of government. If you haven't committed a crime, why does the government need your information to add you to a "list of suspects"? If you compare the Treasury's original mission statement—"to improve, regulate, and provide reports to Congress on the United States's revenue, expenditures, and public credit"—to their current stated mission, it is clear they have gotten off course.

Sources: "Department of the Treasury," George Washington's Mount Vernon, www.mountvernon.org; "Careers at our Bureaus," US Department of the Treasury, home.treasury.gov; "Appropriations Committee Releases Fiscal Year 2023 Financial Services and General Government Funding Bill," appropriations.house.gov.

Agency: Department of Transportation (DOT)

Umbrella Agency: Executive Department.

Year Founded/Founder: President Lyndon B. Johnson took office on November 22, 1963, following the assassination of President John F. Kennedy. Using legislative and political skills he had learned during his more than twenty years in Congress, President Johnson immediately pushed through many laws that President Kennedy had initiated, including the Urban Mass Transportation Act of 1964. Two years later Congress established the landmark law creating a US Department of Transportation. The department's first official day of operation was April 1, 1967.

Mission/Vision Statement: To deliver the world's leading transportation system, serving the American people and economy through the safe, efficient, sustainable, and equitable movement of people and goods.

Number of Employees: 55,000.

Annual Budget: $105 billion.

Subagencies: Commercial Space Transportation Office (AST), Federal Aviation Administration (FAA), Federal Highway Administration (FHWA), Federal Motor

Carrier Safety Administration (FMCSA), Federal Railroad Administration (FRA), Federal Transit Administration (FTA), Maritime Administration (MA), National Highway Traffic Safety Administration (NHTSA), Office of Motor Carrier Safety (FMCSA), Pipeline and Hazardous Materials Safety Administration (PHMSA), Research and Innovative Technology Administration (RITA), Research and Special Programs Administration (RSP), Bureau of Transportation Statistics (BTS), Great Lakes St. Lawrence Seaway Development Corporation (GLS).

Sandy's Take: I have traveled and lived in other countries, and I believe the US has some of the nicest roads and transportation systems in the world. It is a necessary agency, and the service of the different states varies I'm sure, based on personnel. I have found that the DOT doesn't communicate on a local level via returned phone calls or emails, but tends to respond to a congressional inquiry, fixing the problem after receiving a voicemail. My office learns that it has been done when the constituent calls to thank us or we call them to see if the problem is resolved.

Sources: "A Great Day in America: USDOT's 50th Anniversary," US Department of Transportation: Federal Highway Administration, highways.dot.gov; "About DOT," "US Department of Transportation Administrations," and "Budget Highlights 2023," US Department of Transportation, www.transportation.gov.

Agency: Department of Veterans Affairs (VA)

Umbrella Agency: Executive Department.

Year Founded/Founder: The Department of Veterans Affairs was established on March 15, 1989, by President George H.W. Bush, succeeding the Veterans Administration and assuming responsibility for providing federal benefits to veterans and their dependents. Led by the Secretary of Veterans Affairs, the VA is the second largest of the fourteen cabinet departments. It operates nationwide programs of healthcare assistance services and national cemeteries.

History of the Agency:

1930. The Veterans Administration was created by Executive Order S.398, signed by President Herbert Hoover on July 21, 1930. At that time, there were 54 hospitals, 4.7 million living veterans, and 31,600 employees.

1933. The Board of Veterans Appeals was established.

1944. On June 22, President Franklin D. Roosevelt signed the Servicemen's Readjustment Act of 1944. (Public Law 346 was passed unanimously by the 78th Congress). This law offered home loans and education benefits to veterans.

1946. The Department of Medicine & Surgery was established. In 1989, it was succeeded by the Veterans Health Services and Research Administration, which was renamed the Veterans Health Administration in 1991.

1953. The Department of Veterans Benefits was established and succeeded in 1989 by the Veterans Benefits Administration.

1973. The National Cemetery System (except for Arlington National Cemetery) was transferred to the VA.

1988. President Reagan signed legislation to elevate VA to cabinet status.

1989. March 15. VA became the fourteenth department in the president's cabinet.

Mission/Vision Statement: To fulfill President Lincoln's promise, "To care for him who shall have borne the battle, and for his widow, and his orphan" by serving and honoring the men and women who are America's veterans.

Number of Employees: 266,000.

Annual Budget: $135 billion.

Subagencies: Veterans Health Administration (VHA), Veterans Benefits Administration (VBA), National Cemetery Administration (NCA), Board of Veterans' Appeals (BVA).

Sandy's Take: Veterans Affairs has done a lot for veterans and continues to do so. Over the past few years, they have worked to improve their systems that have been in place for a long time, bringing them up to 2024 standards. This has hurt the older veterans, of which there are many. Many veterans don't use technology and have been accustomed to receiving their travel money in a certain way via a kiosk, receiving their reimbursement quickly. Now they must struggle with technology to make their appointments through a call center and file online to get their travel reimbursement. The VA should be considerate of all veterans and accommodate the older and the younger veterans alike. It's the least we can do in return for what our men and women in uniform have sacrificed for us.

Sources: "History," House Committee on Veterans' Affairs, veterans.house.gov; "About the Department," US Department of Veterans Affairs, department.va.gov; "Mission Statement," Department of Veterans Affairs, govinfo.library.unt.edu; "Appropriations Committee Releases Fiscal Year 2023 Military Construction, Veterans Affairs, and Related Agencies Funding Bill," appropriations.house.gov.

Agency: Economic Development Administration (EDA)

Umbrella Agency: US Department of Commerce.

Year Founded/Founder: In 1961, the Area Redevelopment Administration (ARA) was established as a demonstration project and became the first federal program designed to advance area economic development. This pilot program represented a significant adjustment of previous federal macro-economic development policy as it focused on providing federal resources that were based on an understanding of and tailored to meet the unique needs of distressed portions of the country. The ARA was authorized to implement several programs, including those focused on providing business loans, public facility grants and loans, technical assistance, and training assistance. By June 1963, the ARA had exhausted its public facility grant authorization and implemented the public facility program solely with loans for the next two years.

In 1965, Congress passed the Public Works and Economic Development Act of 1965, and President Lyndon Johnson signed it into law on August 26, 1965, (PWEDA; 42 U.S.C. § 3121). It authorized the creation of the Economic Development Administration (EDA) to succeed the previous ARA organization.

Mission/Vision Statement: To lead the federal economic development agenda by promoting innovation and competitiveness, preparing American regions for growth and success in the worldwide economy.

Number of Employees: 202.

Annual Budget: $146.81 million.

Subagencies/Offices: Atlanta Regional Office: Alabama, Florida, Georgia, Kentucky, Mississippi, North Carolina, South Carolina, Tennessee; **Austin Regional Office:** Arkansas, Louisiana, New Mexico, Oklahoma, Texas; **Chicago Regional Office**: Illinois, Indiana, Michigan, Minnesota, Ohio, Wisconsin; **Denver Regional Office:** Colorado, Iowa, Kansas, Missouri, Montana, North Dakota, Nebraska, South Dakota, Utah, Wyoming; **Philadelphia Regional Office:** Connecticut, Delaware, District of Columbia, Maine, Maryland, Massachusetts, New Hampshire, New Jersey, New York, Pennsylvania, Rhode Island, Vermont, Virginia, West Virginia, Puerto Rico, Virgin Islands; **Seattle Regional Office:** Alaska, Arizona, California, Hawaii, Idaho, Nevada, Oregon, Washington, American Samoa, Northern Mariana Islands, Guam, Federated States of Micronesia, Rep. of Marshall Islands, Rep. of Palau.

Sources: "History of EDA," www.eda.gov; "Open Government, Data," www.opm.gov; "Economic Development Administration Fiscal Year 2023 Congressional Budget Request, March 28, 2022," United States Department of Commerce, www.commerce.gov.

Agency: Equal Employment Opportunity Commission (EEOC)

Umbrella Agency: Independent Agency.

Year Founded/Founder: The Equal Employment Opportunity Commission (EEOC) was created by Title VII of the Civil Rights Act when it was signed into law by President Lyndon Johnson on July 2, 1964. It prohibited discrimination in public places, provided for integrating schools and other public facilities, and made employment discrimination illegal. It was the most sweeping civil rights legislation since the Reconstruction. In a nationally televised address on June 6, 1963, President John F. Kennedy urged the nation to take action toward guaranteeing equal treatment of every American regardless of race. Soon after, Kennedy proposed that Congress consider civil rights legislation addressing voting rights, public accommodations, school desegregation, nondiscrimination in federally assisted programs, and more.

Despite Kennedy's assassination in November of 1963, his proposal culminated in the Civil Rights Act of 1964. President Lyndon Johnson signed it into law just a few hours after Congress passed it on July 2, 1964.

The act outlawed segregation in businesses such as theaters, restaurants, and hotels. It banned discriminatory practices in employment and ended segregation in public places such as swimming pools, libraries, and public schools.

The passage of the act was not easy, however. Opposition in the House of Representatives bottled up the bill in the House Rules Committee. In the Senate, Southern Democratic opponents attempted to talk the bill to death in a filibuster. In early 1964, House supporters overcame the Rules Committee obstacle by threatening to send the bill to the floor without committee approval. The Senate filibuster was overcome through the floor leadership of Senator Hubert Humphrey of Minnesota, the considerable support of President Lyndon Johnson, and the efforts of Senate Minority Leader Everett Dirksen of Illinois, who convinced enough Republicans to support the bill over Democratic opposition. When the compromise bill was finally put to a vote in the Senate, it passed 73 to 27. It was noted in the Congressional Record that applause broke out in the Senate galleries.

Title VII of the act created the EEOC to implement the law. The EEOC enforces laws that prohibit discrimination based on race, color, religion, sex, national origin, disability, or age in hiring, promoting, firing, setting wages, testing, training, apprenticeship, and all other terms and conditions of employment.

Mission: Prevent and remedy unlawful employment discrimination and advance equal opportunity for all in the workplace.

Vision: Respectful and inclusive workplaces with equal employment opportunity for all.

Number of Employees: 2,347.

Annual Budget: $464.65 million.

Subagencies: Chair/Commissioner Offices (There are five commissioners appointed by the president and confirmed by the Senate) Office of the Chief Human Capital Officer (OCHCO), Office of Enterprise Data and Analytics

(OEDA), Office of Federal Operations (OFO), Office of General Counsel (OGC), Office of Legal Counsel (OLC), Field Offices (53).

Sandy's Take: The purpose of the EEOC is to administer and enforce civil rights laws against workplace discrimination in all types of work situations (hiring, firing, promotions, harassment, training, wages, and benefits). It now includes classes of individuals who cannot be discriminated against based on their ethnicity, color, gender identity, race, religion, national origin, sexual orientation, age (forty and older), disability, or genetic information. During the pandemic, many employees who applied for religious liberty waivers from their employers to abstain from taking a COVID vaccination were denied, and often with the help of an attorney, an EEOC complaint was filed on their behalf. The EEOC prides itself on "thoroughly" investigating every claim but litigates few complaints because its goal is to (in its words) consider the "wider impact" a lawsuit could have on the EEOC's efforts to combat workplace discrimination. Having lived and worked in an office environment during the pandemic, it's my experience that most EEOC complaints based on religious discrimination were NOT seriously investigated because of the faulty position the government held against individuals who would not comply with vaccinations as a group. In other words, the very class it was supposed to protect became victim to the government's overreach to protect itself! In my view, the EEOC is ineffective because it is so selective of the complaints it investigates. I believe this is based on the Biden Administration's "woke" political views. This is contradictory to its original enactment to protect against real discrimination of the innate civil liberties of individuals guaranteed to individuals by our Constitution. It should, at least, be restructured with new provisions that are kept sacred by strict oversight of the Office of Inspector General, under which it currently operates.

Sources: "Civil Rights Act (1964)," National Archives, www.archives.gov; "EEOC Budget and Staffing History 1980 to Present," and "Fiscal Year 2023 Congressional Budget Justification," US Equal Employment Opportunity Commission, www.eeoc.gov.

Agency: Environmental Protection Agency (EPA)

Umbrella Agency: Independent Agency.

Year Founded/Founder: The American conversation about protecting the environment began in the 1960s. Rachel Carson in 1962 published *Silent Spring*, her attack on the indiscriminate use of pesticides. Concern about air and water pollution had spread in the wake of disasters. An offshore oil rig in California fouled beaches with millions of gallons of spilled oil. Near Cleveland, Ohio, the Cuyahoga River, choking with chemical contaminants, had spontaneously burst into flames. Astronauts had begun photographing the Earth from space, heightening awareness that the Earth's resources are finite.

In early 1970, due to heightened public concerns about deteriorating city air, natural areas littered with debris, and urban water supplies contaminated with dangerous impurities, President Richard Nixon presented the House and Senate with a groundbreaking thirty-seven-point message on the environment. These points included requesting $4 billion for the improvement of water treatment facilities, asking for national air quality standards and stringent guidelines to lower motor vehicle emissions, launching federally funded research to reduce automobile pollution, ordering a clean-up of federal facilities that had fouled air and water, seeking legislation to end the dumping of wastes into the Great Lakes, proposing a tax on lead additives in gasoline, forwarding to Congress a plan to tighten safeguards on the seaborne transportation of oil, and approving a national contingency plan for the treatment of oil spills.

Around the same time, President Nixon also created a council to consider how to organize federal government programs designed to reduce pollution so that those programs could efficiently address the goals laid out in his message on the environment. Following the council's recommendations, the president sent Congress a plan to consolidate many environmental responsibilities of the federal government under one agency, a new Environmental Protection Agency. This reorganization would permit response to environmental problems in a manner beyond the previous capability of government pollution control programs:

The EPA would be able to research important pollutants irrespective of the media in which they appear and their impact on the environment.

The EPA would monitor the condition of the environment—biological and physical—both independently and with other agencies.

With these data, the EPA would be able to establish quantitative "environmental baselines"—critical for adequately measuring the success or failure of pollution abatement efforts.

The EPA would be able to set and enforce standards for air, water, and individual pollutants in concert with the States.

Industries seeking to minimize the adverse environmental impact of their activities would be assured of consistent standards covering the full range of their waste-disposal problems.

As states developed and expanded their pollution control programs, they could turn to one agency for financial, technical, and training assistance.

After hearings that summer, the House and Senate approved the proposal. The agency's first Administrator, William Ruckelshaus, took the oath of office on December 4, 1970.

Mission/Vision Statement: The mission of the EPA is to protect human health and the environment.

Number of Employees: 15,000.

Annual Budget: $11.88 billion.

Subagencies: Office of the Administrator (AO), Office of Air and Radiation (OAR), Office of Chemical Safety and Pollution Prevention (OCSPP), Office of the Chief Financial Officer (OCFO), Office of Enforcement and Compliance Assurance (OECA), Office of Environmental Justice and External Civil Rights (OEJECR), Office of General Counsel (OGC), Office of Inspector General (OIG), Office of International and Tribal Affairs (OITA), Office of Land and Emergency Management (OLEM), Office of Mission Support (OMS), Office of Research and Development (ORD), Office of Water (OW), and 10 regional offices located in the cities of Boston, New York, Philadelphia, Atlanta, Chicago, Dallas, Kansas City, Denver, San Francisco and Seattle.

Sandy's Take: I believe the EPA has become overreaching and is encroaching on Americans' personal rights and freedoms. *It is overreach* when a church owns property and plans to build to expand their ministry only to be denied when the EPA finds a type of plant growing on the property which they consider endangered! This church now has no land on which to expand their ministry. When the EPA is allowed to levy extravagant fines on towns and localities and then force local leaders to pay for unnecessary water systems that are not affordable when there are other options available, *that is overreach*! This agency receives nearly twelve billion taxpayer dollars annually, and many times they use that money to abuse citizens. My take is that the EPA is bad for our freedom and our country. We need to be good stewards of our environment, but our freedoms must remain intact.

Sources: "The Origins of EPA," "Our Mission and What We Do," "What Kind of People Work at EPA?," and "FY 2025 Budget," United States Environmental Protection Agency, www.epa.gov.

Agency: Federal Aviation Administration (FAA)

Umbrella Agency: US Department of Transportation (DOT).

Year Founded/Founder: On May 21, 1958, Senator Almer Stillwell "Mike" Monroney (D-OK) introduced a bill to create an independent Federal Aviation Agency to provide for the safe and efficient use of national airspace. Two months later, on August 23, 1958, President Dwight D. Eisenhower signed the Federal Aviation Act, which transferred the Civil Aeronautics Authority's functions to a new, independent Federal Aviation Agency responsible for civil aviation safety.

Mission/Vision Statement: The FAA's continuing mission is to provide the safest, most efficient aerospace system in the world.

Number of Employees: 48,000.

Annual Budget: $18.6 billion.

Sandy's Take: The FAA is a necessary agency to keep us safe, and air travel is here to stay. I have wondered about the increase of recent plane crashes and near accidents at airports across the country I spoke to a friend who works for the National Transportation Safety Board, and he said there is technology that can prevent these incidents from happening. My friend said he spoke to an FAA agent about this, and they blamed the near misses and other incidents on lack of funding.

They receive $18.6 billion a year. Maybe some oversight should be given as to how they are spending their funding.

Sources: "A Brief History of the FAA" and "About FAA," Federal Aviation Administration, www.faa.gov; "Federal Aviation Administration: Human Capital System Incorporates Many Leading Practices, but Improving Employees' Satisfaction with Their Workplace Remains a Challenge," US Government Accountability Office, www.gao.gov.

Agency: Federal Bureau of Investigation (FBI)

Umbrella Agency: US Department of Justice (DOJ).

Year Founded/Founder: Soon after becoming Attorney General, Charles Bonaparte, an American lawyer and political activist who served in the cabinet of Theodore Roosevelt, the 26th US President, learned that his hands were largely tied in tackling the rising tide of crime and corruption. He had no squad of investigators to call his own, except for one or two special agents and other investigators who carried out specific assignments on his behalf. They included a force of examiners trained as accountants who reviewed the financial transactions of the federal courts and some civil rights investigators. By 1907, when he wanted to send an investigator out to gather the facts or to help a US Attorney build a case, he was usually borrowing operatives from the Secret Service. These men were well trained, dedicated—and expensive. And they reported not to the Attorney General but to the Chief of the Secret Service. This situation frustrated Bonaparte, who had little control over his own investigations.

Bonaparte made the problem known to Congress, which wondered why he was even renting Secret Service investigators at all when there was no specific provision in the law for it. In a complicated political showdown with Congress, involving what lawmakers said was President Theodore Roosevelt's grab for executive power, Congress banned the loan of Secret Service operatives to any federal department in May 1908.

Now Bonaparte had no choice, ironically, but to create his own force of investigators, and that's exactly what he did in the coming weeks, apparently with Roosevelt's blessing. In late June, the Attorney General quietly hired nine of the Secret Service investigators he had borrowed before and brought them together with another twenty-five of his own to form a special agent force. On July 26, 1908, Bonaparte ordered Department of Justice attorneys to refer most investigative matters to his Chief Examiner, Stanley W. Finch, for handling by one of these thirty-four agents. The new force now had its mission—to conduct investigations for the Department of Justice—so that date is celebrated as the official birth of the FBI.

With Congress raising no objections to this new unnamed force as it returned from its summer vacation, Bonaparte kept a hold on its work for the next seven months before stepping down with the retiring President Roosevelt in early March 1909. A few days later, on March 16, Bonaparte's successor, Attorney General George W. Wickersham, gave this band of agents their first name—the Bureau of Investigation. It stuck.

Mission: Protect the American people and uphold the Constitution of the United States.

Vision: Ahead of the threat.

Number of Employees: 35,000.

Annual Budget: $10.8 billion.

Subagencies: "The FBI has nine divisions and three offices at its headquarters in Washington, DC. These divisions provide support services for the FBI's 56 field offices, 400 resident agencies, 4 specialized field installations, and 23 foreign liaison posts."[103] The FBI's divisions include the National Security Branch (NSB), which protects the United States from foreign intelligence operations, espionage, acts of terrorism, and weapons of mass destruction; the Counterintelligence Division (CD), which is part of the NSB and protects the United States from foreign intelligence threats; the Intelligence Branch (IB); the Criminal, Cyber, Response, and Services Branch (CCRSB); the Science and Technology Branch (STB); the Information and Technology Branch (ITB); and the Human Resources Branch (HRB).

The FBI also has programs that investigate a variety of topics, including domestic and international terrorism, foreign counterintelligence, cybercrime, public corruption, civil rights, organized crime and drugs, white-collar crime, violent crimes and major offenders, and applicant matters.

Sandy's Take: This is complicated. The FBI's mission as stated is to "protect the American people and uphold the Constitution of the United States." It is hard to see how this mission is being carried out when so many Americans' constitutional rights are being violated with unlawful searches, seizures, and arrests by the FBI. I know they have done much good, and I'm sure there are still many good agents, but any agency whose mission is to protect the American people should never be weaponized against them.

Sources: "A Brief History: The Nation Calls, 1908–1923," "About: Mission & Priorities," "How Many People Work for the FBI?", and "News: Federal Bureau of Investigation Budget Request for Fiscal Year 2023," www.fbi.gov.

Agency: Federal Communications Commission (FCC)

Umbrella Agency: Independent Agency.

Year Founded/Founder: President Franklin D. Roosevelt signed the Communications Act on June 19, 1934. The law was created to centralize regulatory authority, improve national defense, and create for "the people of the United States a rapid, efficient, nationwide, and worldwide wire and radio communication service with adequate facilities at reasonable charges." To implement these policies, the law created the Federal Communications Commission.

Mission/Vision Statement: The Federal Communications Commission regulates interstate and international communications by radio, television, wire, satellite, and cable in all fifty states, the District of Columbia, and US territories. An independent US government agency overseen by Congress, the Commission is the federal agency responsible for implementing and enforcing America's communications laws and regulations.

Number of Employees: 1,890.

Annual Budget: $390 million.

Subagencies: Offices: Administrative Law Judges (ALJ), Communication Business Opportunities (OCBO), Economics and Analytics (OEA), Engineering & Technology (OET), General Counsel (OGC), Inspector General (OIG), International Affairs (OIA), Managing Director (OMD), Media Relations (OMR), Workplace Diversity (OWD). **Bureaus:** Consumer & Government Affairs (CGB), Enforcement (EB), Media, Public Safety & Homeland Security (PSHSB), Space (SB), Wireless Telecommunications (WTB), Wireline Competition (WCB).

Sandy's Take: The Federal Communications Commission is an independent agency accountable directly to Congress. While the FCC is charged with regulating "interstate and international communications by radio, television, wire, satellite, and cable," the FCC is supposed to maintain jurisdiction over areas of broadband access as well as such areas as media responsibility. In my experience, it's largely a government conglomerate whose bureaucratic arms are too short to reach the citizens it's supposed to serve. It is being funded to offer protection via regulation yet only uses its authority to interfere with over-regulation in areas, which, if left to the states, would cost fewer dollars and provide better service, particularly around broadband.

Sources: "Communications Act (1934)," Living New Deal, livingnewdeal.org; "Open Government, Data," www.opm.gov; "Federal Communications Commission (FCC)," www.usa.gov; "Appendix: Budget of the US Government Fiscal Year 2023," www.whitehouse.gov.

Agency: Federal Deposit Insurance Corporation (FDIC)

Umbrella Agency: Independent Agency.

Year Founded/Founder: On June 16, 1933, President Franklin Roosevelt signed the Banking Act of 1933, a part of which established the FDIC. At Roosevelt's side were Senator Carter Glass of Virginia and Representative Henry Steagall of Alabama, two of the most prominent figures in the bill's development.

Mission/Vision Statement: The mission of the Federal Deposit Insurance Corporation (FDIC) is to maintain stability and public confidence in the nation's financial system.

Number of Employees: Permanent workforce: 5,280; temporary workforce: 2,869; total workforce: 8,149.

Annual Budget: The FDIC does not receive any Congressional appropriation; the agency is funded by premiums that banks and thrift institutions pay for deposit insurance coverage and earnings on investments in US Treasury securities.

Subagencies: Consumer Financial Protection Bureau (CFPB), Federal Financial Institutions Examination Council (FFIEC), Federal Reserve Board (FRB), Federal Trade Commission (FTC), National Credit Union Administration (NCUA), National Technical Information Service (NTIS), Office of the Comptroller of the Currency (OCC), Securities Exchange Commission(SEC).

Sandy's Take: Aside from its role of insuring deposits, the FDIC "regulates" US financial institutions and props up "too-big-to-fail" institutions to avoid bankruptcy that could rock the US financial system. There is little meaning in the term "insurance" even though it is used in the name of this agency.

Sources: "A Brief History of Deposit Insurance in the United States" and "What We Do," FDIC, www.fdic.gov; "Federal Deposit Insurance Corporation (FDIC)," US Equal Employment Opportunity Commission, www.eeoc.gov; "Congressional Budget Justification for Fiscal Year 2023," Office of Inspector General, FDIC, www.fdicoig.gov.

Agency: Federal Election Commission (FEC)

Umbrella Agency: Independent Agency.

Year Founded/Founder: As early as 1905, President Theodore Roosevelt recognized the need for campaign finance reform and called for legislation to ban corporate contributions for political purposes. In response, Congress enacted several statutes between 1907 and 1966.

In 1971, Congress consolidated its earlier reform efforts in the Federal Election Campaign Act, instituting more stringent disclosure requirements for federal candidates, political parties, and political action committees (PACs). Still, the campaign finance laws were difficult to enforce without a central administrative authority.

Following reports of serious financial abuses in the 1972 presidential campaign, Congress amended the Federal Election Campaign Act in 1974 to limit contributions by individuals, political parties, and PACs. The 1974 amendments also established an independent agency, the FEC, which opened its doors in 1975.

Mission/Vision Statement: To protect the integrity of the federal campaign finance process by providing transparency and fairly enforcing and administering federal campaign finance laws.

Number of Employees: 365.

Annual Budget: $81.7 million.

Subagencies: The FEC is composed of six commissioners appointed by the President with the advice and consent of the Senate. The FEC also is allowed three Statutory Officers, the Staff Director, the General Counsel and the Inspector General.

Sources: "Mission and History," Federal Election Commission, www.fec.gov; "Open Government: Data," www.opm.gov.

Agency: Federal Emergency Management Agency (FEMA)

Umbrella Agency: US Department of Homeland Security (DHS).

Year Founded/Founder: FEMA was officially created in 1979 through an executive order by President Jimmy Carter. Its history can be traced as far back as 1803.

Mission/Vision Statement: FEMA's mission is helping people before, during, and after disasters, and they say their core values and goals help them achieve it.

Number of Employees: Over 20,000.

Annual Budget: $3.53 billion.

Subagencies: Office of the Administrator, Office of Civil Rights, Disability Integration and Coordination, Office of External Affairs, Office of the Chief Financial Officer, Intelligence and Threat Analysis, Law Enforcement Engagement and Integration, Office of National Capital Region, Office of National Continuity Programs, Policy and Program Analysis, Office of Professional Responsibility,

Office of Chief Counsel, Mission Support, Office of the Chief Administrative Officer, Office of the Chief Human Capital Officer, Office of the Chief Information Officer, Office of the Chief Procurement Officer.

FEMA has ten regions that cover all fifty states and other territories.

Sandy's Take: FEMA has done a lot of good when it comes to disasters across our nation, and it is needed. But as with any organization, especially one that receives tax dollars, oversight should be required. The last budget report on their website is from 2019. When the American people's money is being spent by the government, there should be accountability. In light of the recent hurricanes and FEMA's slow management of giving help to citizens who were truly experiencing disastrous circumstances, FEMA needs to learn how to serve and handle disasters from the wonderful American citizens who were actually providing assistance to their neighbors. Instead, they were shutting down the locals while people were still stranded and some dying waiting for someone to rescue them. This reminds me of the famous statement that President Ronald Reagan jokingly used a few years ago: "I'm from the government and I'm here to help."

Sources: "About Us," Federal Emergency Management Agency, www.fema.org; "Department of Homeland Security," www.whitehouse.gov; "Federal Emergency Management Agency (FEMA)," www.usa.gov.

Agency: Federal Housing Administration (FHA)

Umbrella Agency: Department of Housing and Urban Development.

Year Founded/Founder: September 1, 2012, marked the seventy-fifth anniversary of the Wagner-Steagall Housing Act, a piece of late New Deal legislation that reflected the government's recognition of adequate housing as an important societal need.

Franklin Roosevelt had been interested in housing issues when he was governor of New York. He brought his support for housing reforms to the federal level when he became president in 1932. The Home Owner's Loan Corporation (HOLC) was created in 1933 to provide mortgage relief to homeowners at risk of losing their homes through foreclosure. The HOLC also developed a comprehensive housing plan that served as the basis for the National Housing Act of 1934. This law created the FHA–insured banks, mortgage companies, and other lenders, thereby encouraging the construction of new homes and the repair of existing structures.

It was FDR's hope that the law would also spur employment in the construction industry. Although the 1934 National Housing Act and the FHA met the needs of existing homeowners and those Americans financially able to purchase homes, it did little to address the housing needs of the poor, including many African Americans living in slums.

Mission/Vision Statement: The goal was to create liquidity and stability for the mortgage and real estate markets, to provide families access to credit, to keep them in their homes, and to offer homebuyers a new way to buy homes—by offering longer-term, affordable financing. The agency's mission has not changed since that time. As part of this mission, FHA continues to play a countercyclical role, serving as a backstop to the private mortgage market.

Number of Employees: Permanent workforce: 9,442; temporary workforce: 599; total workforce: 10,041.

Annual Budget: FHA primarily operates from its self-generated income, but it did receive 27 million federal dollars in 2023.

Subagencies: Office of Housing—Federal Housing Administration (FHA), Government National Mortgage Association (Ginnie Mae), Office of Public and Indian Housing (PIH), Office of Community Planning and Development (CPD), Office of Fair Housing and Equal Opportunity (FHEO), Office of Lead Hazard Control and Healthy Homes (OLHCHH), Center for Faith-Based and Neighborhood Partnerships (CFBNP).

Sandy's Take: Any program that comes under a federal agency tends to have strings attached that limit an individual's freedom when buying a home. FHA is no different.

Sources: "FDR and Housing Legislation," Franklin D. Roosevelt Presidential Library and Museum, www.fdrlibrary.org; "Role of the Federal Housing Administration (FHA) in Addressing the Housing Crisis," Senate Hearing

111–394, www.govinfo.gov; "About Us," US Department of Housing and Urban Development, www.hud.gov; "US Department of Housing and Urban Development (HUD)," US Equal Employment Opportunity Commission, www.eeoc.gov.

Agency: Federal Labor Relations Authority (FLRA)

Umbrella Agency: Independent Agency.

Year Founded/Founder: The Federal Labor Relations Authority is an independent administrative federal agency created by Title VII of the Civil Service Reform Act of 1978, also known as the Federal Service Labor-Management Relations Statute (5 U.S.C.), sponsored by Senator Abraham Ribicoff (D-CT).

Mission/Vision Statement: Protecting rights and facilitating stable relationships among federal agencies, labor organizations, and employees while advancing an effective and efficient government through the administration of the Federal Service Labor-Management Relations Statute.

Number of Employees: 116.

Annual Budget: $31.76 million.

Subagencies: Components: Authority Office of the General Counsel, Federal Service Impasses Panel. **Offices:** Collaboration and Alternative Dispute Resolution Office (CADRO), Office of Administrative Law Judges (ALJ), Office of Case Intake and Publication (CIP), Office of the Executive Director (OED), Office of Inspector General (OIG), Office of the Solicitor General (OSG).

Sandy's Take: In my opinion, this agency and others like it are a waste of our taxpayer dollars. Others include the American Federation of Government Employees (AFGE), the largest federal employee union representing 750 thousand federal and DC government workers; the National Federation of Federal Employees (NFFE), which is the oldest union in America, representing over 110 thousand federal workers; and the National Treasury Employees Union (NTEU), which represents employees in 35 federal agencies and offices. When President Biden sent 75 percent of the federal workforce home during COVID to work remotely, apparently no one took into consideration what it would take to get everyone back to work when the time came. I remember getting the memo from the Biden administration announcing how proud they were that they had been in "negotiations" with the FLRA and were hoping to reach an agreement that would satisfy the federal employees for them to return to work. Federal employees should be treated like anyone else when it comes to their job: if they don't show up for work, they should get fired! They are supposed to be there to serve the people, and yet our president was required to make deals with them. Congress needs to act to ensure the federal workforce is there for the American people, and not just a job! Fire their butts and replace them with people who are willing to do their job!

Sources: "Introduction to the FLRA and "Mission," US Federal Labor Relations Authority, www.flra.gov; "S.2640–Civil Service Reform Act: 95th Congress (1977–1978)," www.congress.gov; "Open Government: Data," www.opm.org.

Agency Name: Food and Drug Administration (FDA)

Umbrella Agency: Department of Health and Human Services (HHS).

Year Founded/Founder: The Food and Drug Administration was founded on June 30, 1906, by Harvey Washington Wiley and is the oldest comprehensive consumer protection agency in the US federal government. Since 1848, the federal government has used chemical analysis to monitor the safety of agricultural products, a responsibility inherited by the Department of Agriculture in 1862 and later by the FDA. Although it was not known by its present name until 1930, FDA's modern regulatory functions began with the passage of the 1906 Pure Food and Drugs Act, a law a quarter-century in the making that prohibited interstate commerce in adulterated and misbranded food and drugs. Harvey Washington Wiley, chief chemist of the USDA Bureau of Chemistry, had been the driving force behind this law and headed its enforcement in the early years, providing basic elements of protection that consumers had never known before that time. Since then, the FDA has changed along with the United States's social, economic, political, and legal changes. Examining the history of these changes illuminates the evolving role that the FDA has played in promoting public health. It offers lessons to consider as we evaluate current regulatory challenges.

Mission/Vision: The FDA is responsible for protecting public health by assuring the safety, efficacy, and security of human and veterinary drugs, biological products, medical devices, our nation's food supply, cosmetics, and products that emit radiation.

Number of Employees: 18,000.

Annual Budget: $6.5 billion (2022).

Subagencies: FDA is an agency within the Department of Health and Human Services and consists of nine center-level organizations and thirteen headquarter (HQ) Offices. It also includes the Center for Biologics, Evaluation, and Research (CBER), the Center for Devices and Radiological Health, the Center for Drug Evaluation and Research (CDER), the Center for Food Safety and Applied Nutrition (CFSAN), the Center for Tobacco Products (CTP), the Center for Veterinary Medicine (CVM), the National Center for Toxicological Research (NCTR), and the Office of Regulatory Affairs (ORA).

Sources: "Food and Drug Administration (FDA)," www.usa.gov.

Agency: Food and Nutrition Service (FNS)

Umbrella Agency: US Department of Agriculture (USDA).

Year Founded/Founder: The foundation for the Supplemental Nutrition Assistance Program (SNAP), was first built in 1933 as part of the Agricultural Adjustment Act (AAA). The program, referred to as the Federal Surplus Relief Corporation, was established in the midst of the Great Depression, when prices for crops fell dramatically. At this time, farms across America were struggling with excess supply. To support farmers, the federal government bought basic farm commodities at discounted prices and distributed them among hunger relief agencies in states and local communities. Secretary of Agriculture Henry Wallace created the Food Stamp Program in the United States to formalize this food distribution and avoid duplicating efforts by local relief agencies. The initiative, called the "Food Stamps Plan," was implemented in 1939 under the administration of President Franklin D. Roosevelt as a key component of the New Deal program. On February 7, 2014, President Obama signed the 2014 Farm Bill (also known as the Agricultural Act of 2014) into law. The legislation made many changes to SNAP, which the FNS has begun to implement.

Original Mission: To provide children and needy families better access to food and a more healthful diet through food assistance programs and comprehensive nutrition education efforts.

Present Mission: To increase food security and reduce hunger by providing children and low-income people access to food, a healthful diet, and nutrition education in a way that supports American agriculture and inspires public confidence.

Number of Employees: 1,346.

Annual Budget: $111 billion.

Subagencies: Nutrition Assistance Program(SNAP) Farmers Market Nutrition Program (FMNP), Senior Farmers Market Nutrition Program (SFMNP), Women, Infants and Children (WIC), Child Nutrition Programs, Child and Adult Food Program (CACFP), Fresh Fruit & Vegetable Program, National School Lunch Program, School Breakfast Program, Special Milk Program, Summer EBT, Summer Food Service Program, Patrick Leahy Farm to School Program, USDA Food Distribution Program, Commodity Supplemental Food Program, Food Distribution on Indian Reservation Program, Emergency Food Assistance Program, USDA Food in Schools Program.

Sandy's Take: As I have researched these food programs, I have found that many appear to be duplicates of another program. What I have listed here is not exhaustive. While some of these programs are needed programs, are we being efficient in how we are executing them?

Sources: "Center for Nutrition Policy and Promotion (CNPP),"and "Statement by Secretary Vilsack on the President's FY 2023 Budget Food and Nutrition Service, US Department of Agriculture, www.fns.usda.gov; "The History of SNAP," Snap to Health!, www.snaptohealth.org; "Open Government: Data," www.opm.gov.

Agency: US Forest Service (USFS)

Umbrella Agency: US Department of Agriculture (USDA).

Year Founded/Founder: Federal forest management dates to 1876, when Congress created the Office of the Special Agent in the US Department of Agriculture to assess the quality and conditions of forests in the United States. In 1881 the department expanded the office into the Division of Forestry. A decade later, Congress passed the Forest Reserve Act of 1891, authorizing the president to designate public lands in the West into what were then called "forest reserves." Responsibility for these reserves fell under the Department of the Interior until 1905, when President Theodore Roosevelt transferred their care to the Department of Agriculture's new US Forest Service. Gifford Pinchot led this new agency as its first chief, charged with caring for the newly renamed national forests.

Mission/Vision Statement: The USDA Forest Service's mission is to sustain the health, diversity, and productivity of the nation's forests and grasslands to meet the needs of present and future generations.

Number of Employees: 30,000.

Annual Budget: $9 billion.

Subagencies: Office of the Chief: Civil Rights, International Programs, Law Enforcement & Investigation, Legislative Affairs, Office of Communication. **Business Operations:** Budget and Finance, Grants & Agreements, Procurement & Property Services, Chief Information Office, Casualty Assistance Program, Controlled Correspondence Unit (CCU) Enterprise Program, Human Resources Management (HRM), Job Corps (JC), Mission Area Senior Program Management (MASPM), Office of Safety and Occupational Health (OSOH), Office of Regulatory and Management Services (OIRA), Strategic Planning and Resource Assessment (SWOT). **National Forest System:** Biological and Physical Resources (BPR), Celebrating Wildflowers, Ecosystem Management Coordination (EMC), Engineering, Forest Management, Geospatial Technology and Applications Center (GTAC), Lands and Realty Management (LRM), Minerals & Geology Management (MGM), National Applications Liaison Office (NALO), National Forest Genetics Laboratory (NFGEL), National Partnership Office (NPO), National Technology and Development Program (NTDP), Office of Sustainability and Climate (OSC), Policy Office; Rangeland Management; Recreation; Heritage & Volunteer Resources; Soils; Wild Horse and Burro; Wilderness and Wild & Scenic Rivers. **Research and Development:** State, Private, and Tribal Forestry (STPF), Conservation Education (CEP), Cooperative

Forestry, National Seed Laboratory (NSL) Fire & Aviation Management (FAM), Forest Health Protection (FHP), Office of Tribal Relations (OTR) Urban and Community Forestry (U&CF).

Sandy's Take: I appreciate the Forest Service and their mission to care for our nation's forests and grasslands. There are times, though, when I sense that they care more for the forests and grasslands than the people who live around them. Our district has a community that is very rural with only one exit out of it. It is located near one of these US-controlled properties. The residents have asked them to allow a road that would give them a second exit in case of fire or other disaster. It has been denied for twenty-one years due to trying to "preserve" the land for the habitat. What about the people? The Forest Service's mission is to "meet the needs of the present and future generations." The list of subagencies and programs here is extremely long, but I listed them to emphasize how large one agency can become. It would be interesting to truly know if our taxpayer dollars are being well spent. Again, I remind you that our nation is $35 trillion in debt (perhaps more by the time you read this)!

Sources: "Our History," "Meet the Forest Service," "About the Agency," and "US Forest Service, Fiscal Year 2023 Budget Justification," US Forest Service, US Department of Agriculture (USDA), www.fs.usda.gov.

Agency: Immigration and Customs Enforcement (ICE)

Umbrella Agency: US Department of Homeland Security (DHS).

Year Founded/Founder: Rep. Richard K. Armey (R-TX-26) sponsored and introduced the Homeland Security Act on June 24, 2002 (by request). In March 2003 the Homeland Security Act set into motion what would be the single-largest government reorganization since the creation of the Department of Defense. One of the agencies in the new Department of Homeland Security was the Bureau of Immigration and Customs Enforcement, now known as US Immigration and Customs Enforcement, or ICE.

Congress granted ICE a unique combination of civil and criminal authorities to better protect national security and public safety in answer to the tragic events on 9/11. Leveraging those authorities, ICE's primary mission is to promote homeland security and public safety through the criminal and civil enforcement of federal laws governing border control, customs, trade, and immigration.

ICE now has more than twenty thousand law enforcement and support personnel in more than four hundred offices in the United States and around the world. The agency has an annual budget of approximately $8 billion, primarily devoted to three operational directorates: Homeland Security Investigations (HSI), Enforcement and Removal Operations (ERO), and the Office of the Principal Legal Advisor (OPLA). A fourth directorate, Management and Administration, supports the three operational branches to advance the ICE mission.

Mission: Protect America through criminal investigations and enforcing immigration laws to preserve national security and public safety.

Vision: DHS is the nation's premier law enforcement agency, mitigating transnational threats and safeguarding our nation, communities, lawful immigration, trade, travel, and financial systems.

Number of Employees: 20,000.

Annual Budget: $8.4 billion.

Subagencies: ICE has two primary and distinct law enforcement components: Homeland Security Investigations (HSI) and Enforcement and Removal Operations (ERO), in addition to three supporting divisions: Management & Program Administration, Office of the Principal Legal Advisor (OPLA) and Office of Professional Responsibility (OPR).

Sandy's Take: DHS and its agencies have one of the most difficult jobs in America today, especially with the massive influx of immigration- and drug-related crimes that affect not only our borders but all of America. I was in a meeting a few weeks ago with one of our local sheriffs from a small rural community. He told me that they had made a random traffic stop for a broken taillight and found an illegal alien driving with enough fentanyl in the car to kill the entire town. Is ICE fulfilling its stated mission?

Sources: "Honoring the History of ICE 2003–2023," ICE, and www.ice.gov; "About Us," US Immigration and Customs Enforcement (ICE), www.ice.gov; "Appropriations Committee Releases Fiscal Year 2023 Homeland Security Funding Bill," appropriations.house.gov.

Agency: Institute of Peace (USIP)

Umbrella Agency: Quasi-official (This institute performs specific governmental services. Due to its status, they are not quite a government agency but also not a private business.)

Year Founded/Founder: Congress established the US Institute of Peace in 1984 following years of proposals for the creation of a national "peace academy," most notably from both a nationwide grassroots movement and World War II combat veterans elected to legislative office.

The congressional leaders included Senator Mark Hatfield of Oregon—who had commanded Navy landing crafts on the beaches of Iwo Jima and Okinawa and had led the first American team to survey the destruction from the atomic bombing of Hiroshima—and Senator Spark Matsunaga of Hawaii, who had been twice wounded and awarded the Bronze Star in World War II's North Africa and Italy campaigns.

Hatfield and Matsunaga led Congress's passage of the United States Institute of Peace Act, signed into law by President Ronald Reagan. The act established USIP as "an independent, nonprofit, national institute."

Mission/Vision Statement: To serve the people and the government through the widest possible range of education and training, to promote international peace and the resolution of conflicts among the nations and peoples of the world without recourse to violence.

Number of Employees: 300.

Annual Budget: $54 million.

Sandy's Take: This agency started out like many agencies: with good intentions. But if you look at their website today, you will find that they are spending millions of our taxpayer dollars advancing special-interest ideology. In my view, our taxpayer dollars have no place there.

Sources: "The Origins of USIP," and "Staff," "FY 2023 Budget in Brief," United States Institute of Peace, www.usip.org.

Agency: Internal Revenue Service (IRS)

Umbrella Agency: US Department of the Treasury (USDT)

Year Founded/Founder: Taxation without representation was the seed of the American Revolution. Colonists rebelled against Britain's punitive taxes because they had no voice in Parliament. On July 4, 1776, the Declaration of Independence severed ties with England. The Revolutionary War ended in 1783, and a new nation was born.

On February 21, 1787, Congress approved a Constitutional Convention to revise the Articles of Confederation, Article I, Section 8, Clause One of the Constitution states that "the Congress shall have the power to lay and collect taxes, duties, imposts, and excesses, to pay the debts and provide for the common defense and general welfare of the United States." On September 2, 1789, Congress established the Department of the Treasury and appointed Alexander Hamilton as its first Secretary.

In 1862, President Lincoln signed into law a revenue-raising measure to help pay for Civil War expenses. The measure created a Commissioner of Internal Revenue and the nation's first income tax. It levied a 3 percent tax on incomes between $600 and $10,000 and a 5 percent tax on incomes of more than $10,000. Heeding public opposition to the income tax, Congress cut the tax rate in 1867. From 1868 until 1913, 90 percent of all revenue came from taxes on liquor, beer, wine, and tobacco. In 1872, the income tax was repealed.

To see the complete timeline and interesting history of taxes visit https://www.irs.gov/irs-history-timeline.

Mission/Vision Statement: Provide America's taxpayers top-quality service by helping them understand and meet their tax responsibilities and enforce the law with integrity and fairness to all.

Number of Employees: 83,807.

Annual Budget: $14.1 billion.

Subagencies/Oversight Agencies: The Government Accountability Office (GAO) (an agency that works for Congress and the American people), Office of Management and Budget (OMB), Treasury Inspector General for Tax Administration (TIGTA), Electronic Tax Administration Advisory Committee (ETAAC), Internal Revenue Service Advisory Council (IRSAC), Taxpayer Advocacy Panel (TAP), IRS Oversight Board, Senate Committee on Finance.

Sandy's Take: When the 16th Amendment was ratified in 1913 and became a part of the Constitution, it granted Congress the authority to issue an income tax without having to determine it based on population. The IRS assumed authority for being the recipient of monies to fund an ever-expanding government that spends without budgetary restraints and without regard to its citizens' right to earned income. In its present state, I believe the income tax is every bit as unlawful as the taxes imposed on those who rose in rebellion against taxation without representation, and it should be abolished. Above all, the term "service" is the greatest misnomer ever given to a bureaucratic agency. In my experience, its stated mission of helping its citizens "meet their tax responsibilities and enforce the law with integrity and fairness" is a far cry from the experience of most Americans.

Sources: "The Agency, Its Mission, and Statutory Authority," Internal Revenue Service (IRS), www.irs.gov; "IRS Budget in Brief Fiscal Year 2023," home.treasury.gov.

Agency: Office of Refugee Resettlement (ORR)

Umbrella Agency: Administration for Children and Families (ACF).

Year Founded/Founder: The US Congress enacted the first refugee legislation in 1948 following the admission of more than 250 thousand displaced Europeans. This legislation provided for the admission of an additional 400 thousand displaced Europeans. Later laws provided for admission of persons fleeing Communist regimes, largely from Hungary, Poland, Yugoslavia, Korea, and China, and in the 1960s Cubans fleeing Fidel Castro arrived en masse. Most of these waves of refugees were assisted by private ethnic and religious organizations in the US, which formed the basis for the public-private roles in US resettlement efforts today.

The continuing outflow of refugees in the aftermath of the Vietnam War and communist revolutions in Southeast Asia generated political support for expanded and regular refugee admissions. Senator Edward Kennedy (D-MA) introduced bill S.643 on March 13, 1979. The Senate passed such a reform unanimously in late 1979, and President Jimmy Carter signed the Refugee Act of 1979 early the next year. The new law superseded the Immigration and Naturalization Act of 1965 and raised the annual ceiling for refugees from 17,400 to 50,000, created a process for reviewing and adjusting the refugee ceiling to meet emergencies, and required annual consultation between Congress and the president on refugee admissions.

Mission/Vision Statement: The Office of Refugee Resettlement provides resources for refugees, asylum seekers, and other new arrivals to the US to assist with their integration into their new community.

Number of Employees: Unable to find this information.

Annual Budget: $1.36 billion.

Subagencies: ORR's resettlement programs fall under the following topics: Refugee Health Overview, Refugee Health Promotion, Health Insurance, Emotional Wellness, Services for Survivors of Torture, Services to Afghan Survivors Impacted by Combat, and Health Resources. Note: I have not been able find the organizational structure for the Office of Refugee Resettlement.

Sandy's Take: I include this agency because of its relevance today, as our country is being flooded with millions of migrants. It's important to note the significance of the ORR's budget and the general lack of transparency in their reporting. There is also very little information about their structure and organization. While the Refugee Act of 1980 raised the annual ceiling for refugees from 17,500 to 50,000 annually, in 2024, according to CBS News, Border Patrol agents recorded 124,215 illegal migrant crossings in January; 140,638 in February; 137,473 in March; and 128,894,000 in April.[104] This is unsustainable!

Source: "History," US Department of Health & Human Services, Office of Refugee Resettlement, www.acf.hhs.gov; "Refugee Act of 1980," Immigration History, www.immigrationhistory.org; "Report to Congress on Proposed Refugee Admissions for Fiscal Year 2023," US Department of State, www.state.gov; "Southwest Land Border Encounters," US Customs and Border Protection, www.cbp.gov.

Agency: Office of Personnel Management (OPM)

Umbrella Agency: Independent Agency.

Year Founded/Founder: OPM's history begins with the Civil Service Act, signed in 1883. This act ended the spoils system (a practice in which a political party, after winning an election, gives government jobs to its supporters, friends, and relatives), and established the Civil Service Commission. The Commission, led by the energetic Teddy Roosevelt, laid the foundations of an impartial, professional civil service based on the merit principle—that employees should be judged only on how well they can do the job.

In 1978, the Civil Service Commission was reorganized into three new organizations: the Office of Personnel Management, the Merit Systems Protection Board, and the Federal Labor Relations Authority. Each of these new organizations took over a portion of the Civil Service Commission's responsibilities, with OPM responsible for personnel management of the government's civil service.

Mission/Vision Statement: OPM prides itself as champions of talent for the federal government. It leads federal agencies in workforce policies, programs, and benefits in service to the American people. OPM executes, enforces, and administers the laws governing the civil service, including those related to merit-based and inclusive hiring. OPM is responsible for the administration of the Civil Service Retirement System and the Federal Employees Retirement System covering 2.8 million active employees, including the United States Postal Service, and nearly 2.7 million annuitants, survivors, and family members.

Number of Employees: 5,907

Annual Budget: $415.6 million.

Subagencies: Federal Executive Boards (FEBs) operate in twenty-eight US cities and provide a forum for collaboration and information exchange between federal field agencies. In this way, field agencies may share best practices and lessons learned or may coordinate efforts when different agencies adopt programs with similar goals.

Sandy's Take: OPM is the agency that vets and has the final say in the hiring of personnel for *all* agencies. While I'm sure there are highly qualified people being hired by OPM, my experience working with agency employees is that many of the people who were approved for hire can't communicate effectively, are unaware of their agency's rules and regulations, and in general do not demonstrate the basic skills essential to do their jobs. Where is our merit-based hiring? We're hurting all Americans by hiring personnel based on the color of their skin or gender orientation rather than their ability to do the job.

Source: "US Office of Personnel Management," www.opm.gov.; www.usa.gov/agencies/federal-executive-boards.

Quite frankly, writing this chapter and placing all the information on paper for you to see has been exhausting. When I consider that this is only a fraction of the agencies that have been created by our government, I am overwhelmed. We are truly being controlled by the Administrative State, which spends our tax dollars as it choose. If the government finds another problem that needs solving, they just start a new agency, program, board, or commission and tax us more to pay for it. We must take back our freedom, demand that our Representatives start working for us, insist on accountability from all federal agencies and shut down those agencies that provide no benefit for the American people.

To see all the agencies found in my research, please go to my website at www.GovernmentServantOrMaster.com or use your smart phone to access the website through the QR code.

Our God, will you not judge them? For we are powerless before this vast number that comes to fight against us. We do not know what to do, but we look to you.

2 Chronicles 20:12

Chapter Five
Real Stories of Agency Abuse

While working for Congress, my colleagues and I have resolved thousands of cases for constituents who had been trying for months and sometimes years to get help from a federal agency. These cases have ranged from IRS cases where people couldn't get their refunds, to the Bureau of Prisons where someone's family was not receiving basic humane care, to the Department of State to help free a constituent from a foreign country where they were being held hostage, and everything in between. For this book, I have chosen only a few stories to illustrate the realities of agency abuse. The names have been changed to protect the privacy of those involved. All stories are used with the permission of both the Congressional Representative in office at the time of this writing and the individual constituents.

Mr. Bobby's Story: A Man Without a Country.

Bobby was born overseas because of an affair between an American soldier and a local national in the country where the soldier was on active duty at the time. This soldier was already married, but his wife could not have children, so an agreement was made between the birth mother, the soldier, and his wife to adopt Bobby and bring him to the States. He entered the US at the age of six months and has now lived here for sixty-eight years. He went to school locally, played football, got his driver's license at sixteen, and has worked here and paid taxes since he started working. He received a passport and has traveled overseas in his lifetime with no problem. That was until about fourteen years ago when he went to the DMV to get his license renewed.

When he arrived at the DMV, they had just locked their doors and told him to return the next day. Bobby thought nothing of it and returned the following day to renew his license. Unbeknownst to him, he was getting ready to embark on a journey that would launch him into a world of a "man without a country."

When he returned to the DMV, he was told that his driver's license had expired by one day and that he would have to provide proof of citizenship by bringing his birth certificate. Both of his parents were already deceased, but they had given him a box with his adoption papers in it, so he went home, retrieved the box, and came back to the DMV.

When he gave the clerk his German birth certificate, she told him she couldn't accept it since he was born overseas. She needed proof that he had entered the country legally. He provided them with an ID card with his six-month-old baby picture and the dated stamp of entry when he had been legally admitted into the US. But that wasn't enough for the DMV. They needed proof that he was a citizen and that Americans had truly adopted him.

Since his adoption papers were in a foreign language, he had them translated into English. This is when he first learned that his adoptive soldier father was his biological father! He thought his problem was fixed since he was the biological son of an American citizen, which would make him an American automatically, right? No, he was told he would still need to apply for citizenship before he could get his license renewed.

This started a process of Bobby walking through the steps to become a US Citizen: (1) You must determine if you are already a US citizen, (2) find out if you are eligible to become a US citizen, and (3) fill out the USCIS N-400 application for naturalization. Bobby walked through each step; when he completed the N-400 application and paid his $400 fee, he was given a date and time to come for an interview at the Department of Homeland Security (DHS). He arrived at his interview, and when he was called, a gentleman looked over his paperwork and stated, "You're already a US citizen; you don't need to be naturalized!" Of course, Bobby was dumbfounded and confused but also elated to learn that this long process was over, and he was finally recognized as a US citizen. Unfortunately, Bobby didn't know to request a document verifying his US Citizenship.

Bobby again returned to the DMV, anticipating that he would now be given a license, but to his dismay he was told again by DMV personnel that they could not grant him a driver's license because he had no documents to prove his citizenship. He was devastated! He was already several years into this journey and did not know what to do next! That's when someone told him that his congressman could possibly help him, and he called us.

We began the tedious process of contacting the DMV, DHS, and USCIS to learn all we could about his status. Except for DMV, who has a record of his expired license, each of the agencies told us they had no record of Bobby in their database or that he had gone through the process to become a citizen. While we have tried to approach this problem from every angle possible with no good results, the other day, Bobby called and told me that his friend was standing in a local DMV and watched as several illegal aliens came in with paperwork they had received from someone, and each of them was granted a driver's privilege card with no problem at all. Bobby has tried to get a temporary driver's privilege card in the past so he can legally drive, but they have refused to grant his request. Unfortunately, he has been driving on an expired driver's license for nearly fourteen years. He lives alone in a rural area and has no other means of transportation for work. He lives in fear every day that he will get in trouble, but he doesn't know what to do!

At the time of this writing, Bobby has filed a FOIA request to try and find the records for his USCIS case so he can regain his citizenship. Recently I was able to reach out to the Virginia Department of Transportation and request an exception for Bobby based on his adoption papers, which have now been translated by a USCIS approved translator, proving he was adopted by American parents. If we are not successful, he will be required to go through the process all over again of applying for naturalization to become a citizen of the only country he has ever known. He has lived here since he was six months old, his father was an American, and yet he has fewer rights than illegal aliens walking across our border!

Mr. Samuel's Story: Community School of the Arts Loses Tax-Exempt Status Due to IRS Error.

Samuel and three other family members opened their music school in 2006 as a personal vision and an extension of their faith. Samuel was appointed by the board of directors to be its director and principal music teacher. While the school was originally organized as a Kindermusik program, the Community School of the Arts (CSA) still focuses on the arts as a tool for wellness while promoting intergenerational and therapeutic participation in a broad range of programs, including dance and drama.

CSA is tax-exempt under Internal Revenue Code (IRC) 501(c)(3) for charitable contributions and for purposes of receiving grants. Tuition is kept at a minimum so children and adults of all socioeconomic levels (even students supported through Medicaid) can take advantage of this creative arts program, the only one of its kind in their community.

Samuel employs an accounting professional to handle his annual tax reporting and generally relies on his accountant's expertise to report accurately and on time. You might imagine Samuel's shock when he received a notice from the IRS that his tax-exempt status had been revoked for failing to file taxes three years in a row!

Samuel's immediate response was to send copies of his past three years' returns to the IRS Service Center as he was instructed, along with a certified receipt of mailing and return receipts requested (RRR). He was sure these documents would clear up any misunderstanding and prove that he had indeed filed his taxes for all three years. His accountant sent each year's returns separately, as requested by the IRS. Based on the dates shown on the RRs, these packages had been received in a haphazard manner, one right away but the other two after several months. It was unclear why, because they were sent the same day in packages addressed to the same service center.

Samuel started to worry and asked the IRS the following question: What happened to the other returns CSA filed? He received no response.

Samuel realized that CSA's fundraising efforts were being forced to a standstill until this mistake could be cleared and their tax-exempt status reinstated. After several months of getting literally no answer from a citizen taxpayer request to the Taxpayer Advocate Service (TAS), Samuel called our office for help. When we received a package of copies of his tax returns, we opened an official congressional inquiry into the issue and, surprisingly, were assigned the same advocate Samuel had been working with before, Ms. Tammy at the TAS.

After several more months of no response to our congressional inquiry, I phoned Ms. Tammy to ask why this mistake couldn't be resolved with copies of signed and dated returns for the three years in question, which the IRS had asked for. She said she would also need a copy of the board's decision to make Samuel their director, so we provided that.

After another long wait, she told us that without a copy of a certified receipt for the three years of returns in question, CSA would need to reapply and pay a fee of up to $850 to be reinstated as a 501(c)(3) organization, if the IRS deemed them eligible for reinstatement. In other words, the burden of proving their returns were filed in a timely manner was totally upon CSA, even though the IRS had copies of the filing dates in hand.

By this time, fundraising season was in full swing, and donors who had been faithful to give substantially to CSA for operation expenses simply backed away. Samuel and his wife started searching through boxes of paperwork that had been moved from their former address for any postal proof that the IRS had received their returns. After months of searching, a rag-tag copy of a receipt for one of the years was found, and we sent it to TAS, hoping it would prove that one of the years' annual returns had been filed.

At this point, CSA only had about two weeks before students would be enrolling in summer classes, and Samuel had been unable to raise funds for more than a year and a half. Finally, after another week and a half passed, their tax status was reinstated in writing. As grateful as we were and as happy an occasion as that was, that was not the end of the story.

The IRS had somehow ignored their own need to apologize in writing for revoking CSA's tax-exempt status. While the school was teetering on the brink of closing its doors, the IRS had gotten busy calculating outstanding penalties and interest to the tune of thousands of dollars for the years they deemed "unfiled." They began sending CSA notices that these penalties were to be paid immediately. Again, we had to return to the IRS with copies of the returns in hand—not once, but three times—for the outstanding penalties and interest to be removed.

Finally, as we started to believe the issue had been resolved, we realized that many of the letters CSA had received from the IRS charging them penalties were being sent to their old and new addresses. After three formal requests for an address change *before* CSA asked for congressional help, and another four formal requests filed by our office on behalf of CSA after their tax-exempt status was reinstated, we finally received notice that their address had been changed. This made it possible for their organization to finally be placed back on the tax-exempt organization registry so they could again receive donations. Even so, sadly, many of their donors had been scared enough by this fiasco that they have never since contributed to CSA.

This school's addition to the Tax-Exempt Organizations List happened in April 2022, a full two and a half years from when their tax-exempt status was revoked and nearly a year after it was reinstated. There has never been an explanation about what happened to their original returns or an apology to Samuel, his wife, or his organization for the trouble the IRS caused.

Ms. Christina's Story: Mama Can't Travel with Her Baby Because SSA Won't Give Baby ID.

Christina contacted our office soon after she had a baby because she was trying to travel abroad. Her story began while she and the baby were still in the hospital when she was asked to complete paperwork to apply for her baby's Social Security card. She filled out the paperwork for her newborn's application and was told it had been sent to the Social Security Administration (SSA) for the number to be assigned. Somehow, the card was lost, never finding its way to her home via the US Postal Service.

Her initial contact with our office was in August 2021 to ask if we could help get her infant son's Social Security card so she could apply for his passport for a family trip in the spring. Because she had never received his Social Security card by mail, she had tried repeatedly to contact the SSA but could never reach anyone by phone. As we often hear, her calls would either go unanswered or go into a circular call-messaging system, or there would be an answer and a hang-up.

Once we were able to contact the field office closest to her home, we were told that her designated location for SSA help was a different field office and that we should follow up with them to request help. After numerous calls to the second field office, we finally got word that the young child had been issued a Social Security number. Still, our constituent would need to apply for a replacement card since Christina had never received the first one by US postal mail.

Even though all the field offices were closed to appointments with American citizens during the COVID pandemic, we understood the application would need to be filed with the field office in person, requiring the mother's identification and the child's vaccination record.

Our congressional office had experienced great difficulty getting "face-to-face" appointments for our constituents since January 2021, so we called the field office ourselves to be sure we could get an appointment for her and have confirmation of the date and time in hand. Christina had pulled together all the required paperwork and identification to take with her to the appointment. We confirmed the date and time in writing with the manager and a claims staffer on duty.

A week later, the office phone rang about fifteen minutes before her 9:00 a.m. appointment. On the other end of the line was the tearful young mother saying that a federal armed guard at the field office would not allow her to enter the building for her appointment. We let her know we had a written confirmation of the appointment and would call the field office so they would let her enter, but when we called, no one answered.

I pulled on my coat and grabbed my keys to drive to the field office (close to our office) with written confirmation in hand. Then Christina called again to say she had just called the local police, who had already arrived, to convince the federal guard to allow her and her baby into the building for their appointment.

Once inside the SSA offices, she filed the required paperwork for the replacement card. After two weeks it arrived at her home, but that was only after our office called to correct a misspelling of the address to which it was to be delivered. Once the baby's Social Security card was in hand, our office helped Ms. Christina expedite her son's passport application so they could travel that spring. At the time of this writing, we still have no explanation for what happened to the original card.

I will say that after this incident, I drove down to the local SSA office to talk with their employees and see what we needed to do to have a better working relationship. Sadly, I was also greeted by an armed guard. I told him who I was and that I represented the congressman's office. I asked if I could come in and speak to the employees who were supposed to be working on behalf of the representative's constituents. He pointed at the red sign on the door and told me I needed to call the number on the sign to schedule an appointment. I explained to him that we had been calling that number for months and most of the time our calls went unanswered.

After this incident, I started researching why all the SSA offices were closed and had an armed guard at the door. I was able to speak to DC-based SSA employees when I was there for training and asked them, "When will your offices be open again?" They responded, "We are open, just not to the public." I was shocked to hear them say that and asked, "Who do you work for? Don't you work for the public?" They didn't know how to answer me. I walked away thinking that so much of our federal government is completely broken and no longer remembers who they are there to serve.

You might find it interesting that on January 20, 2021, President Biden released an executive order on "Protecting the Federal Workforce and Requiring Federal Mask-Wearing." It stated, "Unless it is physically impossible or poses a threat to critical national security interests, generally speaking, occupancy in federal workplaces should be no more than 25 percent of normal capacity during periods of significant or high community transmission."[105] So 75 percent of the federal workforce was sent home and was supposedly working remotely. As of this writing, many have still not returned. The Federal Employees Union is negotiating terms of return.

Adoptive Parents Fred and Connie's Story: IRS Allows Adopted Children to Be Wrongfully Claimed as Dependents by Birth Parents

Fred and his wife Connie adopted three beautiful children from the foster care system in the county where they lived. But the process of adoption through the attorney they hired produced a lot of unanswered questions and a subsequent long nightmare of the IRS disputing tax returns that claimed the children as dependents.

Fred contacted our office to ask if we could help him respond to the IRS notice that his refund had not been processed and their request to furnish proof that the children shown on his tax return were indeed his dependents.

With this request, he needed to furnish school records, medical records, vaccination records, and a host of other documents to prove he and his wife had supported the children for the previous tax filing year. This was provided, but then the IRS wanted each child's birth certificate and all information needed to support the Social Security numbers used on the tax return. This began a long quest for correspondence and phone calls to the attorney's office—which was supposed to have all this information in hand, but didn't.

The adoption process of Fred and Connie's children had taken place during the pandemic, during which time a legal assistant in the attorney's office handling the adoptions was said to have died from COVID. Also, several important pieces to wrap up the case had been left undone. One piece was the birth certificate of one of the children born in Texas.

Our office began by requesting a copy of the legal assistant's initial request for the child's birth certificate. Our request was eventually responded to by Texas Vital Records officials, who promised the document could be issued once the correct fees were received. They said the mistake was that one dollar was missing from the fee payment.

A bigger problem was that because we were not the constituent's attorney who had requested the birth certificate, we could not present the initial request because it was secured with a control number to protect against fraudulent use of the record. We had to initiate our own request on behalf of Fred and Connie, but we could not apply the previous payment to the request because it was not ours.

We ended up having a dialogue with the Texas state government that lasted for weeks. We had to contact the Secretary of State's office for the State of Texas to get help. They were willing to help, and we finally received the birth certificate, but only after several more months of waiting.

Once we had the third child's birth certificate in hand, we could then request the children's Social Security cards be issued in their new adopted names. This took another several weeks of requests and waiting. Finally, they were issued, and we could see light at the end of the tunnel. The IRS accepted all this documentation to prove the children's status, and the tax refund was distributed to Fred's family.

Nice ending, right? Well, not exactly. The following spring, when Fred and Connie filed their tax return for that year, it was rejected by the IRS. This was because their adopted children's Social Security numbers on their return had popped up on someone else's return filed earlier. That someone else turned out to be the birth parents! The unscrupulous couple had entered the children's Social Security numbers on *their* return to get the earned income tax credits for *themselves*. Not only that, but they had also filed their returns to the IRS on the first date federal tax returns could be submitted. They had beaten Fred and Connie to the punch! So, Fred and Connie's refunds—which would have included the monies from the children-associated tax credits—had already been processed and paid out to the birth parents.

We went to the IRS to report this crime of fraud committed by the birth parents. We also asked what could be done to circumvent all the steps already taken in the previous year to prove the children as dependents.

Our request fell on deaf ears. We were told that the IRS only handles tax returns, and that only the SSA can issue numbers to be entered on the tax returns. One does not have any oversight over the other. The only advice we got was to send the IRS a letter about the problem—the very same problem we had just solved the previous year. There was also the matter that the children's Social Security numbers were obviously still in the hands of the birth parents. To prevent them from ever illegally using the children's Social Security numbers again, we would have to get them changed and assigned to their official adoptive names. This request was made, but for whatever reason, the SSA field office handling the request ignored it for several months. More hurry up and wait.

I finally called to ask about the delay and was told some surprising new misinformation: their office couldn't be assured the children's card numbers *could* be changed. It turned out that the staffer handling the change assumed the manager had already sent the information to Baltimore to have the cards reissued with new numbers, but nothing had been sent, so nothing had been done. When the "right hand doesn't know what the left hand is doing," it results in inefficient service to the American people.

Once we had this information in hand about how that SSA field office had dropped the ball, we again became the squeaky wheel, the process sped up quickly, and the cards were reissued in the children's new names with new numbers. These new cards in hand, Fred and Connie resubmitted their tax return, it was accepted, and they got their rightful refund.

This past tax year, Fred and Connie had no issue filing their federal return or having the refund accepted for processing. But our office was left asking ourselves how often this happens to other adoptive families and whether it's even reported. Tax dollars are being paid fraudulently to birth parents in such cases. I would guess this kind of fraud and mismanagement costs taxpayers untold millions of dollars each year. It's another aspect of the IRS's inefficient management that needs to be addressed to prevent this from happening to other adoptive parents.

Ms. Debby's Story: Social Security Administration Denies Her American Citizenship and Right to Medicare and Spousal Benefits Due to Agency Error

Debby has lived in the United States her entire life, although she was born in Canada to American parents. She would be sixty-five in just a few months. She had already sent a copy of her original birth certificate to the SSA as proof of her citizenship to claim Medicare and spousal benefits. She had been married for forty-two years to a gentleman who was permanently disabled in a farming accident.

Debby applied for benefits in February of that year. She waited eight months, only to receive a letter from the SSA saying that she was ineligible to receive the benefits because she had not worked enough quarters (three months equals one quarter), and every citizen is required to work a total of forty quarters to collect Social Security benefits. They also said she was not an American citizen, although she actually was, because both her parents were Americans.

Debby had also hit the proverbial brick wall in what has been described as "the black hole" of recorded messages in trying to respond to the SSA's request for Form FS-240, the Consular Report of Birth Abroad form. The report she had received contained an error in her birthdate. She was still waiting for the Department of State's assistance to correct it. Debby had been unsuccessful in her attempts to speak to anyone at the number she was given to request a corrected FS-240 or to reach the Washington National Records Center in Maryland to which she was referred.

After numerous phone calls, delayed periods of waiting on hold for more than two to three hours at a time, and then hang-ups, she was frustrated to the point of asking our office for help.

After we made many unsuccessful calls to the consular's office (the same one Debby had reached out to for the corrected FS-240), we contacted the local SSA field office to get an in-person appointment with the claims expert. We wanted to see if we could simply provide her birth certificate and other requested documentation that the SSA had initially requested, even though we had already provided them.

Once we had an actual list of the required specific information detailing additional birth information about her American parents, which had already been provided to SSA at least once before, Debby met with a claims specialist at the SSA field office, who processed her claim without further delay.

Neither Debby nor our office ever received the corrected FS-240, nor were we ever given any explanation why the original birth documents provided were insufficient. Her benefits began five months after her claim was processed, a full thirteen months after her initial application for benefits.

This is a story that can be told over and over again. We experience it in our office on a regular basis, where agencies either lose documents or just say they never received them, even when the constituent has proof they were received.

Mr. and Mrs. Evans' Story: Vague and Complex Medicare Part D Rules Result in Lifetime Penalties.

Mr. and Mrs. Evans (both in their mid-seventies) came to our office in desperation. They had tried for many months to resolve the issue presented to them when they discovered they each had been penalized for *not* accepting Medicare Part D for prescription medications.

During the fall open enrollment, at a time of year when making decisions about healthcare is common, representatives of Medicare C (Medicare Advantage or MA) contacted the Evanses and sold them a policy that, at the time, sounded better than their current one. It's important to note that these plans usually do *sound* better because they tout "extra benefits" that are not included in regular Medicare coverage. They also carry several limitations for care outside a certain geographical area. The Evanses quickly learned that the policy did not meet their needs and covered less than what was sold.

At the time they requested help from our office, they were in a quandary about both the failure of their MA coverage and the penalties they were being charged, now that they had opted for Part D prescription coverage.

When Mr. and Mrs. Evans enrolled in Medicare Part A and Part B, they never decided not to accept Part D because the option was never presented to them by anyone (neither by Mr. Evans's former employer nor the representatives of Medicare). Neither Mr. or Mrs. Evans was made aware of annual cumulative penalties for not accepting Part D at the time they chose to receive Medicare (both at age 65). (It's important to note that Part D penalties are calculated at 1 percent per month or 12 percent per year with no cap. In addition to a monthly premium, these Part D prescription plans must list large copays for brand-name drugs in their formularies to be approved under Medicare provisions.)

Upon the realization that these penalties nearly tripled the monthly cost of each of their Part D plans, Mr. and Mrs. Evans tried directly calling the Centers for Medicare & Medicaid Services (CMS), which administers the initial acceptance for coverage of all Medicare C and Medicare Part D plans. Of course, this couple could not reach CMS representatives directly, even after numerous calls. This is a story we often hear from citizens struggling to simply talk to this powerful agency that makes decisions on the healthcare of millions of senior citizens. They make these decisions based on complicated provisions not promoted or explained by any elected official or any governing body other than their own.

Because of these penalties, we began to realize that unless Mr. and Mrs. Evans were granted a waiver (for which they had already filed) from these very stiff penalties, it made no sense for them to now opt for Part D, even at a time they might be facing a greater need for it.

Our office referred this couple to an insurance broker who was well-versed in Medicare coverage to help them sort out their best options, including supplemental plans to Part B, which he advised. At the time of this writing, this couple is now being told that because they made more than one change to their MA plan, they must now wait until the open enrollment period beginning October 15 to change their MA plan to a supplemental plan. They are also being told they must wait to opt out of Part D, which carries sixty-eight months' worth of penalties for prescription coverage for each of them!

We are speaking with the insurance broker to help unravel the complex rules thousands of senior citizens face when they are required to make decisions associated with Medicare Part D. They are rarely informed that there are stiff penalties if they don't sign up for Part D when they are first eligible.

In the meantime, we have contacted CMS to request a copy of a letter apparently written to the constituents but never received by them, in reply to their waiver request to reduce or remove these penalties. This waiver request is in the form of an appeal to Medicare Part D's Qualified Independent Contractor, C2C Innovative Solutions.

If C2C issues an unfavorable redetermination decision, then Mr. and Mrs. Evans may file an additional request for reconsideration to reduce or remove the late-enrollment penalties. This request for reconsideration is to another independent review entity or "IRE," an "independent" Medicare contractor based in Florida. Both review entities are fully organized under the provisions of Medicare with no outside oversight of elected officials or governing authority but their own.

At this time, our office is still waiting for a response from CMS regarding a copy of the letter written in response to Mr. and Mrs. Evans' waiver request. Unless new information changes the facts, this couple will need to continue to pay these penalties until they are eligible to disenroll in the MA plan and Part D, some seven months from now. At our calculation, this will mean an additional $1,500 in penalties, not including prescription copays and premiums for Part D coverage!

This is another example of the ineptness and unfairness of a system many Americans find themselves trapped in.

Mr. Harry's Story: Injured and Permanently Disabled, Penalized Financially, and Harassed for a Mistake Made by the Department of Labor.

Harry was working in Washington, DC, when he was seriously injured while working on the Capitol Building. He was 100 percent disabled and for ten years collected disability. When he turned sixty-five, he decided to file for Social Security and filled out the appropriate paperwork to do so.

We first spoke to Harry when he called our office in November 2021. He was distraught and asked for help with problems he was having with the Department of Labor (DOL). They had been harassing him for approximately three years and were demanding he pay an enormous amount of money. They stated Harry had been overpaid in the amount of $45,505.50 over a period of six years, by no fault of his own, but by the DOL agency's mistake. He stated that he had received a letter from the DOL and was told that he would need to pay the debt in thirty days to avoid penalties and interest, or the overpayment would be recovered by being withheld from his "continuing compensation." I will share the entire letter so you can understand how bizarre it sounds that they would force him to repay money for a mistake they made!

Dear Mr. Harry,

This letter is in further reference to debt number ▮▮▮▮▮▮▮▮ for the period 06/01/2014 through 08/15/2020 in the amount of $45,550.05 that was declared in your case by preliminary overpayment determination dated 11/09/2021. The overpayment occurred because you received benefits from the Social Security Administration as part of an annuity under the Federal Employees Retirement System (FERS) concurrently with Federal Employee Compensation Act (FECA) benefits, therefore, an offset was required.

Your case has been carefully studied and any additional evidence or arguments submitted have been given full consideration. We have determined that you were without fault in the creation of the overpayment because you relied on misinformation given in writing by OWCP (or by another government agency which you had reason to believe was connected with the administration of benefits) as to the interpretation of a pertinent provision of the FECA or its regulations. There is documentation to substantiate that the misinformation was actually communicated to you, and there is no evidence in the case file to demonstrate that you knew, or should have known, the proper course of action to be followed.

However, even though you have been found to be without fault, it has been determined that the circumstances of your case do not warrant waiver of the overpayment. The attached overpayment memorandum explains the basis for this decision.

The overpayment will be recovered in the manner described in the enclosed overpayment payment instructions. You have the right to inspect and copy the Office of Workers Compensation Programs (OWCP) records with respect to this debt and to dispute any information contained and those records concerning the debt.

This represents a formal decision with regard to your overpayment. If you disagree with this decision, you should carefully review the attached appeal right and pursue this avenue if appropriate to your situation. Note that even if an appeal is requested, interest will be charged, and collection actions will continue unless and until this decision is overturned.

Sincerely,
Federal Employees Program

The letter also included information for the overpayment instructions and who to make the check or money order to, which was not the Department of the Treasury but the US Department of Labor.

He was given the following information:

1. "Interest will begin to accrue as of the date of this letter, at the rate of the US Treasury note."
2. Interest charges will be waived if the debt is paid within thirty days.
3. They gave him several ways that his bank account or wages could be garnished to pay for the debt by several other federal agencies: Department of the Treasury, Office of Workers Compensation, and Office of Personnel Management.

And finally, they ended with: "If we do not receive payment or some indication that you intend to make payment within thirty days, your overpayment will be considered a delinquent debt and one of these courses of action will be taken."

I don't know how this letter made *you* feel, but it made me extremely angry! Where in any court of law should an innocent person be required to pay the penalty for someone else's mistake? The Department of Labor made this mistake, not Mr. Harry! This is an Administrative State agency robbery of Harry, which is unconstitutional! The DOL is run by unelected bureaucrats who write the laws, enforce them, and adjudicate them, which is also unconstitutional! But I digress.

When Harry received this letter, he immediately tried to appeal. He followed the instructions that were in the letter and tried for two weeks to appeal on his own but received no answers to his phone calls or emails. He then hired a lawyer, knowing he had only thirty days to appeal, thinking they would surely respond to his lawyer—but no, they didn't respond!

On the thirty-first day, he received correspondence from DOL that they had not heard from him, so the time to appeal was past. He must pay the debt immediately or his compensation would be garnished. They started taking money out of his account, and the penalties and interest started racking up. During all this, his wife died from COVID-19 complications, and he was diagnosed with throat cancer.

We contacted the DOL through email with little to no response. Finally, I made a phone call and tried to plead with the manager for the DOL liaisons to our office, Ms. C, who kept saying, "Ms. Adams, it is the law, and there is nothing we can do about it." I explained the hardships that Harry was going through. Her only suggestion was that he fill out the Overpayment Action Request Form which would require him to list every single asset he owns so *they* (the DOL) could determine if it was a hardship for him. So, the DOL made a law, enforced the law, and adjudicated the law. The bottom line is that when they made a mistake, Mr. Harry, the American citizen, paid for it. Unbelievable!

Today, what started out as a $545 monthly payment coming out of Harry's compensation has increased to almost $800 due to penalties and interest. What started out as a $45,550.50 overpayment has now climbed to a staggering $58,000.00 repayment!

Harry is being penalized with penalties and interest for a mistake he did not make. This is wrong on every level, and it *must* be stopped! I spoke to Mr. Harry recently, and he expressed that he is tired and has just resigned to the fact that the DOL will continue to make him pay for their mistake.

Ms. Betty's Story: Brought Back from the Dead Each Year to Pay Her Taxes.

Betty contacted our office on April 18, 2022, seeking help with filing her 2021 taxes. She told us that the IRS had locked all her records, saying the person with the Social Security number she was trying to use was deceased. She went on to say that she had been having this problem with the IRS since 2015.

When Betty reached out to us, she had already been to the SSA office twice in an attempt to get it straightened out! They made copies of her Social Security card and her driver's license. The previous year, they had done the same thing and even wrote a letter for her to attach to her file that she was "indeed, alive and well and standing right in front of them." But here she was again, in 2021, being told by the

IRS that she was dead and that she would have to go back to the SSA and have them prove she was alive! Our office's caseworker contacted the Tax Advocate Service (TAS) to see if they could expedite restoring her deceased status to alive. (TAS is a service that acts as a mediator between the IRS and the congressional office.)

TAS responded, saying, "Unfortunately, we will not be able to assist immediately as TAS does not make these corrections. We will still have to contact the IRS to have the corrections made. It will not be as simple as us just removing the indicator from your constituent's account and her filing her return electronically. The options available to your constituent would be to either file a paper return or she can file once the account is corrected. Once they make the correction, it takes a couple of weeks for the correction to post. If she is due a refund, she will not be penalized. She has three years from the due date of the return to still file and claim her refund."

Betty chose to send in a paper file on April 22, 2022. A few days later, she texted our caseworker, stating that she had received four letters from the IRS, all identical. Then she received an email from USPS stating that she had four more letters from the IRS on their way. (Talk about inefficiency and a waste of taxpayer dollars!)

On May 26, 2022, our office received a notification that TAS had sent in the two transactions needed to correct the "being deceased" issue, but one did not go through. It was resent, and we were told that the refunds should be released on or before June 13.

On June 13, we were notified that an IRS worker had corrected the issue with the IRS that had shown that Betty was deceased. They would send the case to a team to monitor it for the refund. However, while they were fixing the issue of her being deceased, they were telling her she had another issue with her 2020 taxes because the system was showing her return had not been received. Betty's records indicated that they had received the $58 check she had sent, along with the top copy of the 1040, showing her name and address, marked "received on May 16, 2021." We resolved this for Betty, but how many times can the IRS mess up one person's taxes? You just can't make this stuff up!

Betty expressed frustration that the IRS was asking for all her records again—the very same records she had sent before and then gave to our office, which we also sent to them. Betty said, "If we operated our affairs the way the IRS does, we would go to jail!"

In short, this saga has been a problem off and on since 2015. The fact that a government agency that has been put in place to serve the people can just say you're dead and then refuse to answer your phone calls or emails when you try to call and get it worked out is unacceptable.

I just spoke with Betty, and she stated that she is preparing her taxes for 2024 and hopes that all the work our office has done will help the IRS get their records straight this year. She also said that if she is declared "deceased" again, we will be the first to know!

A Story of Small Town USA: Federal Agencies Leave Citizens Without Clean Water and Hold a Town Hostage with Overbearing Costs, Regulations, and Restrictions.

One of the local towns in our district in rural Virginia, which has 1,660 citizens and encompasses only 1.8 square miles, recently faced a clean-drinking-water crisis brought about in part by an earthquake. The Environmental Protection Agency (EPA) promptly stepped in and increased their standards, placing the town in a position of serious violation of disinfection byproduct standard guidelines.

The EPA applied pressure on the Virginia Department of Health, who then placed the town under a consent order to fix the disinfection byproduct issue. The small town was given a short period of time to complete the fix or face possible penalties. Some of these penalties were excessive. One townsperson and elected official told me that the fine was more than $32,000 per day, which would be nearly a million dollars a month. The town's annual budget was only $1,644,000, so the hardship was evident and pressing! Most citizens in the town were retired or on financial assistance.

At the same time, the Virginia Department of Health (VDH) also placed the local water authority under a consent order for the same reason. The local water authority provides water for the town utility system. The VDH felt pressure from the EPA to improve all systems simultaneously, even though it would interrupt the critical water supply for the people of the town.

The town had met all requirements and was working diligently to meet their deadlines. They spent over a million dollars but, unfortunately, ran into numerous hurdles that took time and money away from installing systems to deal with the water quality issue.

The town needed to find the best location to drill a well to dilute water quality and help fix their water problem. It was determined that the best location for the well was in the town park. The problem was that the town had received a grant from the US Department of Agriculture (USDA) of $75,000 for a playground and pavilion. In exchange, the National Park Service (NPS) required jurisdiction over the land. (There are always strings attached when accepting federal dollars.) This meant the town had to get permission from the NPS to drill the well. The town believed that the NPS, since they had jurisdiction, should be able to give them permission to use it, but months were wasted while different federal and state agencies went back and forth trying to decide whose permission was required. In the meantime, the citizens were dealing with the issue of bad water. The NPS finally allowed the town to proceed with the project of a well on the site and agreed that they would work with the town on replacement property.

The town bid out the well construction package twice. The first round of bids received zero contractor response. When contractors were contacted to determine why they did not bid, they responded that the standards spelled out in the EPA and VDH grant loan package requirements, such as the Davis Bacon Wage rates and American iron and steel requirements, created a work situation that would be difficult to bid on.

The project was rebid, and one contractor submitted a cost of $1.3 million, which was $820,000 above VDH and town engineer estimates. This is also much more than a town with a total general fund budget of $1.6 million could afford without assistance.

I recently spoke with the town mayor. He told me that the town engineers finally took matters into their own hands for the health and safety of the townspeople. An advanced treatment process of nanofiltration was added, and chlorine and fluoride were added to the water before distribution after treatment. The water immediately began passing the standard tests after they installed this treatment process. With this solution, the town resolved the issue on their own. Ironically, instead of praising the town for fixing their problem, the EPA was upset that the town had not followed their guidelines. The mayor also told me about the long, frustrating, and painful process of being hounded by so many agencies who seemed to be more concerned about their own interests than the interests of the health and safety of the townspeople.

So, there you have it, one small American town, with 1,660 citizens in 1.8 square miles, bullied by four federal agencies and one state agency! They prevented the town from using their own resources to keep their people safe by delaying the process of getting the work done, imposing so many standards that, when they finally got permission to use the land, the price was too high for any contractor to want to bid on the project. They then left them stranded, seeking alternate sites without guaranteeing their site would be approved. They threatened extreme and excessive fines that were not even feasible for a town of their size, yet we're supposed to believe these agencies are there to serve us!

The town now has clean water for its citizens, but only because it decided to use common sense and the wisdom of engineers who live there and actually care about the water they drink.

Ms. Mary's Story: Social Security Administration Employee Gives Misinformation Causing Massive Fines.

The following case is still ongoing because we just received it in the last couple of weeks, but I want to share it with you.

Mary contacted our office not long ago because she had been misinformed by the Social Security Administration personnel regarding her receipt of her late husband's benefits even though she had remarried. She was told that she was allowed to receive them because she had remarried after the age of sixty. She was grateful and didn't worry about it until she received a notice from the SSA stating that she had been overpaid and would be required to return the money. The agency stated that she was *not* at fault, but the letter they sent stated, "Even though the SSA was at fault in making the overpayment, that fact does not relieve the claimant or any other individual from repaying the overpayment."

I have included part of the letter below for you to see on the next page.

What shocks me when we receive cases like this is that agencies have no problem admitting they've made a mistake but rarely take responsibility for it! They almost always pass the punishment onto the American citizen.

Where is our representation that is supposed to protect us from this kind of abuse? Congress forfeited that protection when it abdicated its responsibility and gave authority to these agencies in the Administration Procedures Act, as discussed earlier. There is very little oversight. This must change so that Americans

> **FINDINGS OF FACT AND CONCLUSIONS OF LAW**
>
> After careful consideration of the entire record, the undersigned makes the following findings:
>
> 1. **The claimant was overpaid benefits in the amount of $46,007.00 during the period March 2014 to September 2017** ~~████████~~.
>
> The claimant was paid Title II wife's insurance benefits from March 2014, through September 2017, on the earnings record of her former spouse, ~~████████~~ She was paid benefits in the amount of $46,007.00, but at the time of her payment was remarried and therefore was not entitled to the benefits.
>
> 2. **The claimant was not at fault in causing the overpayment (**~~████████████~~ ~~████~~**)**.
>
> Fault as used in *without fault* applies only to the individual. Although the Social Security Administration may have been at fault in making the overpayment, that fact does not relieve the claimant or any other individual from whom the Administration seeks to recover the overpayment from liability for repayment, if the claimant is not without fault. In determining whether the individual is at fault, the undersigned will consider all pertinent circumstances, including the claimant's age and intelligence, and any physical, mental, educational, or linguistic limitations (including any lack of facility with the English language) she has (20 CFR 404.507).
>
> In this case, the evidence of record reveals that the claimant disclosed her remarriage to SSA at the time of filing her application of Title II wife's insurance benefits on the earnings record of her former spouse, ~~████████~~. However, the claimant was given erroneous information from SSA that she could receive wife's benefits even though remarried. When the SSA Claim's Representative put the claimant's information into the system to process her claim, it would not allow her claim to go through, so her current marriage date was removed and put it in the Remarks section, which allowed her claim to be processed and her to be put in pay status.
>
> The claimant therefore, is not at fault for the overpayment, as she disclosed her remarriage and there was no way she could have prevented or would have known that SSA had incorrectly paid her. Her acceptance of the overpayment was secondary to her reliance on erroneous information from an official source within the Social Security Administration regarding a pertinent legal provision (20 CFR 404.510a).
>
> 3. **Recovery of the overpayment does not defeat the purpose of Title II of the Act (20 CFR 404.508(a) and (b))**.

can regain their rights and freedoms and stop being the scapegoat for every agency that makes a mistake.

Mary's case is just getting started. I don't know how it will end, but I know it will not be the last. Our office will work hard to get the repayment waived for Mary, because she should not be required to pay for the federal government's error. Sometimes the problem seems too big to fix, but we must keep fighting!

Mr. Tim's Story: Internal Revenue Service Leaves Employer Hanging Over Promised Employee Retention Tax Credits.

Mr. Tim owns and operates a popular cafe specializing in hamburgers and craft beer. When the COVID-19 epidemic hit, the federal government mandated the closure of many establishments in early 2020. Tim thought his business was finished, but he kept the doors open. Why? He was told the government would issue him quarterly tax credits if he continued operating during the crisis—in essence, he became an "employment arm" of the federal government.

This was a time of extreme hardship for the business, as employees and clients were concerned about exposure to the virus. However, Tim took the risk to keep his business and support his employees and customers, assuming that, on the government's statement, when he applied for the tax credits beginning in the second quarter of 2020, he would be allowed claims for his employee retention by the Internal Revenue Service.

Through Automatic Data Processing, a global payroll management system used by nearly every small business in the country, Tim filed his payroll records to claim this tax credit. After filing for the three quarters in 2020, he began trying to reach the IRS to ask when he could expect his tax credits to be processed. After months of no response, he contacted his US Senator. After nearly a year of casework and a promise that his tax credits were forthcoming, he was contacted by a local IRS agent to verify his claims—the one who had promised to file amended returns on his behalf because of an apparent error in his initial claims on IRS Form 941.

After several more months of waiting, Tim was told by the IRS his claims could not be found in their system. He contacted our office in August 2023 to ask if we could help investigate the delays he was experiencing with his claims, now totaling some $180,000. Our office discovered through information from the same TAS advocate who had handled his case with the Senator's office that his case was closed at the beginning of 2023 for "non-receipt of documents." Ironically, he was being told by his caseworker at the time that his claim was being processed for payment.

During this period of waiting, the IRS arbitrarily imposed a moratorium in September 2023 on the processing of ERTC payments due to massive fraud perpetrated in early claims. When asked whether Tim's claims during this period could be processed, our office was told that because his claims "were filed" *before the moratorium*, they could be processed, but the IRS could make "no promises" that they would be.

In January 2024, our office was told that the moratorium had been lifted, and a special investigative arm had been established to process all the residual claims filed during the moratorium. As of July 2024, that investigative unit had still not given us a date when these claims would be paid. Our office recently sent a letter to Tim's county treasurer stating that he was waiting on these payments to pay his unpaid local taxes so he could remain open for business. After almost four years, the claims are still awaiting payment processing, and there is no assurance that the IRS will ever resolve the matter.

The IRS made a promise that ff Tim would keep his business open and retain his employees, they would give him a tax credit, but here he is four years later holding the financial burden caused by their not keeping their promise. Sadly, our office is aware of at least twenty more businesses in our district that are experiencing this same problem.

Mr. Sam's Story: Lost Green Card and Bureaucratic Red Tape.

USCIS = United States Citizenship and Immigration Service
SSA = Social Security Administration
Green Card = Government-issued Lawful Permanent Resident ID card
(Alien number)

Mr. Sam, a Belgian immigrant, came to the United States with his mother and brother after his father initially immigrated a year before at the invitation of a local company looking to hire experienced machinists in 1966. Sam was eight years old and, along with all his family members, was issued green card (lawful alien) status in 1967.

As fate would have it, many years later, during a fishing trip in 2008, Sam dropped his wallet into the murky waters of a lake on which he was fishing. In his wallet were all his credit cards and identifying documents, including his green card. Sam began to have these important cards and documents reissued, knowing he would need to prove his lawful permanent resident status. Although it took several years, he eventually pulled together the needed documentation (including school records and an initial Social Security application for a number issued to him in 1975 to work in the US). He did this with the help of an attorney in order to request the reissuance of his green card. Of course, he was met with the usual delays associated with information issued by the USCIS, but eventually was told his alien number included with his initial I-90 request was not valid or found in the USCIS system. He even produced the sequential green card numbers of his mother, brother, and father, but USCIS still declared that his own number was "unverifiable."

By 2023, and soon reaching age sixty-five, Sam came to our office seeking our help through the introduction of his present employer, who was trying to help him prepare for retirement and request Medicare benefits. It seemed reasonable that since Sam had worked since 1975 with the same Social Security number and had a continued record of employment paying into FICA, along with having paid state and federal taxes with that number, it would be a simple matter to verify the number through the SSA. However, during the time Sam has been in the US, several changes were made for immigrants who claim Social Security and Medicare benefits. The most important among those changes was that alien status needs to be verified by a green card that's been reissued within the previous ten years. At this point, our office went back to USCIS on Sam's behalf to show verified school records with his alien number used to admit him as a student in the local public school system and, again, original paperwork to show SSA's initial request in 1975 of "evidence" authenticating his green card number and alien status. Still, USCIS responded to us saying his alien number is "unverifiable."

As of this writing, and after spending nearly six thousand dollars in attorney's fees, Sam is still being rejected by the SSA for Medicare benefits until he can prove his alien status with a green card number, which is still unverifiable by USCIS. He is now filing yet another Form I-90 (a form of renewal or replacement of a green card), which is being reviewed by another attorney recommended by our casework director.

This has been a lengthy process, but our office is hoping to know in some weeks whether this new I-90, under updated immigration regulations, will enable Sam to receive a replacement green card that can serve as ID acceptable to the SSA as proof of eligibility for his Medicare benefits and ultimately his retirement benefits.

After being excited for many years about becoming an American citizen, Sam has become discouraged to the point that he's unsure whether this country is one whose citizenship he wants. His opinion is that our bureaucratic record keeping is so lax for those who've immigrated legally that he's wondering whether he wants to continue to fight for citizenship when so many illegal aliens are awarded benefits paid for through his tax dollars—while he is now being considered ineligible for his own—after being here legally and paying into FICA since 1975.

American Small Business Owners Being Treated as Criminals.

Early one morning in late March 2024, a gentlemen met one of my staff at our office door before we opened at to show us a letter he'd received from his small local bank. It stated that there was a new law that "requires certain new and existing small corporations and limited liability companies to disclose information about their 'beneficial owners.'"

We did some research to give our constituent a little more information and help calm his worries over this letter, and we discovered that this new "beneficial ownership information" (BOI) is required to be reported to Financial Crimes Enforcement Network (FinCEN) and carries stiff penalties for not doing so. The civil penalty for not reporting is set at a whopping $591 a day, and a criminal penalty may be as high as $10,000 and up to two years' imprisonment, effective January 25, 2024. These fines were established when the Corporate Transparency Act (CTA) sponsored by Rep. Carolyn B. Maloney (D-NY, Dist. 12), mandating the reporting of this information, became law in 2021.

According to the law that was passed (H.R. 2513), a beneficial owner is an individual who

1. Exercises substantial control over a corporation or limited liability company,
2. Owns two percent or more of the interest in a corporation or limited liability company, or
3. Receives substantial economic benefits from the assets of a corporation or limited liability company.

The bill's purpose is to generally address the disclosure of corporate ownership, the prevention of money laundering, and the financing of terrorism.

What I've read from the bill seems to clarify that FinCEN could force any LLC, nonprofit, small business, or anyone else trying to make an honest living to disclose their personal information.

The gentleman who visited our office said that he was a retired farmer and didn't want to give this information to them because frankly, "It was none of their business." He was also retired and hardly worked his farm. He complained that it was an overreach of government. He wondered if there was anything that could be done to protect an American's rights and privacy.

Right after the visit from our local farmer, I received an email from a friend, a recently retired FBI agent, who raised the same concern over this bill. We spoke on the phone, and she told me that she was very familiar with FinCEN. She warned that the names of the small businesses and their owners that would be placed on this list would be considered "suspects" to be investigated. She encouraged our office to try to repeal the bill that had been passed. It is time for Congress to do its job and represent and protect the American people from the tyranny of these federal agencies! They are completely out of control, and they are affecting our freedom!

This week, I received another constituent call saying they had also received a letter from their bank informing them of the requirement for their small LLC to register with FinCEN. I obtained the letter they received, and I have inserted it below so you can see that I am not making this up.

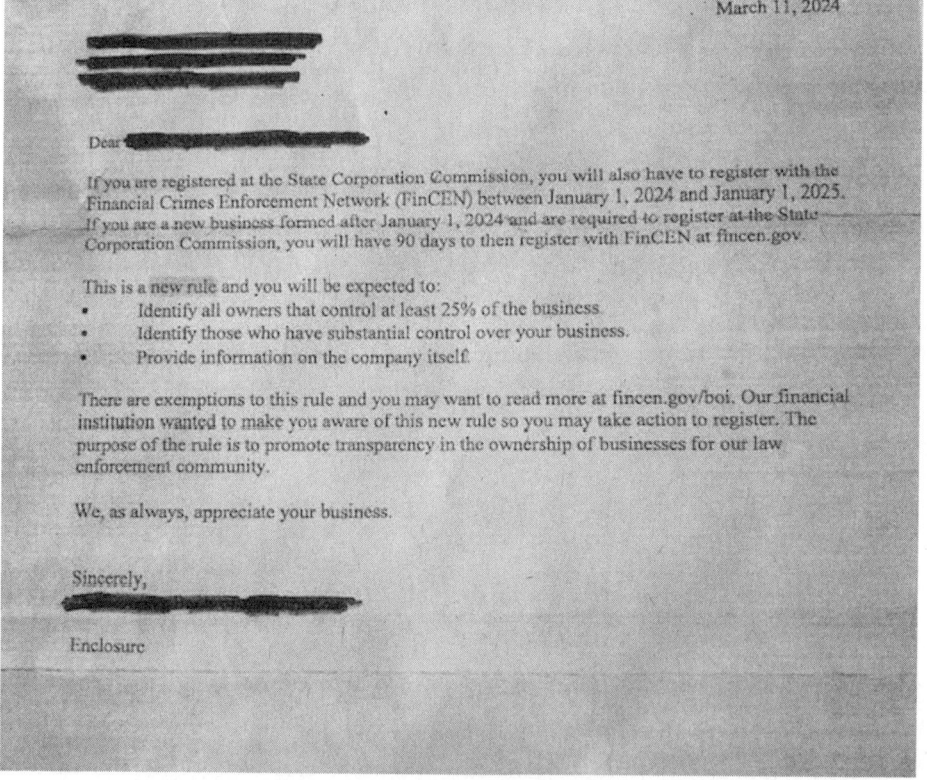

We now also know that at least one state (Alabama) accepted a civil lawsuit against the government and has ruled that this federal mandate to register is unconstitutional. At this writing, we are still within the year in which this reporting must happen, and at least one congressman has taken this encroachment of the government to task. We must be vigilant and hold our representatives accountable and let them know they must represent us and protect us from this growing tyrannical government!

In the past three years, my team and I have resolved, or at least tried to resolve, nearly 6,500 constituent cases in our district alone. Many of these cases should never have come to our office. If the agencies had been doing the work they were put in place to do, by answering the phone calls and emails of the American people who needed help, they would not have needed to call us.

Of course, the congressman is there to represent and protect his constituents from the abuse of the federal government. That is what our office tries to do every day! It is not getting better, though. If Congress doesn't do its job, clean up the mess they've created, and start shrinking the size of government, our country will no longer exist as we have known it.

Today, as I finish this chapter of stories, our office has a current caseload of 634 active cases. Each one represents a real person with a real problem with a federal agency that is unwilling to help them. So, they are flocking to their congressional representative's office to get help.

Just yesterday, I met with my staff members, who again expressed frustration over the growing problem of agency staff who no longer seem to take a "Congressional Inquiry" seriously. Too often, phone calls and emails go unanswered. A simple issue that used to take days to resolve can now take six months to a year. The question is, what can be done about it?

The rest of this book will focus on what you can do as an individual citizen and what our representatives in Congress must do to rein in our runaway bureaucracy and stop the abuse of the American people.

> **Dishonest scales are detestable to the Lord, but an accurate weight is his delight.**
>
> **Proverbs 11:1**

Chapter Six
What Can You Do?

Every government degenerates when trusted to the rulers of the people alone. The people themselves, therefore, are its only safe depositories.
Thomas Jefferson, Notes on the State of Virginia.[106]

I imagine that by now you feel a bit discouraged and maybe even hopeless after reading about the behemoth in chapter four, especially when you realize those pages represent only a fraction of the federal government agencies, and then saw the abuse of the American people in chapter five. You might think that the problem is too big and that there is nothing we can do about it. The "ship has already sailed!"

But I've heard a statement often attributed to Francis Bacon: "Knowledge is power, but ignorance is death," and I believe it's true. We must empower ourselves by being knowledgeable about our founding. Our founding documents are like a plumb line that a builder uses to see if a wall is straight up and down. If a wall is not plumb, it is dangerous and must be realigned, reinforced, or torn down. We must measure our government, our representatives, and their actions according to the plumb line of the Constitution. If we don't understand the importance of this plumb line and its significance in keeping us safe, our nation is in danger of crumbling to the ground! But how can citizens hold the government accountable if they have never read the Constitution?

Again, "Knowledge is power, but ignorance is death." We don't have a choice; we must know the Declaration and the Constitution personally and ensure it is taught to and understood by every student in every school in America. We must require its teaching and understanding by every immigrant who is seeking citizenship in our country, and we must demand the understanding of it by every person seeking to hold office and represent fellow Americans in Congress or any other elected position on a federal, state, or local level.

We have a generation rising to lead this nation that has never studied the Declaration of Independence or the Constitution and is simply enamored by the thought of being in a place of power and position! This is dangerous, and this ignorance will bring certain death to our nation.

Unfortunately, many representatives in Congress have no clue what the Declaration or the Constitution says, and quite frankly, I don't believe they care. Again, this is ignorance that will bring about the death of our nation!

So "knowledge is power, but ignorance is death!" That phrase is very significant as we ask the question, "What can you or I do?"

By reading this book, you have already taken an important step toward increasing your knowledge. You've started on your journey of learning about the Declaration of Independence and why it was written, and the Constitution, the standard and plumb line for the structure of the government that our Founding Fathers laid out for us. Thank you so much for doing that!

After reading this book, I hope that you have gained some knowledge about

1. Your country: how and why it was founded,
2. How your government was structured to operate,
3. What your constitutional rights and responsibilities are as an American citizen,
4. The government's unconstitutional exertion of extreme power over American citizens through the Administrative State,
5. Congress's abdicating its constitutional responsibility to give adequate oversight to federal agencies,
6. How large the government has become, and how if "we the people" and Congress don't do something about it, we will soon be destroyed, and

7. The importance of reading and understanding the founding documents, knowing where we came from, and why we must remain faithful to the Constitution.

But that is not enough! I hope you will join me and go further.

For the remainder of this chapter, I want us to focus on our responsibility as citizens and what we must do to turn the government around and get it moving in the right direction.

Our Founding Fathers had opinions on the importance of educating citizens in order to remain free. George Washington stated the following in his eighth annual address to Congress: "In a republic, what species of knowledge can be equally important and what duty more pressing on its legislature than to patronize a plan for communicating it to those who are to be the future guardians of the liberties of the country?"[107] He also said, "The power under the Constitution will always be with the people."[108] It is important that we teach our children about our history because they will determine the future of our country. Remember, we are the sovereign of this nation. What will we do with our power?

James Madison remarked in his second annual address to Congress, "It is universally admitted that a well-instructed people alone can be permanently a free people."[109] If we know our constitutional rights and responsibilities, we can hold our Representatives accountable and remain a free people. Educating ourselves about our country's founding and the people's power to control what happens in this country is absolutely vital. But if we are uninformed or misinformed, there is nothing we can do.

Wall Builders, an organization dedicated to teaching America's forgotten history and heroes, surveyed how uninformed Americans are about the Constitution and our country in general. I would like to share the survey here to give you a glimpse of America's constitutional ignorance.

America's Constitutional Ignorance

- 86% of Americans can't name the Right of Petition (1st Amendment).
- 61% don't know of the Right to Assemble (1st Amendment).
- 27% believe students should be punished by teachers or administrators for posting political opinions they disagree with on social media (1st Amendment).

- 46% of Americans think institutions should disinvite a speaker who might offend listeners (1st Amendment).
- 12% of Americans think the Constitution specifically ensures the right to own a pet.[110] *(This is not in the Constitution, but you can have a pet because you're free.)*

Perhaps the most shocking and revealing statistic is that *57% of Americans have never read the Constitution*! If Americans don't know what the Constitution says, how can they defend it? As Thomas Jefferson warned, "If a nation expects to be ignorant and free, in a state of civilization, it expects what never was and never will be."[111]

You are probably reading this book because you are concerned about our country or have experienced abuse from the government and want to do something to help. In the next section I'm going to share some things that you can do to make a difference. As you read, it may feel a little overwhelming, but each point is important, and I want you to see the big picture. I recognize you may not be able to do it all, but all of us can do something.

Educate Yourself and Take Action

1. Read the Constitution (the "plumbline") and know it from top to bottom. Then you will recognize when the government is doing something it shouldn't be doing.
2. Get to know your elected representatives—local, state, and federal—build a relationship with them, and make sure they are aware that you understand the Constitution and their responsibility to it.
3. Pay attention to what is happening in Congress and hold your Representatives accountable when they go against the Constitution. You can follow your Representative and their votes through this website: www.congress.gov.
4. Share a copy of this book with your family and friends.
5. Teach your children the Constitution and the Founding Fathers' design for our country.

6. Every American has two US Senators and one Congressman who represents them. Contact your Senate and Congressional District Offices and make an appointment to visit your Senator or Representative when he or she is in the district. Politely ask the members or staff speaking for them the following questions:

    a. Have they read and studied the Declaration of Independence and the Constitution, and when did they last review them while considering their proposed legislation?

    b. Ask if the legislation they are trying to pass into law aligns with the Constitution and if their legislative assistants are required to ensure the legislation they prepare for him/her to vote aligns with the Constitution.

    c. If they answer yes, thank them, and ask if they can give you a recent example of how they have done that. If they say no or insinuate that the Constitution is outdated or irrelevant, then do everything in your power to get your representative voted out of office. They don't belong there.

7. If you can, make an appointment to visit Washington, DC, to speak to your Senators and Representatives and ask them the same questions.

8. Do the same with your local and state representatives.

9. Go to your local schools and ask to see the curriculum being taught to the students about our nation's founding and structure of government. Ask if students are studying original sources in their history and civics classes. If they are, thank them. If not, express your concern and disapproval. Ask if teachers are giving revisionist history. If they are, you should express your concern and disapproval.

10. Finally, *vote* every time there is an election, this includes the primaries and every election that takes place in your community, not just every four years in November.

I recently read an article in *Newsweek* that discussed the average American young person's lack of knowledge of the US Constitution:

Younger Americans are woefully ignorant of what is in the US Constitution. This ignorance is a major cause of our current national discontent as our citizenry increasingly has no idea how our government works.

A survey of more than one thousand liberal arts colleges by the American Council of Trustees and Alumni found only 18 percent of these colleges require a class in US history or government for graduation. The same report found that nearly 10 percent of college students believed Judge Judy was on the Supreme Court. Forty percent did not know Congress had the power to declare war. . . .

The way forward is clear. A renewal of civic education can reverse America's civic deficit and restore widespread awareness of our history and government. It is time for students, parents, colleges and universities, and lawmakers to confront the crisis in civic education. Of the one thousand Americans surveyed in the 2018 State of the First Amendment survey done by the Freedom Forum, only one was able to name all five First Amendment rights: freedom of speech, freedom of religion, freedom of the press, freedom of peaceful assembly, and freedom to petition the government. Even worse, 40 percent could not identify a single First Amendment right.[112]

Our republic cannot survive if this lack of knowledge continues. Our young people, our future leaders, must understand how the government is supposed to work according to the Constitution! As President George Washington once said: "The power under the Constitution will always be with the people."[113]

But if the people are unaware of the power the Constitution gives them, then the door remains open to modern-day despots and tyrants who would usurp that power for themselves. It is also fair to say that the failure of the Constitution will also always be with the people! If we fail to educate our citizens properly beginning at an early age, the Constitution will be moot, and "we the people" will be the ones to blame.

Now, I understand that life is busy. We often feel we can't take on any more. Maybe you're a busy mom just trying to meet everyone's needs, a business owner struggling to make payroll, a pastor trying to lead your congregation in the right direction, an activist who is involved in all things politics, or a politician trying to serve your constituents well. It doesn't matter who you are, but it does matter that we all do something. I'm asking you to choose one to three actions from the list above that will stretch you and start doing them consistently. This is not an exhaustive list of things that you can do. There may be other specific areas that you are passionate about. Just do something! Don't be silent!

I hope and pray that you now realize your power as an individual American citizen and will use it to restore stability and constitutional governance to our representative government.

Follow me to the next chapter to learn what Congress can do and how we can encourage them to do it.

> Let the favor of the Lord our God be on us; establish for us the work of our hands—establish the work of our hands!
>
> **Psalm 90:17**

Chapter Seven
What Can Congress Do?

All legislative Powers herein granted shall be vested in a Congress of the United States, which shall consist of a Senate and House of Representatives.

Article I of the Constitution of the United States of America

Not too long ago, our youngest son found out that the concrete block walls in the basement of his house were bowing in, causing structural liability for his entire home. Something had to be done immediately to save it. I found it interesting as he showed me the steps the engineers took to carefully return his home to a place of safety.

First, they assessed every wall to determine how far out of plumb it was. They did this by applying a plumb line to it. Second, they had to remove structures connected to the walls over the years, such as water lines, dropped ceilings, and more. Third, they had to drill into the ground all the way to the foundation to set steel beams on the foundation footers and secure the bottom of each beam by pouring concrete to keep it in its proper place. Fourth, they placed a bracket with an adjustable bolt at the top of each beam. Finally, the bolts attached at the top of the brackets are now being slowly adjusted to apply steady pressure on the beams. In time, this will force the wall back into plumb. Once there, the beams will remain to ensure the strength and plumb of the wall and the safety of his home.

Beams secured in place to the foundation footers.

Beams placed against a bowing wall.

Bracket and bolt in place to pressure the beam against the bowed wall.

Bolt that must be slowly adjusted over time to finish bringing the beam and wall into plumb.

As my son described this process to me and I began to research and study for this book, I couldn't help but notice the parallel between a home's foundational structure and our country's structural foundation.

As we have walked through this book together, we have learned that we were given a beautiful thing: a constitutional republic built on a solid foundation of the Declaration of Independence and the US Constitution. Thanks to this solid foundation, the citizens of the United States are no longer under the rule of a tyrannical king. We are the sovereign and in control because we choose who represents us. In turn, those representatives go to Washington to ensure that the Constitution is followed and that our lives, liberties, and pursuits of happiness are protected.

But we have also learned that along our nearly 250-year journey our representatives have not always followed the Constitution. For the past hundred-plus years, the government has grown out of control, and we are now left holding the bag of abuses that will not go away unless things are brought back into proper alignment. Our walls are now dangerously bowed, and the structural integrity of our country is at stake unless something is done immediately to restore and align its walls with the plumb line of the Constitution.

Just as my son had to bring engineers into his home to assess and repair the damage, we must do a similar exam of the structure of our country and take action to ensure a return to our foundational principles.

Let's begin, shall we?

Assessing the Damage

Let me share where my assessment began and what caused me to go a step further than just being upset about the detour from our constitutional plumb line.

When I began writing this book, I wrote out of pure shock and anger from what I saw with my own eyes. As I led a team for a congressional district office, I watched one constituent after another be wrongfully fined, penalized, accused, ignored, belittled, disrespected, and threatened by the unelected bureaucrats in the federal agencies.

I got mad! To me, this treatment screamed that it was unconstitutional on every level! Constitutional rights were being violated, but we struggled to figure out how to defend them. It was not uncommon for one of my colleagues or me to come out into the hallway of our small office and share—or more appropriately, rant—about the abuse of yet another constituent and try to figure out what we could do to fix their problem! You know, the representative is supposed to do just that: represent his constituency and protect them from the abuse of the federal government by upholding the Constitution and the rights of the people they serve. We were doing our best to do that, and our boss supported us in doing so, but it almost seemed as if we were fighting a losing battle.

That is when I started researching during my personal time to try and understand how these agencies had gained so much power and control over us. How could they do this, and where did they get their authority? I brought this to my boss's attention, who shared my concern. I then began searching to see if other congressional members shared this concern or if they were complicit and just okay with it.

I started my research by speaking to fellow district directors as I attended meetings in DC and engaged with hundreds of them from across the country. I asked if they were experiencing the same abuses from agencies as we were, and they said they were, some more than others. What bothered me, though, was that it seemed that most accepted this as the "norm" and felt there was nothing that could be done. They were appalled by it but resigned to it. I also asked about their representative or senator's opinions. Again, it just seemed that everyone thought it was a problem that had been going on for so long, and there just wasn't much we could do to fix it.

I guess I am one of those people who sees injustice and says, "No way!" I decided I wanted to try and do something about it. Yes, I know it's a huge task, and I have been laughed at, told I'm wasting my time, and told that things will never change, but I moved forward anyway.

As you saw in chapter four, I researched to find out how many agencies there are. As I searched, I found many agencies have subagencies, and then there are programs, committees, commissions, and boards. It was clearly impossible for me, even to this day, to know exactly how many federal agencies there are. New agencies are being added by both the agencies themselves and Congress on an ongoing basis.

I have hundreds of pages of research on what I could find online. I couldn't fit it all in this book, so I created a GovernmentServantOrMaster.com website, where you can find the information I do have. I encourage you to go and scroll through the hundreds of agencies so you can see the behemoth that our government has created and the many unnecessary "structures" that need to be removed to get America back on track to being sound.

I doubt that any member of the House or Senate, if they were honest, could give us an accurate count today of every agency that they are required to give oversight to. According to the current 118th Congressional Committee on Oversight and Accountability, Congress is supposed to be giving oversight to *all* federal agencies. Please find the mission statement for the Congressional Committee on Oversight and Accountability for the 118th Congress below, with the link to the entire plan.

<u>Authorization and Oversight Plan</u>
Committee on Oversight and Accountability
US House of Representatives
118th Congress

Our mission statement is to ensure the efficiency, effectiveness, and accountability of the federal government and all its agencies. We provide a check and balance on the role and power of Washington—and a voice to the people it serves.

Genuinely good government requires a commitment to expose waste, fraud, and abuse. We ultimately report to hardworking taxpayers to ensure their investment in government is spent effectively, efficiently, and transparently.

We identify problems, shine light on the situation, and propose reforms to prevent abuses from being repeated.[114]

If you open the link (found in the endnotes), you will find that they list all the items they oversee. I will list the topics so you can see how impossible it is for this committee to do what it aspires to do when applied to every agency, subagency, board, committee, and commission of the federal government as it is today.

- Lapsed Authorizations
- Expiring Authorizations This Congress
- Waste, Fraud, Abuse, and Mismanagement

- The Federal Workforce (They've been "working" from home since January 20, 2021, by Executive Order No. 13991, and are still not completely back to work.)
- Federal Regulation and the Regulatory Process (They've given this to the Agencies to do.)
- The Government Accountability Office (Lists of high risk agencies particularly vulnerable to waste, fraud, abuse, or mismanagement or in need of transformation.)
- Inspectors General
- GSA Real Property Disposal
- Whistleblower Protection (People coming to our office are often afraid to speak out in their agency for fear of retribution. That is tyranny!)
- Federal Financial Management
- Government Contracting
- Grant Reform
- Cybersecurity and Data Privacy
- Information Technology and Management
- Open Government and Transparency
- United States Postal Service (One of the agencies with the largest number of issues and complaints in our caseload.)
- Government of the District of Columbia
- National Archives and Federal Records
- Office of Government Ethics
- Select Subcommittee on the Coronavirus Pandemic

I truly believe that Chairman James Comer has the best intentions to follow through with the above mission. But how is this possible when the number of agencies, subagencies, boards, committees, and commissions is not fully known to Congress and is constantly growing?

Each is supposedly required to give an annual report to Congress or to whomever they're told to report to, but the reports are at times misleading. I have seen some of those reports and know that they can include any information, whether true or not. I know this because some of the numbers of unresolved cases I have seen reported for all fifty states can't possibly be true, because our office alone had more unresolved cases than the agency listed for the entire country.

This is *not* an effective, transparent, or efficient way to give oversight, and it must change!

In the past three years, our congressional office alone has resolved nearly 6,500 cases. That means 6,500 individual citizens have been forced to come to us with a problem that these agencies have either refused to help them with or have even suggested, "Call your congressman," and then hung up the phone! This is after the constituent has waited anywhere from one to four hours on the phone to talk to someone! Many times, the phone call goes unanswered. Congress supposedly put these agencies in place to help with citizen issues and provide "effective and efficient" service. But our congressional office is just one of 435, not to mention the 100 Senate offices.

If our office has had that many cases, imagine how many there would be if we added them all up from every congressional office. Furthermore, how many people even know they can call their congressman or senator to ask for help with an issue they're having with a federal agency? I'm sure some people feel hopeless and give up because they don't know what to do. We hear that all the time. Until I started working for Congress, I didn't know that I could contact my congressman!

We have problems that need to be corrected, or our entire governmental structure is in danger of collapsing. In the meantime, Americans' rights are being violated, and too much of Congress is MIA, or at the very least, scurrying around going to all its committee meetings, social meetings, and special interest meetings while the work for the people is neglected.

The Constitutional Plumb Line

As we have applied the constitutional plumb line and assessed our progress throughout this book to determine whether our foundational walls are structurally sound, it is obvious that they are seriously bowed.

Our first step was assessing. My assessment is minuscule compared to what needs to be done, but I have found that as I have shined the light on some of the problems, other issues come to light as the situation is addressed. We all know that if you walk into a dark room and turn on the light, many more bugs are present than those you see scurrying for cover.

I want to limit what I address further to the Administrative State, a.k.a. the federal agencies.

Article I of the Constitution, particularly Section 8, clearly defines the federal government's powers and the need to leave all other powers to the "states or the people." I don't believe we could adequately list the ways in which we have wandered off course, but let's name a few of the obvious structures that need to be removed before we can begin to set our correctional beams on our foundational footers.

Structures to Remove from our Bowed Walls

The Administrative Procedures Act (APA) was passed on June 11, 1946. It gave all three powers to federal agencies: legislative, executive, and judicial. (We covered this in detail in chapter three.) While some of the items listed in the APA are necessary, these agencies must be under the authority of our elected representatives, not unelected bureaucrats. This power needs to be rescinded and returned to Congress. But how can this be done? Is it possible?

As I continued searching to see if anyone in Congress knew this, I stumbled upon something very encouraging. I literally typed in the question, "Can Congress take back the power given to federal agencies?" Immediately, I found an article entitled "How Can Congress Reassert Control over Federal Agencies?" I just about fell over! I had been searching for a sign that someone was doing something but obviously had not googled the right words. The article was about Senator Mike Lee's (R-UT) speech on May 18, 2017, in which he gave an update on the Article 1 Project (A1P) he had introduced in 2016.

He stated the A1P's goal: "To develop, advance, and ultimately enact an agenda of structural reforms to strengthen Congress by reclaiming the legislative powers that have been ceded to the executive branch." He said that the "core of our mission is restoring congressional authority over regulations and regulators."

Lee went on to say:

Many Americans now feel that they are not in control of their own government. It's because they aren't. The administrative state is designed to be insulated from politics—that is, it's designed to be insulated from the will of the people. This vast, unaccountable morass of programs, agencies, and commissions are all easily captured by the powerful and well-connected, and all dedicated to the regulation of the minutiae of everyday life.

But we can push back. If we are able to pass even one of the legislative reforms I've outlined—the REINS Act, the Separation of Powers Restoration Act, or the Agency Accountability Act—then we will have made real progress toward returning power to the people.[115]

— Senator Mike Lee

In a nutshell, through the Article 1 Project, Senator Lee offers some of the structural beams that need to be installed to return Congress to its original constitutional purpose and prevent the executive branch and unelected bureaucrats from making laws without accountability from the American people and their representatives.

What are those beams, and how will they help?

Setting Our Steel Beams on the Foundation Footers

1. The REINS Act (Regulations from the Executive in Need of Scrutiny Act)

    "The REINS Act . . . would help restore the balance between the executive and legislative branches by requiring Congressional approval for any new regulation that would impose $100 million or more in compliance costs on the American people."[116]

2. The Separation of Powers Restoration Act

    "The bill amends the APA and requires judges who are hearing challenges to agency actions to review all relevant questions of law "de novo" [from the beginning]. In other words, the bill would end the dysfunctional status quo that tilts the legal playing field in favor of federal bureaucracies. If passed, this legislation would place federal law into the hands of legislators empowered to write it and judges empowered to interpret it, just as the Constitution contemplates."[117]

3. The Agency Accountability Act

"[This act] makes federal agencies accountable again by directing most fines, fees, and unappropriated proceeds to the Treasury, instead of letting federal agencies keep and spend money as they see fit."[118]

As excited as I am to know that there are a few good representatives and senators in Congress who are aware of the serious problems we're facing and have even stepped out with bold legislative solutions, getting these beams set in place will take a lot of courage from more than just a few good men and women. It will take a bipartisan effort and an honest evaluation of how far off plumb we are. It will require an all-hands-on-deck approach to set each beam in place. It will take a keen awareness of the imminent danger of the government walls collapsing and crushing the people. It will take every member of Congress asking themselves if they believe the Constitution is the supreme law of the land they are committed to defending. That's what every one of them took an oath to!

I know this might seem like an impossible task, since Congress is more divided than ever before. Common sense and the ideals and principles that our country was founded upon are being challenged at every turn. Our foundational walls are caving, and we must find a way to get the constitutional beams of reining in the executive branch, restoring the separation of powers, and demanding accountability from the federal agencies securely set on the foundation footers again. The battle cannot be about peripheral issues, special interest groups, or any power that wasn't given to Congress by the authority of the Constitution. Congress must get back to doing the work of the people! However, this effort will also require significant citizen involvement and a resolute determination to hold our representatives accountable by engaging them in what they're doing in Washington.

There are other beams that are needed, but these three—reining in the executive branch, restoring separation of powers, and holding agencies accountable—will start moving the foundational walls back into their proper place and put power back in the hands of the people through their personal representatives.

A majority of Congress is needed to place the beams on the foundation footers. Who in Congress will join the members who have courageously stepped forward with a plan to save our country?

Once we have the beams in place and the foundational walls are being brought back into constitutional alignment, we have one more task to do, and this might be as hard as the last one to accomplish.

Placing Brackets and Bolts to Apply Constant Pressure:

Whose job will it be to apply the pressure?

Once the structural beams are in place, it will take continued pressure to realign and strengthen our foundational structure and bring our walls into plumb. Only then will we be in a position of strength that can securely take us into the future. Failure to do so will lead to the collapse of this great nation!

It will take the members of Congress staying strong and educating themselves by reading and knowing the Constitution and legislating accordingly. It will also take citizens who are constitutionally educated and engaged in what their representatives are doing. We must intentionally educate our children, who are our next generation of leaders.

If my son had ignored the obvious caving of the walls of his home and refused to pay the price, do the work, and put in the time and effort to fix the problem, his home would have been condemned, and his family would have become homeless. But he acknowledged that there was a problem. A problem can't be fixed if it isn't acknowledged!

The same is true for our country. Our walls are caving in. It will cost us all something to get the work done. Applying the needed pressure will take time, effort, and conviction, but we must first recognize that we have a problem. Congress and the American people must be willing to apply pressure for the long haul. We didn't get here overnight, and our problems won't be fixed overnight. But if we don't fix them, we will be "homeless!"

I commend Senator Lee and others who have joined him in his efforts! He has acknowledged that we have a problem, identified the most pressing problems, and put forward some great solutions to start the work to restore our foundation and save our "home," our great United States of America.

Let's join him!

What Other Lawmakers are saying about Senator Lee's Article ONE Act

Sen. Lee Introduces ARTICLE ONE Act to Reclaim Congressional Power

June 9, 2023

WASHINGTON – Sen. Mike Lee (R-UT) introduced the ARTICLE ONE Act, a bill that would reclaim significant legislative powers delegated to the executive branch by the National Emergencies Act of 1976.

When Congress passed this act in 1976, it gave the president of the United States the ability to exercise unilateral power like a king. Now, there are more than forty ongoing national emergencies that were never approved by Congress and have no expiration date.

"This kind of lawmaking-by-proclamation runs directly counter to the vision of our Founders and undermines the safeguards protecting our freedom," said Sen. Lee. "It's high time that Congress reclaimed its legislative power and restored constitutional balance to our Republic."

Of the bill, **Rep. Chip Roy (TX–21)** said, "The presidency was never meant to have monarchical power over the American people; that's why the Framers of our Constitution designed a system of checks and balances. For far too long, however, presidents from both sides of the aisle have ignored Congress and undermined the constitutional order by abusing the virtually unchecked power to declare national emergencies. The ARTICLE ONE Act reasserts Congress's authority over emergency declarations and rebalances federal power between the legislative and executive branches as the Framers of the Constitution intended for it. I am proud to join my friend Senator Mike Lee in reintroducing this bill and am glad to have Representative Steve Cohen join me in this bipartisan initiative."

Of the bill, **Sen. Richard Blumenthal (D–CT)** said, "Requiring the reauthorization of emergency declarations after thirty days will reassert Congress's role in governing our nation during times of crisis. If we continue to sit on the sidelines, our institution will ignore its constitutional responsibility, undermining our fundamental separation of powers."

Of the bill, **Sen. Mike Braun (R–IN)** said, "The Biden administration has gotten into the bad habit of forcing their unpopular measures through executive order that otherwise would not make it through the congressional legislative process. I'm proudly cosponsoring this bill that reclaims and solidifies the legislative branch as the lawmaking authority in America."

Of the bill, **Rep. Steve Cohen (D–TN)** said, "When I was chairman of the Judiciary Subcommittee on the Constitution, Civil Rights, and Civil Liberties, I held hearings on the National Emergencies Act and built bipartisan support for its reform. Our government is defined by checks and balances. But right now, Presidents can tap into emergency powers without any meaningful political check, time limit, or public rationale. We need to restore the balance of power and make sure that emergency powers are used only in emergencies and that Congress is integral to the process. I'm pleased to join with my colleague in the House, Congressman Chip Roy, and Senators Mike Lee and Richard Blumenthal in this continuing bipartisan effort. An emergency declared during the Carter Administration should not still be in effect."

The ARTICLE ONE Act would automatically end all future emergency declarations made pursuant to the NEA after thirty days unless Congress affirmatively votes to extend the emergency. Currently, Congress can cancel an emergency declaration only by passing a resolution that can withstand a presidential veto. The bill's full name is the "Assuring that Robust, Thorough, and Informed Congressional Leadership is Exercised Over National Emergencies Act."[119]

When the foundations are destroyed, what can the righteous do?

Psalm 11:3

Chapter Eight
Final Thoughts—Is There Still Hope?

The Founding Fathers discoursed endlessly on the meaning of "republicanism." In 1787, John Adams defined it as "a government in which all men, rich and poor, magistrates and subjects, officers and people, masters and servants, the first citizen and the last, are equally subject to the laws.[120]

In chapter two, I shared some important questions I asked myself before launching this book project. My job brought me into constant observation of and constituent advocacy over government abuse of the American people. It is our job to hold our government accountable; if we don't, we deserve the government we get.

Through my research and writing, I believe I have discovered answers. I want to share them with you, now that we better understand our government's structure and role. I hope we also better understand our important responsibility as American citizens.

What is the government's role supposed to be in relation to the American people?

The Declaration of Independence and the US Constitution make it clear that our government was created to serve the people. Our Founders' design of government was a republic, which means that ordinary citizens have the power to choose their own representatives who govern at their will. In other words, the government works for us.

The government is supposed to provide for the common defense and provide for its citizens' general welfare (life, liberty, and pursuit of happiness). This does not mean they provide me with money or food because I am too lazy to work. There is a place for benevolence, but it is for those who cannot help themselves. Churches and other civic and benevolent organizations have historically engaged actively in this kind of benevolence. See Article 1, Section 8 (Chapter 2, Part 2) for a complete list of the government's responsibilities.

Is the government supposed to have total control over our lives in every area, or did our Founding Fathers lay out a specific and limited role for those who govern?

As we have seen repeatedly throughout this book, our Founding Fathers understood the importance of a limited government that was subject to the people and warned that excess government would lead to oppression and hardship. While the government's control should be limited, we have gradually allowed it to increase its influence and power until it has come dangerously close to having total control over almost every aspect of our lives.

I have laid out how we can take that control back. We must educate ourselves by knowing the Constitution, our rights, and our responsibilities as American citizens and must become engaged with our representatives so *they know* that *we know* what permissions they have.

From whom do these agencies receive their authority?

We have addressed how government agencies received their authority when the APA was passed and how the Supreme Court empowered the agencies with the Chevron Deference ruling in 1984.

Does Congress have the constitutional authority to start and empower an agency and permit it to create rules and regulations that inhibit our personal liberty without giving adequate oversight?

Congress has the constitutional authority to start an agency to help our country run more efficiently. However, according to the separation of powers as articulated in the Constitution, Congress does not have the authority to allow those agencies to make laws, enforce them, and adjudicate those laws. Congress does not have the authority to create any law that violates our constitutional rights. The Constitution is the supreme law of the land!

When agencies infringe on the liberty of the American people, who must give oversight and correction to ensure they are not abusing the people with unconstitutional rules and regulations?

Congress must provide oversight, yet this is not happening adequately because Congress has delegated its power to agencies and funded this runaway government for decades instead of reining it in and holding it accountable. Simply put, the size and power of government agencies have gotten out of control. Abuse will stop when Congress returns to its Constitutional checks and balances. Then the Administrative State will no longer have the power to abuse us.

Does the American citizen really have any say in how the government functions?

Yes! Yes! Yes! We do have a say, but we must be active in our role and take responsibility by educating ourselves constitutionally and staying on top of what is happening at all levels of government: local, state, and federal!

We must register to vote and exercise that privilege whenever we have the opportunity. Roughly one-third of eligible Americans are not registered to vote. Many have lived their entire lives and have never bothered to exercise this amazing privilege. The right to vote is what secures what our Declaration of Independence calls the "right to liberty."

Do we still have the right to "petition the government for a redress of grievances," as stated in the First Amendment, or is that ignored today?

We have the right to "petition the government for a redress of grievances." This begins most effectively through relationships with our local, state, and federal representatives. That relationship exists not just so we can pat our representatives on the back, which is important and often appropriate, but also so we can deliver the proverbial "strong kick in the pants" when they are legislating inappropriately.

Our influence is only felt and impactful when there is a relationship with those in power.

The right to "petition the government for a redress of grievances" is often ignored! People who contact our office do so because they are experiencing that very reality. But, let me be clear, it is ignored most by "we the people." We don't take advantage of the privileges afforded to us by the First Amendment and are too often disengaged until we find ourselves victims of the government.

BREAKING NEWS!

I want to close this book with some very encouraging news!

On June 28, 2024, the Supreme Court of the United States (SCOTUS) ruled to limit federal agencies' broad regulatory authority.

By a vote of 6–3, the justices overruled their landmark 1984 decision in *Chevron v. Natural Resources Defense Council*, which gave rise to the doctrine known as the Chevron Doctrine. Under that doctrine, if Congress has not directly addressed the question at the center of a dispute, a court was required to defer to the agency's interpretation of the statute, as long as it was reasonable. In a thirty-five-page ruling by Chief Justice John Roberts, the justices rejected that doctrine, calling it "fundamentally misguided."

In response to appeals heard by SCOTUS on *Relentless v. Department of Commerce* and *Loper Bright Enterprises v. Ralmondo*, Roberts explained in his majority opinion for the court that the Chevron Deference is inconsistent with the APA. The APA, Roberts noted, directs courts to "decide legal questions by applying their own judgment" and therefore makes clear that agency interpretations of statutes—like agency interpretations of the Constitution—are not entitled to deference. Under the APA, Roberts concluded, "It thus remains the responsibility of the court to decide whether the law means what the agency says."[121]

Is There Hope?

Yes, there is hope! As we have learned, Congress can reclaim its constitutional authority. It has the power to reduce the size of the government. It has all the authority vested in it by the Constitution to turn our country around. But sometimes it lacks the political will to do so.

Congressional members need more persuasive pressure from the people! Many special interest groups are always shouting in our representatives' ears about what they want Congress to do. Sometimes, that is the only thing they hear because most citizens are *silent*! We must realize that we need to speak up to be heard. Politicians will listen and respond when constituents speak loudly and consistently in their offices and at the voting booth. Your voice and your vote can make all the difference in the world. But you must use both. Speak up! What you and I do will determine the state of our government for our children and for future generations of Americans. Whether or not the government is our servant or master truly depends on you and me!

> *Governments are instituted among men, deriving their just powers from the consent of the governed.*
>
> **Thomas Jefferson, The Declaration of Independence**

> *Every government degenerates when trusted to the rulers of the people alone. . . . Influence over government must be shared among all the people.*
>
> **Thomas Jefferson, Notes on the State of Virginia**[122]

> Blessed is the nation whose God is the L ORD.
>
> **Psalm 33:12 (NIV)**

Endnotes

1 Forbes, "Thoughts on the Business of Life," Forbes Quotes, https://www.forbes.com/quotes/3611/

2 John Adams, "John Adams to Abigail Adams, 3 July 1776," Founders Online, National Archives, accessed September 30, 2024, https://founders.archives.gov/documents/Adams/04-02-02-0016.

3 "Congressman Good Opposes the Inflation Reduction Act," Congressman Bob Good, August 12, 2022, https://good.house.gov/media/press-releases/congressman-good-opposes-inflation-reduction-act.

4 Congress.gov, "Family and Small Business Taxpayer Protection Act," Congressional Record, Vol. 169, No. 7, Daily Edition, accessed November 8, 2024, https://www.congress.gov/congressional-record/volume-169/issue-7/house-section/article/H76-1.

5 USHistory.org, "The Declaration of Independence Lesson Plan: Indictment against King George III," USHistory.org, accessed September 30, 2024, https://ushistory.org/declaration/lessonplan/doi_indictment.html

6 Jesse Greenspan, "How the Proclamation of 1763 Sparked the American Revolution," HISTORY, October 7, 2013, updated June 26, 2023, https://www.history.com/news/remembering-the-proclamation-of-1763.

7 Kelly Altman, "27 Grievances of the Declaration of Independence," Quizlet, accessed October 9, 2024, https://quizlet.com/582148799/27-grievances-of-the-declaration-of-independence-flash-cards/

8 "Great Britain: Parliament—The Quebec Act: October 7,1774," The Avalon Project, Yale Law School, accessed September 30, 2024, https://avalon.law.yale.edu/18th_century/quebec_act_1774.asp.

9 Ted Brackemyre, "The Quebec Act: British Legislation in Canada and the American Outcome," U.S. History Scene, accessed September 30, 2024, https://ushistoryscene.com/article/quebec-act/.

10 Michael Troy, "Episode 045: Governing from Salem," American Revolution Podcast, May 20, 2018, https://blog.amrevpodcast.com/2018/05/episode-045-governing-from-salem.html.

11 "Massachusetts Circular Letter to the Colonial Legislatures; February 11, 1768," American Battlefield Trust, accessed September 30, 2024, https://www.battlefields.org/learn/primary-sources/massachusetts-circular-letter-colonial-legislatures-february-11-1768#:~:text=In%20response%20to%20the%20Townshend,without%20their%20representation%20in%20government.

12 National Humanities Center, "Legislative Petition Opposing the Quartering Act, 1767." from "Colonists Respond to the Quartering Act of 1765," Making the Revolution: America 1763-1791, accessed September 30, 2024, https://americainclass.org/sources/makingrevolution/crisis/text4/quarteringactresponse1766.pdf

13 The Claremont Institute, "He Has Endeavoured to Prevent the Population of These States [. . .]," Founding.com, https://founding.com/he-has-endeavoured-to-prevent-the-population-of-these-states-for-that-purpose-obstructing-the-laws-for-naturalization-of-foreigners/.

14 Nina Sankovitch, "It Wasn't All About Taxes: Royal Tampering with the Colonial Courts and the American Rebellion," The History Reader, accessed September 30, 2024, https://www.thehistoryreader.com/us-history/it-wasnt-all-about-taxes-american-rebels/#fn2.

15 USHistory.org, "The Declaration of Independence."

16 Sankovitch, "It Wasn't All About Taxes."

17 Scot Faulkner, "Eating Out Their Substance: Ever-Expanding and Intrusive Presence of Tax Collectors, and the Declaration of Independence," Constituting America, accessed September 30, 2024, https://constitutingamerica.org/90day-dcin-eating-out-their-substance-ever-expanding-intrusive-presence-of-tax-collectors-and-the-declaration-of-independence-guest-essayist-scot-faulkner/.

18 Constitutional Rights Foundation , "Quartering of Soldiers in Colonial America: What Really Happened?," Teach Democracy, accessed November 8, 2024, https://teachdemocracy.org/images/pdf/quarteringofsoldiersincolonialaamerica.pdf.

19 Matthew A. Bryan, "Thomas Gage," In The Digital Encyclopedia of George Washington, eds. Anne Fertig and Alexandra Montgomery, Mount Vernon Ladies' Association, 2012–, https://www.mountvernon.org/library/digitalhistory/digital-

encyclopedia/article/thomas-gage#:~:text=A%20year%20later%2C%20Gage%20 ordered,and%20Concord%20in%20April%201775.

20 The Claremont Institute, "He Has Combined with Others to Subject Us [. . .]," Founding.com, accessed September 30, 2024, https://founding.com/he-has-combined-with-others-to-subject-us-to-a-jurisdiction-foreign-to-our-constitution-and-unacknowledged-by-our-laws-giving-his-assent-to-their-acts-of-pretended-legislation/.

21 Jamestown-Yorktown Foundation, "The Quartering Acts," JYFMuseums.org, accessed September 30, 2024, https://www.jyfmuseums.org/learn/teacher-resources-programs/classroom-resources/the-quartering-acts#:~:text=Quartering%20in%20 1777,accommodation%20among%20the%20city's%20residents.

22 Library of Congress, "Timeline: 1770 to 1772," Documents from the Continental Congress and the Constitutional Convention, 1774 to 1789, Library of Congress, accessed September 30, 2024, https://www.loc.gov/collections/continental-congress-and-constitutional-convention-from-1774-to-1789/articles-and-essays/timeline/1770-to-1772/.

23 The Editors of Encyclopaedia Britannica, "Navigation Acts," Encyclopaedia Britannica, accessed October 10, 2023, https://www.britannica.com/event/Navigation-Acts.

24 Jayne, E. Triber, "Britain Begins Taxing the Colonies: The Sugar & Stamp Acts," National Park Service, accessed September 30, 2024, https://www.nps.gov/articles/000/sugar-and-stamp-acts.htm.

25 West Virginia Association for Justice, "A Forgotten History: Trial By Jury and the American Revolution," West Virginia Association for Justice, accessed September 30, 2024, https://www.wvaj.org/?pg=TrialbyJuryAmericanRevolution#:~:text=In%20the%20Declaration%20 of%20Causes,Independence%20included%20%22depriving%20us%20in.

26 "The Coercive (Intolerable) Acts of 1774," In The Digital Encyclopedia of George Washington, eds Anne Fertig and Alexandra Montgomery, Mount Vernon Ladies' Association, 2012–, https://www.mountvernon.org/library/digitalhistory/digital-encyclopedia/article/the-coercive-intolerable-acts-of-1774.

27 John Adams, "I. Heads of Grievances and Rights, 9 September 1774," Founders Online, National Archives, http://founders.archives.gov/documents/Adams/06-02-02-0041-0002.

28 Smithsonian Art Museum, "Massachusetts Government Act," Smithsonian American Art Museum, accessed September 30, 2024, https://americanexperience.si.edu/glossary/massachusetts-government-act/.

29 Ranger Val and Ranger Bill, "The Declaration of Independence: What Were They Thinking?" National Park Service, updated June 30,2021, https://www.nps.gov/fost/blogs/the-declaration-of-independence-what-were-they-thinking.htm.

30 The Claremont Institute, "He Has Plundered Our Seas, Ravaged Our Coasts. . ." Founding.com, accessed September 30, 2024, https://founding.com/he-has-plundered-our-seas-ravaged-our-coasts-burnt-our-towns-and-destroyed-the-lives-of-our-people/.

31 PBS, "King George III," The American Experience, PBS, accessed September 30, 2024, https://www.pbs.org/wgbh/americanexperience/features/adams-king-george-III/.

32 The Claremont Institute, "He Has Constrained Our Fellow Citizens Taken Captive on the High Seas [. . .]," Founding.com, accessed September 30, 2024, https://founding.com/he-has-constrained-our-fellow-citizens-taken-captive-on-the-high-seas-to-bear-arms-against-their-country-to-become-the-executioners-of-their-friends-and-brethren-or-to-fall-themselves-by-their-hands/.

33 The Gilder Lehrman Institute of American History, "Lord Dunmore's Proclamation, 1775: A Spotlight on a Primary Source by John Murray and Lord Dunmore," The Gilder Lehrman Institute of American History, accessed September 30, 2024, https://www.gilderlehrman.org/history-resources/spotlight-primary-source/lord-dunmores-proclamation-1775.

34 "Declaration of Independence: A Transcription," National Archives, updated August 27,2024, https://www.archives.gov/founding-docs/declaration-transcript.

35 "Articles of Confederation (1777)," National Archives, updated October 23, 2023, https://www.archives.gov/milestone-documents/articles-of-confederation.

36 Government Publishing Office, "Articles of Confederation: 1777-1789," Ben's Guide to the US Government, accessed September 30, 2024, https://bensguide.gpo.gov/articles-of-confederation-1777-1789.

37 Lou Frey Institute, "How Did the US Constitution Address the Weaknesses of the Articles of Confederation?" Civics360.org, accessed September 30, 2024, PDF, https://civics360.org/uploads/Byqet2E87/fjcc_aocandconstitution_c15_activityform.pdf (page removed from site).

38 Mount Vernon Ladies' Association,"6 Key Players at the Constitutional Convention," George Washington's Mount Vernon, accessed September 30, 2024, https://www.mountvernon.org/george-washington/constitutional-convention/6-key-players-at-the-constitutional-convention.

39 Government Publishing Office, "States and Dates of Ratification," Ben's Guide to the US Government, accessed September 30, 2024, https://bensguide.gpo.gov/j-states-ratification?highlight=WyJjb25zdGl0dXRpb24iLCJjb25zdGl0dXRpb24ncyJd#:~:text=Maryland%3A%20April%2028%2C%201788,Virginia%3A%20June%2025%2C%201788.

40 Hillsdale College, "Promote the General Welfare: A How to . . .", Constitution Minute, Hillsdale College, August 30, 2013, https://blog.hillsdale.edu/dialogues/promote-the-general-welfare-a-how-to.

41 Digital History, "The Three-Fifth Compromise," Digital History, accessed September 30, 2024, https://www.digitalhistory.uh.edu/disp_textbook.cfm?smtID=3&psid=163.

42 Congress.gov, "ArtI.S6.C1.2 Privilege from Arrest," Constitution Annotated, accessed September 30, 2024, https://constitution.congress.gov/browse/essay/artI-S6-C1-2/ALDE_00013354/.

43 Congress.gov, "ArtI.S6.C2.1 Overview of Federal Office Prohibition," Constitution Annotated, accessed September 30, 2024, https://constitution.congress.gov/browse/essay/artI-S6-C2-1/ALDE_00013136/.

44 Charlie Dunlap, "The Supreme Court, Affirmative Action, and the Military: Some Observations," Lawfire, Center on Law, Ethics and National Security, Duke Law, July 24, 2023, https://sites.duke.edu/lawfire/2023/07/24/the-supreme-court-affirmative-action-and-the-military-some-observations/#:~:text=After%20all%2C%20the%20Court%20said%20in%20Parker,of%20its%20own%20during%20its%20long%20history.%E2%80%9D.

45 Care of the Armed Forces , Legal Information Institute, Cornell Law School, accessed November 8, 2024, https://www.law.cornell.edu/constitution-conan/article-1/section-8/clause-14/power-to-govern-and-regulate-land-and-naval-forces

46 Legal Information Institute, "Power over Places Purchased," Legal Information Institute, Cornell Law School, accessed September 30, 2024, https://www.law.cornell.edu/constitution-conan/article-1/section-8/clause-17/power-over-places-purchased.

47 Legal Information Institute, "Habeas Corpus," Legal Information Institute, "ArtI.S8.C14.1 Legal Information Institute, Cornell Law School, accessed November 8, 2024, https://www.law.cornell.edu/wex/habeas_corpus.

48 Congress.gov, "ArtI.S9.C7.1 Overview of Appropriations Clause," Constitution Annotated, accessed September 30, 2024, https://constitution.congress.gov/browse/essay/artI-S9-C7-1/ALDE_00001095/.

49 Legal Information Institute, "ArtI.S9.C8.1 Overview of Titles of Nobility and Foreign Emoluments Clauses," Legal Information Institute, Cornell Law School, accessed November 8, 2024, https://www.law.cornell.edu/constitution-conan/article-1/section-9/clause-8/overview-of-titles-of-nobility-and-foreign-emoluments-clauses

50 Greg Abbott, "Governor Abbott Renews Border Security Disaster Proclamation in June 2024," Office of the Texas Governor, June 28, 2024, https://gov.texas.gov/news/post/governor-abbott-renews-border-security-disaster-proclamation-in-june-2024.

51 US Supreme Court, *Springer v. Government of Philippine Islands*, 277 U.S. 189, 202 (1928) Justia, accessed November 8, 2024, https://supreme.justia.com/cases/federal/us/277/189/.

52 John Fonte, "National Conservatism, Freedom Conservatism, and Americanism," Imprimis 53 no. 6/7 (June/July 2024), https://imprimis.hillsdale.edu/national-conservatism-freedom-conservatism-and-americanism/.

53 Laura Clark, "The First State of the Union Address: Way Shorter, Way Less Clapping," Smithsonian Magazine, January 20, 2015, www.smithsonianmag.com/smart-news/first-state-union-address-way-shorter-less-clapping-180953954/.

54 Merriam-Webster, s.v. "Corruption of blood," accessed September 30, 2024, https://www.merriam-webster.com/dictionary/corruption%20of%20blood

55 Brian Taylor, "How Many U.S. Military Bases in the World?" Online-Military-Education.org (blog), February 23, 2023, https://onlinemilitaryeducation.org/blog/356-how-many-us-military-bases-in-the-world.html.

56 Embassy WorldWide, "List of Diplomatic Missions in United States & American Diplomatic Missions Abroad," Embassy WorldWide, accessed September 30, 2024, https://www.embassy-worldwide.com/.

57 US Governmental Services Administration, "GSA Properties," US General Services Administration, accessed September 30, 2024, https://www.gsa.gov/real-estate/gsa-properties.

58 Convention of States ACTION, "Progress Map: States that Have Passed the Convention of States Article V Application," Convention of States ACTION, accessed September 30, 2024, https://conventionofstates.com/states-that-have-passed-the-convention-of-states-article-v-application.

59 "The Constitution of the United States: A Transcription," National Archives, https://www.archives.gov/founding-docs/constitution-transcript .

60 National Constitution Center, "15.3 Visual Info Brief: 27 Amendments to the Constitution," National Constitution Center, accessed September 30, 2024, https://constitutioncenter.org/education/classroom-resource-library/classroom/15.3-visual-info-brief-27-amendments-to-the-constitution.

61 Ashbrook Center, "Debates over the Bill of Rights in the First Congress," Teaching American History, accessed September 30, 2024, https://teachingamericanhistory.org/resource/house-debates/0817-2/.

62 Renée Lettow Lerner and Suja A. Thomas, "The Seventh Amendment," National Constitution Center, accessed September 30, 2024, https://constitutioncenter.org/the-constitution/amendments/amendment-vii/interpretations/125.

63 Nicholas J. Dilley, "'Constitutional Amendments' Series—Amendment VIII—'Freedom From Excessive Bail, Fines, and Cruel Punishments,'" The Reagan Library Education Blog, August 22, 2022, https://reagan.blogs.archives.gov/2022/08/22/constitutional-amendments-series-amendment-viii-freedom-from-excessive-bail-fines-and-cruel-punishments/.

64 Annenberg Public Policy Center, "11th Amendment," The Annenberg Guide to the United States Constitution, accessed September 30, 2024, https://www.annenbergclassroom.org/11th-amendment/#:~:text=The%20amendment%20specifically%20prohibits%20federal,known%20as%20%E2%80%9Csovereign%20immunity.%E2%80%9D.

65 The White House, "Thomas Jefferson: The Third President of the United States," The White House, accessed September 30, 2024, https://www.whitehouse.gov/about-the-white-house/presidents/thomas-jefferson/.

66 *Erratum.*

67 Legal Information Institute, "14th Amendment," Legal Information Institute, Cornell Law School, accessed September 30, 2024, https://www.law.cornell.edu/constitution/amendmentxiv.

68 Sarah Pruitt, "When Did African Americans Actually Get the Right to Vote?," HISTORY, A&E Television Networks, January 29, 2020, https://www.history.com/news/african-american-voting-right-15th-amendment.

69 Joseph R. Fishkin, William E. Forbath, and Erik M. Jensen, "The Sixteenth Amendment," National Constitution Center, accessed September 30, 2024, https://constitutioncenter.org/the-constitution/amendments/amendment-xvi/interpretations/139#:~:text=The%20Sixteenth%20Amendment%2C%20ratified%20in,government's%20largest%20source%20of%20revenue.

70 Dan Culp, "Why should senators be elected by the state legislature instead of the people?," Quora, accessed September 30,2024, https://www.quora.com/Why-should-senators-be-elected-by-the-state-legislature-instead-of-the-people.

71 Center for American Women and Politics, "Teach a Girl to Lead: Women's Suffrage in the U.S. by State," Rutgers, August 2014, PDF, accessed September 30, 2024, https://tag.rutgers.edu/wp-content/uploads/2014/05/suffrage-by-state.pdf.

72 Ronald Reagan Presidential Library and Museum, "Constitutional Amendments – Amendment 20 – 'Date Changes for Presidency, Congress, and Succession,'" Ronald Reagan Presidential Library & Museum, National Archives, accessed September 30, 2024, https://www.reaganlibrary.gov/constitutional-amendments-amendment-20-date-changes-presidency-congress-and-succession.

73 Nathan Murphy, "24th Amendment: Definition, Summary & Court Cases," Working Scholars, Study.com, updated November 21, 2023, https://study.com/learn/lesson/24th-amendment-summary-history-court-cases.html.

74 Rock the Vote, "The 26th Amendment: An Explainer," Rock the Vote, accessed September 30, 2024, https://www.rockthevote.org/explainers/the-26th-amendment-and-the-youth-vote/.

75 Evan Andrews, "The Strange Saga of the 27th Amendment," HISTORY, A&E Television Networks, updated September 1, 2018, https://www.history.com/news/the-strange-case-of-the-27th-amendment

76 Larry P Arnn, "Constitution 101: The Meaning and History of the Constitution," Hillsdale College, accessed September 30, 2024, https://online.hillsdale.edu/courses/constitution-101.

77 Frank J. Goodnow, "The American Conception of Liberty," ed. Jason R. Jividen, Teaching American History, Ashbrook Center, accessed September 24, 2024, https://teachingamericanhistory.org/document/the-american-conception-of-liberty/.

78 Lloyd De Jongh, "America is a Constitutional Republic," X, July 1, 2024, https://mobile.x.com/LloydDeJongh/status/1807642933941706953.

79 Digital History, "The Oldest Written National Framework of Government," Digital History, accessed September 24, 2024, https://www.digitalhistory.uh.edu/disp_textbook.cfm?psid=3231&smtid=2#:~:text=The%20U.S.%20Constitution%20has%20the,had%20been%20adopted%20since%201970.

80 Ballotpedia, "Administrative State," Ballotpedia, accessed October 19, 2023, https://ballotpedia.org/Administrative_state; Edward L. Rubin, "Law and Legislation in the Administrative State," Columbia Law Review 89, no. 3 (April 1989): 369-426; Mark Mancini, "The Political Problem with the Administrative State," Journal of Commonwealth Law 55 (2020), https://www.journalofcommonwealthlaw.org/article/17361-the-political-problem-with-the-administrative-state.

81 Jonathan Turley, "The Rise of the Fourth Branch of Government," Washington Post, May 24, 2013, https://www.washingtonpost.com/opinions/the-rise-of-the-fourth-branch-of-government/2013/05/24/c7faaad0-c2ed-11e2-9fe2-6ee52d0eb7c1_story.html.

82 Oxford Languages, s.v. "Despotism," accessed via Google search on September 30, 2024.

83 Merriam Webster, s.v. "Despotism," accessed September 30, 2024, https://www.merriam-webster.com/dictionary/despotism.

84 Jeannie Ricketts, "A Very Brief History of Federal Administrative Law," Oklahoma Bar Association, originally published in Oklahoma Bar Journal 88 (November 18, 2017), https://www.okbar.org/barjournal/nov2017/obj8830ricketts/#:~:text=Congress%20created%20the%20first%20federal,to%20perform%20other%20related%20duties.

85 Editors of Encyclopaedia Britannica, "Regulatory Agency," Encyclopaedia Britannica, January 10, 2024, https://www.britannica.com/topic/regulatory-agency.

86 National Archives, "Interstate Commerce Act 1887 National Archives , accessed November 8, 2024.https://www.archives.gov/milestone-documents/interstate-commerce-act.

87 Center for Effective Government, "A Brief History of Administrative Government," Center for Effective Government, https://www.foreffectivegov.org/node/3461 (site discontinued).

88 Center for Effective Government, "A Brief History."

89 Students of History, "New Deal Alphabet Soup Agencies," Students of History, accessed September 24, 2024, https://www.studentsofhistory.com/the-new-deal-alphabet-soup#:~:text=Franklin%20D.,or%20just%20%22Alphabet%20 Agencies.%22.

90 Editors of Encyclopaedia Britannica, "New Deal," Encyclopedia Britannica, September 5, 2024, https://www.britannica.com/event/New-Deal.

91 Roni Elias, "The Legislative History of the Administrative Procedure Act ," *Fordham Environmental Law Review* 27, no. 2 (2015), PDF, https://ir.lawnet.fordham.edu/cgi/viewcontent.cgi?article=1732&context=elr#:~:text=against%20the%20 abuse%20of%20administrative,reflected%20a%20significant%20political%20 compromise.

92 Administrative Procedure Act, Pub L. No. 79-404, PDF, https://www.justice.gov/sites/default/files/jmd/legacy/2014/05/01/act-pl79-404.pdf.

93 History.com Editors, "Great Society," HISTORY, A & E Television Networks, updated August 28, 2018, https://www.history.com/topics/1960s/great-society.

94 Center for Effective Government, "A Brief History."

95 Center for Effective Government, "A Brief History."

96 *Chevron U.S.A., Inc. v. NRDC,* 467 U.S. 837 (1984).

97 Legal Information Institute, "Chevron Deference," Legal Information Institute, Cornell Law School, accessed September 24, 2024, https://www.law.cornell.edu/wex/chevron_deference.

98 Peter J. Wallison, *Judicial Fortitude: The Last Chance to Rein in the Administrative State* (New York: Encounter Books, 2018).

99 Peter J. Wallison, "Justice Kavanaugh and the Administrative State," American Enterprise Institute, October 10, 2018, https://www.aei.org/economics/justice-kavanaugh-and-the-administrative-state/.

100 James Madison, "The Particular Structure of the New Government [. . .]," *The Federalist Papers,* No. 47, The Avalon Project, Yale Law School, accessed September 30, 2024, https://avalon.law.yale.edu/18th_century/fed47.asp

101 Department of Defense, "About," Department of Defense, accessed November 8, 2024, https://www.defense.gov/About.

102 Financial Crimes Enforcement Network, "What We Do," FinCEN, accessed November 8, 2024,o https://www.fincen.gov/what-we-do.

103 Department of Justice, "A FBI Organizational Structure and Investigative Jurisdiction," Justice Manual, Department of Justice, accessed November 8, 2024, https://www.justice.gov/jm/organization-and-functions-manual-9-fbi-organizational-structure-and-investigative-jurisdiction.

104 Camilo Montoya-Galvez, "Illegal Crossings at U.S. Southern Border Reach Lowest Point of Biden Presidency," CBS News, October 7, 2024, at https://www.cbsnews.com/news/u-s-mexico-border-migrant-crossings-reach-new-biden-era-low.

105 Memorandum: COVID-19 Safe Federal Workplace: Agency Model Safety Principles. (M-21-15), January 24, 2021, PDF, https://www.whitehouse.gov/wp-content/uploads/2021/01/M-21-15.pdf.

106 Thomas Jefferson, *Notes on the State of Virginia*, electronic edition (Chapel Hill: University of North Carolina at Chapel Hill, 2006), Documenting the American South, https://docsouth.unc.edu/southlit/jefferson/jefferson.html.

107 George Washington, "Eighth Annual Address to Congress," The American Presidency Project, accessed September 30, 2024, https://www.presidency.ucsb.edu/node/200398.

108 "From George Washington to Bushrod Washington, 9 November 1787," Founders Online, National Archives, https://founders.archives.gov/documents/Washington/04-05-02-0388.

109 James Madison, "December 5, 1810: Second Annual Message," Miller Center, University of Virginia, accessed September 30, 2024, https://millercenter.org/the-presidency/presidential-speeches/december-5-1810-second-annual-message.

110 WallBuilders, "Constitution Hub," WallBuilders, May 29, 2023, https://wallbuilders.com/resource/constitution-hub/#_edn9.

111 Robert M.S. McDonald, ed., *Light and Liberty: Thomas Jefferson and the Power of Knowledge* (Charlottesville, VA: University of Virginia Press, 2012), 1-18, https://www.jstor.org/stable/j.ctt6wrk2j.6.

112 Timothy S. Goeglein, "The Consequences of Constitutional Ignorance: Opinion," Newsweek, March 24, 2023, https://www.newsweek.com/consequences-constitutional-ignorance-opinion-1789650.

113 "From George Washington to Bushrod Washington."

114 Committee on Oversight and Accountability, US House of Representatives, 118th Congress "Authorization and Oversight Plan," February 2023, PDF, https://oversight.house.gov/wp-content/uploads/2023/02/118th-Authorization-and-Oversight-Plan.pdf.

115 Mike Lee, "How Can Congress Reassert Control Over Federal Agencies?," Mike Lee: US Senator for Utah, May 18, 2017, https://www.lee.senate.gov/2017/5/how-can-congress-reassert-control-over-federal-agencies.

116 Mike Lee, "How Can Congress Reassert Control?"

117 Mike Lee, "How Can Congress Reassert Control?"

118 Mike Lee, "How Can Congress Reassert Control?"

119 Mike Lee, "Sen. Lee Introduces ARTICLE ONE Act to Reclaim Congressional

Power," Mike Lee: US Senator for Utah, June 9, 2023, https://www.lee.senate.gov/2023/6/sen-lee-reintroduces-article-one-act-to-reclaim-congressional-power.

120 John Adams, "Defence of the Constitutions of Government of the United States," in *The Founders' Constitution*, ed. Philip B. Kurland and Ralph Lerner, web edition (Chicago: University of Chicago Press), vol. 1, chap. 4, document 10, https://press-pubs.uchicago.edu/founders/documents/v1ch4s10.html.

121 Amy Howe, "Supreme Court Strikes Down Chevron, Curtailing Power of Federal Agencies," SCOTUSblog, June 28, 2024, https://www.scotusblog.com/2024/06/supreme-court-strikes-down-chevron-curtailing-power-of-federal-agencies/.

122 Thomas Jefferson, "Quotes: Jefferson and Founding Fathers," Thomas Jefferson Monticello, Thomas Jefferson Foundation, accessed September 30, 2024, https://tinyurl.com/j4xhr8n9.

About the Author

Sandra was born into a pastor's home in Fredericksburg VA, the second of nine children. While raising her family, she trained as a nurse at Indian River State College in Fort Pierce, Florida. Soon after, she moved to Ukraine with her husband and six children to serve as Christian missionaries. After returning home, Sandy and her husband were led to become involved in conservative politics. Since 2021, she has worked for Congress as a District Director.

Sandra has been married for 41 years to Melvin, is the proud mother of six married children, and enjoys twenty-two grandchildren. She and her husband reside in western Virginia.